"This is a remarkable book. Filled with words, it leaves you with no words left to say. Some lovely people met up with hate one day, and with love they responded. Every story of the human journey, every reflection on the appearance of evil, every admonition to triumph over hatred through the power of love—it's all in here, not just in theory but in the story of a beautiful little girl and her daddy, slaughtered while surrounded by angels. It doesn't matter if your heart is open now; it will be open once you read this. It doesn't matter whether your mind is open now; it will be open once you read this. And it doesn't matter whether you believe in the realm of the deathless and transcendence of the human spirit now; you'll be a believer once you read this. Having ended the book, I bow before the spirit of love that survives and lifts all things."

—**Marianne Williamson,** author of *A Return to Love*

"This is a powerful book. Many spiritual teachers and wisdom traditions, both ancient and modern, preach compassion, forgiveness, non-judgment and peace. But rarely do we get the opportunity to bear witness to these ideals being lived when the practitioners are quite literally under fire. In this original, bold, and moving account, Master Charles Cannon and his students demonstrate rare integrity and courage in their convictions. They speak with a spiritual self-confidence that only comes from deep insight into what lies beyond life and death."

—**Andrew Cohen,** author of *Evolutionary Enlightenment*

"Out of the most horrific experience, Master Charles shares a wisdom that is common to all religions at their deepest level, that grace surrounds us if we but open our eyes. I am filled with gratitude."

—**Constant Mews, D.Phil. (Oxon), FAHA**
Director, Center for Studies in Religion and Theology
Monash University, Melbourne, Australia

"The true nature of a human being is revealed in life-threatening situations. *Forgiving the Unforgivable* reveals the nature of the whole human being. This group of people responded to terrorism with compassion and forgiveness after being held captive for forty-eight hours and losing two of their members in the attack. This holistic state of being offers a new way for all of us to be more fully human. The essence of all wisdom traditions is love, compassion and forgiveness. Master Charles shows us how to maintain this focus and experience the unity within all diversity."

—Naila Alam
Founder and Ambassador for Peace CEO, Express Care Inc.

"What is most evident in working with drug-addicted individuals is the self-destructive aspect of this condition or disease. Master Charles has made an enormous contribution to my work in helping thousands overcome their addiction by enlightening me to the importance of self-forgiveness in healing the pain of a divided self."

—Howard Josepher
Founder, President and CEO of Exponents, NYC

"Helping us make sense of the Mumbai terrorist attack, *Forgiving the Unforgivable* demonstrates how a more inclusive philosophical and spiritual perspective can not only heal the wounds of this event, but contribute to a greater understanding that supports peaceful resolutions to warring factions throughout the world."

—Steven Halpern, Ph.D.
Recording artist/sound healer

"This book represents a significant contribution towards learning how to overcome trauma in order to lead meaningful, purposeful, enjoyable lives. Master Charles understands that while forgiveness does not obviate responsibility—the Mumbai terrorists remain responsible for their actions—it does mean that you can stop being a victim, while plumbing the depths of your own humanity. Such understanding of the human heart offers hope for healing a broken world."

—Rabbi Steve Robbins
Kabbalist psychologist and healer
Rabbi of Congregation N'vay Shalom

Forgiving the Unforgivable

Forgiving the Unforgivable

*The True Story of How Survivors
of the Mumbai Terrorist Attack
Answered Hatred with Compassion*

❧

THE POWER OF HOLISTIC LIVING

by Master Charles Cannon

with Will Wilkinson

SelectBooks, Inc.
New York

Modern Spirituality™ and Holistic Lifestyle™ are trademarks
of Synchronicity Foundation, Inc., USA

Synchronicity®, High-Tech Meditation®, Contemporary Meditation® and
Holodynamic® are all registered trademarks of Synchronicity Foundation, Inc., USA.

This edition published by SelectBooks, Inc.
For information address SelectBooks, Inc., New York, New York.

First Edition

ISBN 978-1-59079-218-6

Library of Congress Cataloging-in-Publication Data
Cannon, Master Charles.
  Forgiving the unforgivable : the true story of how survivors of the Mumbai
terrorist attack answered hatred with compassion : the power of holistic
living / by Master Charles Cannon with Will Wilkinson.
       p. cm.
Summary: "The founder of Synchronicity Foundation presents his innovative
spiritual teachings and contemporary holistic lifestyle practices. He and
members of his group who were victims of the 2008 Mumbai terrorist attack
during a pilgrimage explain how Master Charles Cannon's concepts empowered
them to have forgiveness and compassion for terrorists who murdered their
close associate and the man's 13-year-old daughter"--Provided by publisher.
  ISBN 978-1-59079-218-6 (pbk. : alk. paper)
  1. Spirituality. 2. Synchronicity Foundation International. 3.
Forgiveness--Religious aspects. 4. Mumbai Terrorist Attacks, Bombay, India,
2008 I. Wilkinson, Will. II. Title.
  BL624.C3453 2011
  299'.93--dc23
                           2011023592

Designed by Janice Benight

Manufactured in the United States of America
10 9 8 7 6 5 4 3 2 1

To the One in the many.
It is you that I truly adore.

Contents

ৡৡৡ

Foreword

In November 2008, Virginia-based spiritual teacher Master Charles Cannon and twenty-four associates traveling with him found themselves trapped in the Oberoi Hotel in Mumbai when it came under attack by terrorists. A total of one hundred sixty-six people were killed in the Mumbai attacks, including two in Master Charles's group, a father and his 13-year-old daughter. This book documents these events and the aftermath as seen through the eyes of those who survived. The book's main focus however is not on the external events, but on the inner: the survivors' state of consciousness during and after the ordeal and, above all, your consciousness as you read.

This book is about forgiveness but, more essentially, it is about how to live in a certain state of consciousness out of which forgiveness arises naturally and effortlessly. Thus, it is a book of spiritual teachings given against the background of a life-threatening emergency situation, just as the Bhagavad Gita is a book of spiritual teachings given against the background of an impending battle and, perhaps, imminent death. Awareness of the closeness of death has been recognized since ancient times as having great potential for bringing about a spiritual awakening. This is why in some Buddhist traditions monks regularly go to the morgue or cemetery for their meditations.

Forgiveness is one of the most important spiritual concepts, but also one of the most misunderstood. Many people still consider it an act of self-deception, a sugarcoating of evil in an unconscious attempt to improve one's "spiritual" self-image. They say forgiveness is too often associated with absolving the perpetrators of unspeakable acts of cruelty and inhumanity from responsibility for their crimes, attributing these acts instead to other factors such as social conditions ("we are all responsible"), the perpetrators' childhood experiences, or their use of drugs, and so on. These are valid concerns and I would like to address them briefly here.

The question of personal responsibility is, indeed, of crucial importance. If the perpetrator is responsible, how can we forgive? If he or she is ultimately not responsible, how can we not forgive? In the aftermath of their ordeal, one person in Master Charles's group recalled the words Jesus spoke on the cross: "Forgive them, Father, for they know not what they do." Deep within she recognizes the truth of these words. But are these words objectively true?

In certain extreme cases of clinical insanity, the saying "they know not what they do" applies, without question. But what about the Mumbai terrorists, or those who carried out the bomb attack and mass shootings in Norway, or countless other atrocities one could mention here that were orchestrated by individuals and, more frequently, by religious or political factions or governments? The perpetrators usually plan their actions long in advance. They have a rigid belief system or ideology and can explain in seemingly rational terms why they consider their actions to be necessary. Don't they know exactly what they are doing? In what sense could we possibly say, then, that they are not responsible, that "they know not what they do?"

It is not commonly realized—and certainly not taught at school—that there are two ways or modalities of knowing. These two modalities are complementary, not mutually exclusive. Let me give an example.

Almost every day I take a walk in a nearby forest. On a conceptual level, of course, I know that "I, Eckhart, am walking in the forest." I know the names of at least some of the trees and plants and other things that can be known conceptually about the forest and myself walking in it.

Yet, at the same time, there is also a deeper way of knowing the forest. It requires a certain degree of inner stillness, an alertness that brings about a temporary cessation of thinking. On that deeper level of knowing, I can sense the aliveness of the forest and the silent presence of the trees and plants as living energy-fields. I can also sense my own presence, not as Eckhart (which is a story attached to a concept), but as the perceiving and witnessing consciousness beyond name and form. We could call that the knowing through awareness (rather than through concepts). Conceptual knowing has to do with the world of form. The formless dimension is known through awareness. To put it more accurately: awareness IS the formless dimension (another word for which is spirit).

When I interact with other humans, the same applies. To some extent I may relate to them through mental concepts, but my preference is always to relinquish concepts about who they are, to know them through awareness instead, and thus sense the essence of who they are beyond their history—beyond name and form. Reliance on concepts creates a sense of separation, but with awareness comes the realization of oneness. That is where you feel the sacredness of all life.

Now it is a sad fact that many humans still have no access to that deeper way of knowing. They are imprisoned, so to speak, within their limited conceptual reality, which is conditioned by the past. So Jesus's words "they know not what they do" refer to the lack of that deeper dimension of knowing, where we see ourselves in the other, are aware of the sacredness of all life, the oneness of all things. This is where empathy, compassion, and love arise.

Of the millions of humans who are still trapped in complete identification with conceptual thinking and who have not found access to that deeper and more inclusive sense of knowing that comes with awareness, only a relatively small percentage actually engage in acts of physical violence. All of them, however, tend to manifest conflict, unhappiness, and ongoing negativity in their lives.

One of the world's most famous sculptures, Michelangelo's "Pieta," is in St. Peter's Basilica in Rome (where it is ironically protected by bullet-proof glass). It shows the Virgin Mary holding the dead body of Jesus on her lap in a gesture of infinite tenderness. I see it as a powerful and moving universal image that, like all great art, transcends its original religious and historical context. It is an image of an all-embracing compassion, a compassion that arises from that deeper knowing and includes those who are still unconscious—still confined within their conceptual mental prisons—and who inflict suffering on themselves and others, particularly when their rigid mental concepts are fueled by deep-seated accumulations of emotional negativity (what I call the pain-body). But when mental judgment and emotional negativity are transcended in awareness, in that deeper knowing, we are able to forgive the unforgivable, as the men and women whose experiences you read about in this book were able to do so admirably.

However, this book is not primarily about other people's experiences. It is about you. Master Charles invites you again and again to enter that state of awareness as you read. He invites you to relinquish attachment to the stories that define your identity and to discover a deeper, timeless, and formless identity beyond the content of your mind.

Herein lies the essence of all spirituality.

—Eckhart Tolle, author of *A New Earth*

Acknowledgments

To everyone whose contribution made this book possible, you know who you are. You know that I am grateful.

Special thanks to Will Wilkinson, my collaborator, who has helped render the material user-friendly and compelling, and whose inspiration was invaluable.

"Forgiveness is the fragrance the violet sheds upon the heel that crushes it."[1]

—Mark Twain

Introduction

A good friend had a dream recently where he met an actual genie. The genie did the obvious—offered him three wishes. My friend struggled inside the dream, trying to decide, until a voice whispered to him: "Ask for understanding." He didn't understand. In fact, his confusion woke him up and he lay in bed for a long while, fishing for meaning. Then, in a sudden flash of profound insight, he made the connection. "If I choose understanding for my first wish, then I would know what to ask for with the other two!"

When I heard this, I knew I'd found the perfect introduction for this book because the ability to understand lives at the heart of true forgiveness. And understanding forgiveness resides at the center of fulfilled living.

Most of us don't understand what forgiveness really is. We think it's about coming to terms with injury. "He did that to me and he shouldn't have, but I forgive him." We've all struggled to forgive petty injustices, so it's mind-boggling when we hear about someone else doing it in an extreme circumstance.

In 1995, Azim Khamisa's son Tariqu was murdered in a gang-related incident. Azim chose to forgive and followed a path of compassion, not revenge. He created the Tariqu Khamisa Foundation, has written four books, and now offers public presentations and corporate seminars around the world. His message of forgiveness has reached millions.

The 2006 Amish school shooting in Pennsylvania is another chilling but inspiring example. Gunman Charles Roberts killed five young girls before committing suicide. Here's the *Wikipedia* report on how families of the slain children responded. "An Amish neighbor comforted the Roberts family hours after the shooting and extended forgiveness to them. Amish community members visited and comforted Roberts's widow, parents, and parents-in-law. One Amish man held Roberts's sobbing father in his arms, reportedly for as long as an hour, to comfort him. The Amish have also set up a charitable fund for the family of the shooter ... Marie Roberts (widow of the killer) wrote an open letter to her Amish neighbors thanking them for their forgiveness, grace, and mercy. She wrote, "Your love for our family has helped to provide the healing we so desperately need. Gifts you've given have touched our hearts in a way no words can describe. Your compassion has reached beyond our family, beyond our community, and is changing our world ..."[1]

Mr. Khamisa and the Amish families understood that more hating just compounds the original crime. They refused to do what a killer does. They met hatred with compassion.

In November of 2008 I traveled to India with twenty-four associates on a spiritual retreat. We were in the Oberoi Hotel in Mumbai when terrorists attacked. Four of us were wounded, two were killed, and all of us were under siege for over forty-five hours. When we were rescued by Indian Army SWAT teams and interviewed by the international media, we had our opportunity to do what Azim Khamisa, the Amish families, and many others—largely unreported—have done. Like them, we chose differently. We refused to do as our attackers had done. Instead of speaking in the same language, responding to hate with more hate in return, we compassionately forgave them.

Kia Scherr, who lost her husband and thirteen year-old-daughter in the attack, answered a reporter's question this way: "I don't hate the terrorists. I forgive them. And I recall what Jesus said: 'Father, forgive them, for they know not what they do.' They were brainwashed. They believed what they were doing was right. No, I don't hate them, I have compassion for them." Kia took the lead with us to create a non-profit foundation, One Life Alliance, dedicated to honoring the sacredness of life. She accompanied me back to Mumbai in November, 2010 for a memorial program on the second anniversary of the attack, where she met with President and Michelle Obama.

This book is our story of what happened in Mumbai. It's also a response to the thousands of emails and phone calls that flooded in from family, friends, and strangers all over the world who watched the news coverage and heard our message of compassion and forgiveness. They asked, "Who are you and how did you get to be the way you are? You have inspired us and we want to understand ... to know how you did that, so we can do it ourselves." Even some of the media recognized that fighting fire with fire has not been working, that escalating violence through retaliation will never bring peace in our world. By now there are millions of us who know that there has to be another way.

In addition to the story, told by nineteen of us who were there, this book offers a comprehensive and detailed presentation of the holistic model of reality and its principles that we live by. Within this, we offer the understanding that true forgiveness has very little to do with being a "good" person and everything to do with waking up from illusion.

The illusion I am speaking of is the illusion of separation. This is the "reality" filled with "others" who are separate and different from you. There are so many ways we profile each other: race, religion, age, social standing, education, and gender. It's not that we aren't different. We are. Such is the great diversity of unity. But we've let our differences separate us in conflict rather than unite us in harmony. Imagine all the parts of your body being at war with each other! Sometimes they scuffle, but for the most part they get along with each other, regardless of how different they are. Little finger and brain cell are radically different from each other, but it all works together because they are all complementary parts of your one body.

All individuals are unique parts of the one human race. We just don't understand and experience ourselves that way. So, when one human being exhibits their uniqueness, it often rubs another individual in the wrong way. Beliefs and prejudices are triggered. Especially when someone does something that hurts you, it's customary to lash out at the person in return and to seek justice. Within that mindset of separate, conflicting individuals, it seems remarkable that a "victim" could express forgiveness instead of blame and anger towards their attacker. But this is misleading, because it accepts the illusion of separation between us as real, and that the best you can do is to be a kind person within that illusion.

This book is about awakening, waking up from a dream of this pervasive illusion of separation. When you do wake up, forgiveness—as you have perceived it—becomes unnecessary. Why? Because the experience of unity, oneness, and wholeness includes compassion for everyone. This is not some admirable human trait. It's the nature of unified consciousness itself and it is automatically experienced by anyone who actually has that holistic experience. But few of us do, and so, in our illusory separateness, it seems idealistic and admirable to be able to forgive. No, that's simply a limiting perspective. The thrilling alternative is to awaken from the illusion of separation and experience compassion for all.

Throughout the pages of this book you will be guided from the illusion of separation into the experience of oneness. Full awakening takes time. It **is** an experience, by the way, not just a theory. We will pause regularly throughout this book for guided experiences that will help your understanding deepen. For instance, right now, take a moment to pause and embrace this new understanding of compassionate forgiveness. Slow your reading, become aware of your breathing, notice your heart beating ... experience yourself being fully alive in this moment and sense the significance of the journey that is opening before you. From separation to oneness, what an invitation! Wait. Wait. Right here ... and right now ... between these words ... enjoy the spaces out of which they arise. Words ... spaces ... balance ... wholeness ... welcome to the fullness of this moment and the experience of life truthfully lived.

We will be unraveling the illusion of separation together. I advocate meditation as a primary tool for becoming increasingly familiar with the unified, holistic state of experience, and I will introduce you to the benefits of what I call "High-Tech Meditation." But what about later? For instance, when you get a parking ticket? Can you include the meter maid in that holistic understanding? Who do you choose to be in relation to her and that experience, any experience, throughout your day?

Can you accept the totality of what is happening, just as it is? If you can't, there's an obstacle in the way and it's always this illusion of separation, a delusion in your own mind. When Socrates wrote, "The unexamined life is not worth living,"[2] he could have just as easily referred to the unexamined mind. Most people blindly accept their thoughts and beliefs without question. They do not question their thinking to see if it is genuinely truthful. I will be inviting you to examine everything as you read. In fact, you're going to learn how to empty your mind of all those illusory stories that have given your life meaning in separation. When you are empty, the illusion gives way to truthful reality and there is nothing in the way of experiencing the unity of consciousness. You become able to include everyone and everything, all the time. All is indeed one, not as a nice theory, but as your actual experience.

Years ago a friend told me a story about an odd incident that occurred when she was in her twenties. It's a very down-to-earth example of what I'm introducing here. She told me: "I was renting a house with friends. One day, Jane came storming out of the bathroom and started shouting at Suzanne, accusing her of not cleaning the bathtub the night before. Suzanne just got up and cleaned the tub. I don't think she even said anything. A few days later we all found out that another one of our housemates had been the culprit. Jane was really embarrassed and apologized to Suzanne for wrongly accusing her. But Suzanne just shrugged and said something like, 'Well, the tub was dirty and I had the time so I cleaned it.'"

Suzanne understood that "the truth" of the situation was less important than just doing what was needed. She seized the opportunity to do the obvious. In the process, she demonstrated another truth about forgiveness that we will be exploring, which is to be "for giving."

Lost in the illusion of separation, we are takers. Awakening to the reality of unified consciousness, we become givers. When some circumstance presents itself, we don't analyze it for "fairness," we just give whatever we can. Shifting from the identity of an illusory taker to a truthful giver is another way of describing the process of awakening, and that is what is offered in this book.

Awakening. Awakening to experience a dramatically new way of living. That's what happens when any individual actualizes what we call the Holistic Model into a Holistic Lifestyle. This becomes Modern Spirituality in experience and is precisely why we created the Synchronicity Foundation for Modern Spirituality and established our own holistic lifestyle here in Virginia in 1983. We have validated the holistic model of reality in our own lifestyle practice for over 30 years now. While thousands of students have learned and benefited, this book broadcasts the message further, out into a world populated by millions who hunger for experience, not theories. They want the real thing for themselves, not just a description of it. They want something that will change their lives.

Great numbers have sought out masters in all times and all cultures. Those teachers with a substantial, holistic, amplitude of power draw all that they need to them, including students to teach, resources to expand the teaching, and colleagues to work with. Everything magically comes to such a person, including miracles. I feel blessed to have that experience, and to now be presenting our time-tested materials in a way that doesn't require everyone to come to my door in person. That would be prohibitive!

Instead, I present myself through these words, on our website, and in our products and programs. And I am not alone. My Mumbai colleagues stand with me. We speak with one voice throughout these chapters, welcoming you on a journey of evolution in consciousness.

What you are about to undertake is a page-by-page expansion of your own holistic awareness, steadily increasing your experience of what you have always known in essence, that you are one with everyone and everything. This is, of course, already true and you already know it, somewhere deep within yourself. In fact, you have always known it. All that will change is your conscious experience of this eternal truth. As that increases, your life will reflect the understanding back to you as a dramatically enriched day-to-day fulfillment. You will discover yourself being happy for no reason at all and handling daily challenges, not as a "victim in waiting," but as the master of a life holistically and compassionately lived.

PART I

The Principles of the Holistic Model

CHAPTER 1

An Experience
Whose Time Has Come

*"When the heart weeps for what is lost,
the spirit laughs for what it has found."*[1]

—Sufi Aphorism

Saturday, November 22

Ten young men board a small boat in Karachi, Pakistan. They travel 500 miles south to Mumbai, India. Each carries guns, ammunition, grenades, a bomb, and a cell phone. On November 26 they reach their destination. Two of them head for the Oberoi Hotel.

9:00 P.M., November 26

Twenty-four spiritual pilgrims return to the Oberoi after a public meditation session with their teacher, Master Charles Cannon, from the Synchronicity Foundation for Modern Spirituality in Virginia. Some go to their rooms; some go to the Tiffin Restaurant in the hotel for a late dinner.

Around 9:30 P.M. the diners hear a crash, what one later speculates might be a large crystal chandelier smashing to the floor.

Moments later the shooting begins.

Be wakeful.
Be aware.
Consciousness creates itself newly in each moment.
Each experience is an experience
whose time has come.
Our experience—here and now—
is the experience whose time has come.

❧❧❧

KIA:

When the trip to Mumbai, India with the Synchronicity group was being planned, I naturally thought that it would be exciting to go with my husband Alan and my daughter Naomi. But as the trip got closer, I realized that I had responsibilities here at home and it felt more appropriate to have some time to myself. Then my two sons in Tampa, Florida invited me for Thanksgiving.

So, instead of accompanying my husband and my daughter to India, I found myself driving them to Dulles Airport in Washington. There was a real sense of excitement. This was Naomi's first plane trip and the longest time she would be away from home. I knew she was in good hands with her father and the nurturing support of Master Charles and the group from Synchronicity that they were traveling with. Naomi was way beyond excited about all the new experiences that lay ahead.

We left our car in the parking garage maze at the airport and walked around for a while before they had to go through security. I remember feeling a bit distracted and concerned about finding the car and navigating through that maze to get home. Then it was time, so we put our arms around each other in a big three-way hug and said goodbye.

On the drive home I stopped for lunch at a Chinese restaurant that we had all been to before. It felt strange to sit at the table by myself this time. As usual, the fortune cookie was delivered along with the check. I have always enjoyed those silly little messages in fortune cookies, but this one surprised me. It said, "Today your luck has changed forever."

అహి అహి అహి

"The spring we're looking for
is somewhere in this murkiness." [2]

—Rumi

Finding and reading this book is an experience whose time has come for you. You may not understand this, but it doesn't matter. This is the evolutionary moment in your consciousness and it's like a snowball rolling down the hill. You can analyze it, understand it or not, but it keeps on rolling. Your consciousness keeps on evolving.

You can have no experience before it's time. So, relax. You couldn't be more on schedule if you tried. This book and the experiences you will have reading it are coming to you at the perfect time in your life.

Reading this book will be like traveling between check points of awakening, to create a consistently more enlightening experience. There are words and spaces between the words. There are letters and spaces between the letters. I encourage you to pause as you read ... pause to experience. Slow down ... be wakeful ... breathe and be aware. We are here and it is now.

This is very different than grasping for intellectual understanding, then hurrying on, without anything really significant moving within you. There is nothing more important in this book than the words and the spaces before you in this moment. What you seek is not in chapter seven. Savor these words, in this very moment. Experience this enlightening moment by surrendering your desire to become enlightened.

Experience Comes First

Most books explain things. Some also tell you how to apply what you learn in daily life, to gain what you do not have. This book is different. Experience comes first; concepts follow. Yes, this means that you can experience what you long for as you read, rather than waiting until later. This is that kind of book.

This book is a map to Now. The simple truth is that reality is only ever reality here and now. And this moment of your reading is the same moment when I wrote these words.

Be still and know.

Stay with us. Don't sink to the bottom
like a fish going to sleep.
Be with the ocean moving steadily all night,
not scattered like a rainstorm.
The spring we're looking for
is somewhere in this murkiness.
See the night-lights up there traveling together,
the candle awake in its gold dish.
Don't slide into the cracks of ground like spilled mercury.
When the full moon comes out, look around.[3]

—Rumi

Beginning Where I Am

My daily experience of reality is this: I experience blissful consciousness, not as a concept, not thinking the thought, but having the experience without the thought. I enjoy a constant holistic energetic reverberation within the whole of my being. For me, being human means being aware of myself as a blissful, pulsing field of energy. I am this energy, conscious of itself. I am aware within the center of this energetic field that radiates through every aspect of my multi-dimensional consciousness, outward into infinity. From the center of who I am, consciousness permeates everything that I perceive ... and creates my world. I experience my world as it truly is: a vibrating, fluxing, holistic energy field.

This makes driving a challenge! Fortunately, others drive for me. I've learned to walk slowly, to avoid bumping into things. When I am with someone, I see their physical form, the energy field that surrounds them, and I also see deep within their soul, through to the center of their individuated consciousness. The other person is just like me; they are a vibrating field of energy and they are beautiful.

I am talking about you now. You also are a vibrating field of energy. ... And you are beautiful.

Everything I see is vibrating. Everything is sparkling and scintillating, as if charged with tiny diamond light particles within a rosy blue hue. When I focus, I can watch those particles moving and dancing. I've seen them for years; they move like random electrons within the energy field of consciousness, ecstatic, billions of them ... dancing. This is life, existence joyously delighting in itself.

No Escape

When I sleep, I let go of the physical, emotional, and mental levels of awareness to absorb my consciousness into more subtle levels. I generally remain this way for three hours or so, in what most people would call deep sleep. Then I become wakeful again and shift into lucid sleep, more like a meditation, surfing the subtlest dimensions of reality.

Sleep is a long meditation, rather than an escape from reality. In fact, during sleep, I actually increase my awareness of myself as formless consciousness. When I wake up in the morning, I simply put on my body and return to the denser dimensional aspects of daily life.

What I am describing is mystical experience and it has become my norm. It was not always so, but I am now able to sustain this through many of the usual activities that most of us have every day. Of course, the Mumbai terrorist attack was hardly a usual experience! It was a life and death challenge that the twenty-five of us faced. Our ability to handle it the way we did, remaining peacefully present while under siege for over forty-five hours, and expressing compassion towards our attackers rather than hatred, was not because of something extraordinary that we did during that time. We simply brought our "normal" state of being into this radically abnormal circumstance and maintained it.

Developing the ability to do that for yourself is what this book is about.

Accessing the Downloads

When you experience the mystical, spiritual level of human experience over time and become accustomed to it, you learn to pay attention to the "downloads," that is, to insights and information that you intuitively access. This requires a still mind. If you are fragmented and distracted, subtle dimensions are not dominant in your awareness. A mystic has a whole, rather than fragmented, experience and is therefore able to "tune in." Since none of us were resisting the experience we were having in Mumbai, this allowed us to sense and perceive in unusual ways. As you will discover, this holistic awareness proved to be literally life saving.

Not only were we accepting the validity of this experience, we were actively expanding our awareness, in order to participate as fully as possible in the extraordinary experience that was unfolding. Why were we there? Why were four of us wounded and two of us killed while the rest avoided injury and death in a variety of unlikely ways?

From a non-spiritual perspective, onlookers lamented, "Isn't it awful? Isn't it terrible what's happening to these people?" But, from our spiritual perspective we were simply participating in an experience whose time had come. Our soulular history had led us to this, and we were genuinely curious to discover how best to participate in the unfoldment of our destiny together. Not that there wasn't fear, even terror. Certainly, that's the natural, primal human reaction, impossible to avoid. But it didn't control us. This freed us to become aware of what to do and not do moment by moment (as if we had all been granted that first wish of understanding by the genie I mentioned in my introduction)—not just so that we could survive, but so that we could fulfill our destiny. For some, this meant that we lived (relatively free of post-traumatic stress, incidentally). For some, it meant being shot. And two of us died.

This was an experience whose time had come; otherwise it wouldn't have come. No blame, no judgment, no victims, no evil-doers to punish. Just a witnessing consciousness watching the experience that was happening.

Introducing the Holistic Lifestyle

This is a lifestyle, not a belief system.

What we call the "Holistic Lifestyle" is based on the principle of balance, which we will discuss throughout this book. In its simplest application, we learn to balance our physical, mental, and emotional experiences throughout the day. There are techniques for doing this, and they all emerge from a consciousness that is present, aware, focused here and now. I call them "Technologies of Now."

While many of us understand the practicality of maintaining balance, for instance, the pH level in our body, mental clarity, and emotional stability, our culture increasingly celebrates excess. Extreme behavior is rewarded with fame and fortune. Consider what fills the airwaves via mainstream media. Not much news about balance!

As vital as it may be, achieving a semblance of balance within the fragmented, illusory state of human experience is **not** the entirety of the awakening adventure this book maps. Losing weight, getting a pro-motion, and solving your relationship issues are all important. But they are secondary results that can arise from adopting the Holistic Lifestyle and culturing a spiritual experience for yourself. This, when put first and foremost, allows you to fulfill your evolutionary destiny. I hold this as less of a destination than a journey. Instead of seeking to become enlightened, you can learn how to enjoy the enlightening experience of any moment.

This reminds me of a story about a young monk who asked his Mas-ter, "If I meditate for two hours every day, how long will it take me to become enlightened?"

"Five years," replied the teacher.

"And if I meditated for four hours every day?" pressed the eager student.

"Ten years," came the cryptic reply.

Relax. You couldn't be more on schedule if you tried! That applies to every one of us. We are all walking exactly where our feet are, hav-ing the experiences we are meant to have. Consciousness is precisely orchestrating the show. If you are reading this book, and you continue reading it, you are ready for it. Otherwise it wouldn't be happening. When the student is ready, the teacher appears.

Guidance for Your Journey

"My friend, before you wander in Love's street,
Do not forget to take with you a guide
So perilous for your undirected feet
The twists and turns once you are inside."[4]

—Hafiz, from *Before You Wander in Love's Street*

My spiritual teacher was Paramahansa Muktananda. He was one of the most well known of the twentieth century Indian masters because his enlightening state of being was so radically powerful. He awakened thousands, like a Johnny Appleseed of awakening, all across the world. No other master had ever moved out of India to do what he did, not before or since.

I could have gone to an Indian university, but without a master to model the awakened state, my studies would have remained conceptual. This is true in all fields. If you wish to learn anything, it helps to study with a relevant master, whether for cooking, golf, music, spirituality, or other interests.

Based on a lifetime of study and experience, I teach modern spirituality, which can be described in both philosophical and scientific terms. The philosophy articulates holistic models of reality which have been in consensus since the Age of Idealism (although remaining primarily at the academic level until relatively recently). Quantum science explores the totality of reality from subtle to dense dimensions. According to Andrew Zimmerman Jones, the author of *String Theory for Dummies*, "... The many worlds interpretation concludes that there must exist two universes: one in which the particle decayed and one in which it did not. The universe therefore branches off each and every time that a quantum event takes place, creating an infinite number of quantum universes."[5] Throughout the book I will refer to this phenomenon as "the fifty billion theoretical simultaneous universes," just for the sake of round numbers and because it is easier to grasp than "an infinite number of quantum universes."

The roots of human philosophy and the oldest holistic model of reality can be traced back eight to ten thousand years to the origins of the Veda and the Tantra. Both are vast holistic philosophical systems that thoroughly delineate the nature of reality. My Indian teacher taught an update of the original Tantra system called "Kashmir Shavism," which was developed during the ninth to eleventh centuries by the Indian sage Vasugupta Acharya. His seminal work was the *Shiva Sutras*, a revelation of forty-five aphorisms.

The first Sutra in Sanskrit is Chaitanyam Atma, which means "I am consciousness." The second is Jnanam Bandaha, which means "knowledge is bondage." In essence, these two say: "I am consciousness ... one and whole ... until I start thinking about it!"

The Birth of Relative Reality (or, You Are Here)

All holistic models of reality point to that which is beyond experience, that which you cannot know. Gnostics called it The Ultimate Mystery. In Buddhism, it's referred to as The Void, The Pregnant Void. All possibility emerges from this Pregnant Void, this Ultimate Mystery. This is consciousness with its primary intention to fully be itself, to know itself, to experience itself.

But all experience is, by its very nature, relative. To know light, there must be darkness. To know heat, there must be cold. For there to be an "inner," there must be an "outer." So, out of this Ultimate Mystery—where all is eternally One—emerges the seeming duality of the relative field: formlessness and form. Spanda is the Sanskrit word used to describe the initial "flashing forth," the phenomenon science calls "The Big Bang" when this cosmic, relative field initially manifested. This was the origin of relative reality: anti matter and matter, formlessness and form, being and becoming.

And what caused this Big Bang? Intention in consciousness. The primary intention was for consciousness to fully be itself, know itself, and experience itself. The nature of this reality is known in Sanskrit as Satchitananda. "Sat" means that which is eternally existing, free and independent unto itself; "chit" means the awareness of itself existing (or consciousness); and "ananda" means bliss, its innate delight in being. This also describes the nature of holistic reality and the experience of the Holistic Lifestyle.

Obviously, in order to fully be itself, consciousness must fully experience itself. To make this possible, consciousness created this relative field (where we are right now)—a place for all experience to occur. I call this the Creation Game, and it is referred to in the Tantra as Chitshakti Vilas, "the Play of Consciousness."

What Goes Down Must Come Up

Relative reality emerges from the Void. The One becomes the seeming two, wholeness becomes fragmentation, light becomes dark, subtle becomes dense, truth becomes illusion. And consciousness begins to fulfill its primary intention: to experience what it is not, by contracting energy into matter throughout the fifty billion theoretical simultaneous universes and all the life forms involved (including us). The more it contracts, the more it forfeits and limits its self-awareness. (We forget who we are.) This contraction in consciousness or descent is the "involutionary cycle" and once it is fully experienced we shift and ascend or expand in the "evolutionary cycle."

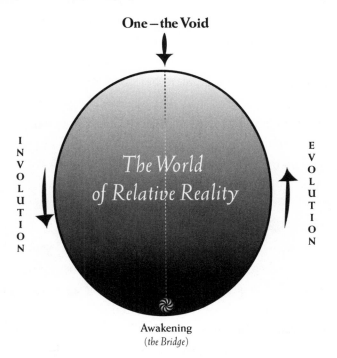

One – the Void

I
N
V
O
L
U
T
I
O
N

The World of Relative Reality

E
V
O
L
U
T
I
O
N

Awakening
(*the Bridge*)

If you are reading this book, you have traversed this downward path of illusion. You have experienced what you are not and you are beginning to experience what you are. Self-awareness has already increased, and you are probably standing on the bridge between involution and evolution.

As you continue to shift from involution to evolution, fragmentation to wholeness, from illusion to truth, you bring your history and your attachments with you. This can sabotage your continuing evolution and frustrate your enlightening experience. So, you need guidance. You need the guidance of someone who has experienced the ascending path and knows that terrain. The holistic guide is like an older brother or sister who is farther down this road and can help you with the parts of the journey that are especially challenging and frightening.

This is no small matter! Your reality is changing; your identity is shifting … and you don't actually understand all of what is happening. This means that you will tend to judge some experiences that come to you as being wrong. "This shouldn't be happening to me!" "This should be other than the way it is!" Really? Here is a moment when your guide can help you learn differently! Just as with anything in life that you are learning, a teacher is helpful. When the student is ready, the teacher appears; you can have no experience before its time.

Mumbai was a teacher for us. Because we accepted the experience, we learned from it and evolved through it. Every member of our party would say without hesitation that they have expanded their awareness and evolved their consciousness because of their experience during that terrorist attack.

The Role of the Ego

I think the ego gets a bad rap. Let's look at it from the perspective of the consciousness that created it. If consciousness created it, it must have some purpose. After all, consciousness created the theoretical fifty billion theoretical simultaneous universes. Would the ego be its first mistake?

The primary intention in consciousness is to fully be itself. In order to be itself, it must experience itself. Therefore it created the relative field where all experience is relative … light and dark, truth and illusion, and so on. In order to experience what it is, it must first experience what it is not. Here is a conundrum indeed! How can it experience what it is not, if in truth it is already all and everything? There isn't anything that it is not! For this reason consciousness must come up with some sort of clever strategy through which it can experience what it is not. That strategy is illusion, and the primary illusion of consciousness is the illusion of separation. The subject (me) becomes different from the object (for instance: you, that chair, the opposing team, a different religion or political party). In this relative reality then, I am the perceiving subject, separate and different from all the others/objects that I perceive.

The ego (your separate identity) is the instrument of illusion and, as such, is totally appropriate within the involutionary cycle. The ego is necessary. It gets you through to the bridge that connects with the evolutionary cycle and the reversal of polarized dominance from illusion to truth. But from the bridge upward, from that awakening onward, the dissolution of the ego is inevitable. After that turning point it is no longer needed, and it is progressively phased out by consciousness. Increasing wholeness disempowers illusion. This means that the more whole you become, the more you experience the Holistic Lifestyle, the more your ego is diminished and the more you shift from the experience of what you are not (in illusion) to the discovery of who you really are (in truth).

This shift and discovery requires that you utilize the ego throughout the whole of the involutionary cycle, until you finally realize that this illusion is not fulfilling. There is something lacking. There must be more than this misery, this oscillation between happiness and suffering. Remember back to when you thought you were content with your life? The career, the entertainment, the family, the toys, all the peak experiences. They were enough. But, you continued to grow through those experiences (and the ego helped you). Now you have arrived at a point where all that just doesn't do it for you anymore. Life is no longer a consistently fulfilling experience. If it were, you would have no interest in this book.

You have reached the bridge.

The ego's only purpose is relative to illusory experience. When illusion is disempowered enough by truth, the ego dissipates, leaving an individuated consciousness expressing itself as whole. Your ego was a fraudulent identity, separate, all along, but necessarily so. When trans-egocentric consciousness develops there is no longer any separation and no further need for the ego.

The moment there is detachment from ego identification, there is an automatic expansion of holistic awareness. This arises from balance. Wholeness, proportional to balance, disempowers the ego as it develops wakefulness. The more balanced you are, the more wakeful you are, the more wholeness you experience, and the more you disidentify with egoic illusions.

The ego has its place, but its days are numbered.

The Learning Process

Those of us in Mumbai brought years of spiritual experience to focus in order to deal with that extreme circumstance. In particular, we used our ability to embrace and integrate peak experiences. That term is usually assigned to pleasurable activities but, believe me, Mumbai was a peak experience!

All of us are familiar with the hangover that often follows some sort of high. On the personal growth path, we've encountered the seminar junkies, those who gobble up one peak learning experience after another but gain no lasting positive change. This is a processing and integration problem. I use and teach a five-fold model that progresses from peak experiences through evolution, illumination, and processing to integration.

Peak experiences are often highly enjoyable. An intensified frequency of vibration impacts you and endorphins flood your body, producing a deeply pleasurable experience. But any peak experience left unprocessed becomes a cliff to fall over. The high must be transitioned into its next natural stage which is evolution. You have become more than you were. Suddenly you are on the cutting edge of your own evolution and this is what creates the momentum for lasting change—if you keep going.

Illumination follows, a further expansion of self-awareness and the downloading of creative insights relating to your peak experience. Every time your consciousness moves to a new peak on the cutting edge of its evolution, it alters its frequency of vibration. This change in frequency then ripples through the whole of your multi-dimensional consciousness and confronts any data that is stored therein, in order to adjust it to the new frequency that has just been introduced. Any old data that is incongruent or disharmonic to the new frequency must be eliminated. If it isn't, dissonance results and eventually the old frequency will reassert itself to cancel out the new one. This explains why New Year's resolutions, made during a peak experience moment, often fail very quickly.

Processing is required. Your consciousness focuses on what it must eliminate. This diminishes the peak sensation, which explains why we prefer peak experiences to processing! But, once it has fully processed (and you can learn how to do that efficiently and swiftly) the pleasure returns to sustain itself at a heightened level. You have now integrated the peak experience and established a new "base line" or default setting for your evolving consciousness.

In fact, integration means that you have substantiated a new level of personal evolution. The intensified frequency of vibration that has rippled through the totality of your multi-dimensional consciousness has eliminated anything that was incongruent with it, and what remains has progressed to an integrated status. You have developed a new level of stability that you can enjoy until the next peak experience arises.

Mumbai was indeed a peak experience! And we processed it exactly the same way we have learned to process every other peak experience. Because of that, the experience has proven to be a positive one, in the long term. We have grown, evolved, and integrated the peak into a new level of expanded holistic awareness that, because of the nature of this particular experience, includes more love, compassion, and forgiveness.

This helps to explain what the press failed to understand when they asked us how we felt about the terrorists and we compassionately replied that we did not hate them and had no interest in revenge or punishment. To have responded in any other way would have been inauthentic for us and would have lowered our frequency of vibration—a giant step backwards.

The Intensity of Light and Dark

During the attack, we heard that a nearby guru declared it was no accident we were there, captives in the hotel. "They are there to hold the light," he said. It's true. As the hours progressed and we continued to process our experiences without judgment, our holistic awareness expanded and our consciousness radiated, increasing peace. In fact, the hotel room I shared with two others who just "happened to be there" when the assault began, filled with light. As the attack intensified, so did our spiritual experience.

My spiritual journey began with a peak experience at age three when I awoke to see an apparition of The Blessed Mother. I have been blessed to commune with Her all my life and she was with me during the siege, Her face appearing many times, and Her presence consistently with me.

It's quite an experience, something like a time-warp where everything slows down. Suddenly, I am peering down a tunnel and everything seems suspended, radically expanded and absolutely clear. From this lucid "place" the apparition emerges, coming through space-time and the dimensionality of consciousness, hallowed and ethereal, and so impactful that I feel it in every cell of my being. She brings a saturating peace, intoxicating and euphoric. When someone talks about rapture and bliss, this is it! Not some time later ... right now!

There are many examples throughout history where universal consciousness has assumed a subtle form and interacted with human beings. We know of this from stories about Moses, Ramakrishna, St. Francis, Bernadette of Lourdes, Shiva, Mother Mary, and many others. And it happens for us mere mortals as well.

One student described an encounter with his master: "All at once the roshi, the room, every single thing, disappeared in a dazzling stream of illumination. I felt myself bathed in a delicious unspeakable delight. For a fleeting eternity I was alone. I alone, was."

Who Are You Really?

Imagine closing your eyes for a moment. The world instantly disappears. You are left with your thoughts, bodily sensations, and feelings. Is this who you are? Or, are you something more? Awake, asleep, or dreaming, who is watching the experience that is happening? To truly understand who you are, you must begin with a truthful perception of reality, which is what we have introduced in this first chapter. Since most people do not have anything remotely approaching that, most people have little idea of who they truly are. They may struggle to discover some sort of identity, but to attempt that before learning about truthful reality leads only to a thousand dead ends populated by a thousand ego substitutes.

A truthful perception of reality is only accessible in the present, the "here and now" moment. Most individuals, most of the time, are ***not*** here and now. Why? Primarily because of the mind and its incessant judgments that what is happening should somehow be other than it is. As a result, they are not fully experiencing the **reality** of the uninterrupted present moment just as it is. If they were, the gateway to a truthful perception of reality would open and they would instantly know who they are, not as a belief but as an experience.

This is the opportunity that we had in Mumbai: to be fully present for a peak learning experience, to process and integrate it into an expanded sense of self. This is also the opportunity that opens before you now in the pages ahead, to develop a truthful perception of reality through the experience of being fully here and now in the moments you are reading.

Remember the words and the spaces between the words. Slow down, breathe, and be aware. The words are consciousness, the spaces are consciousness, you are consciousness. All and everything is consciousness.

There is only one. Be wakeful and present ... within the here and now of truthful reality ... and enjoy this experience whose time has come for you.

❧❧❧

LINDA:

I was totally puzzled about what to take to India so it took me a long, long time to pack. Then, ironically, the airline lost all my luggage! So I bought myself three outfits from a local shop and, as it turned out, this was all I really needed. Even after my luggage finally arrived, I stayed in my new clothes. I discovered that all I really need to bring anywhere is me!

❧❧❧

To better integrate the meaning of this chapter, please visit www.synchronicity.org, go to the "Forgiving the Unforgivable" section, and use the password "one" to access additional material.

CHAPTER 2

The Seeds of Transformation

"The fact that modern physics,
the manifestation of an extreme specialization
of the rational mind,
is now making contact with mysticism,
the essence of religion and
manifestation of an extreme specialization of the
intuitive mind, shows very beautifully the unity
and complementary nature of the rational
and intuitive modes of consciousness;
of the yang and the yin." [1]

—Fritjof Capra

November 26, 2008, 10:05 P.M.

Patty and Bonnie look up from their plates. Their eyes meet and a knowing glance confirms that they both intuitively know something.

"Joe, let's go, now!" They quickly pay the tab and urge their elderly dinner companion to complete his goodbyes. Reluctantly, he mobilizes his walker and trails after them to the elevator.

Bonnie exits on the 11th floor, Patty exits with Joe on the 12th floor. As they shuffle down the hallway, sudden gunfire explodes behind them and screams begin echoing up the open atrium.

If not now, when?
If not you, who?
You have never been here before,
you have never had this experience before,
and you never will again.
Merge your individual consciousness
with universal consciousness
to receive the guidance you need.

కొంకొంకొం

BEN:

I was very excited about flying to India. Even though I had been in a very serious plane crash when I was eight and had suffered some mild post-traumatic stress ever since, flying has never bothered me. I am not afraid of death but being surprised, or attacked, being inflicted with pain ... that is what scares me.

HELEN:

As the departure date for the trip drew near I wondered who I would be rooming with in India. An answer came during meditation: "Naomi."

"Oh good," I thought. "That'll be fun." I already loved Naomi, from previous retreats I'd spent with her and her parents Alan and Kia at the Synchronicity Sanctuary. I knew her youthful presence would keep me from missing my own two young adult children. Naomi had many of the same interests as my kids, plus she had grown up in a meditative environment. I knew that she would be a respectful and enjoyable roommate. A short time later, a Synchronicity email arrived, asking if anyone would like to room with Naomi. Of course, I replied immediately, "Yes!"

This proved to be a great decision. Naomi was young, just thirteen, but wise beyond her years. We got along together effortlessly, sharing scarves and make-up, music, favorite films, meditative insights and Indian sweets. She said I reminded her of her mom, that we were similar in temperament.

What love she and her dad Alan had for each other. It was a joy and an inspiration to behold! I felt blessed to be a 'surrogate' part of their family during our India adventure.

BERNIE:

At the end of one busy day visiting temples we returned to the hotel and instead of going up to my room, I detoured into a delightful essential oil shop within the hotel called Shama Plaza. The owners, Sabeena and Yunus, sold many unique blends of oils and a product called Oudh bark, which you saturate in oil and burn like incense.

A few moments after I got there, Alan arrived and we smelled the varieties of Oudh bark together. He mentioned that one particular scent took him back to the memory of an old, musty temple. He had an odd far off look in his eyes as he spoke. That would make sense to me later.

MUREEN:

Alan had been my mentor for a number of years and we had developed an easy friendship but during this trip he seemed distant in some way. I remember thinking: "Is he leaving?" and then wondering what exactly would he be leaving ... Synchronicity Foundation maybe? That seemed totally unlikely.

That last day on our bus trip to Swami Vishveshwarananda's ashram, Alan suggested that I buy some Tulsi beads. He looked right in my eyes and said that he thought they would be good for me. "They're made from the root of the Holy Basil Plant," he said. So, I bought them and showed Alan on the return bus trip. I thought about going back to where he was sitting to talk a little more, but I didn't. I wish now that I had.

I always think of Alan whenever I touch those beads.

HELEN:

The daily meditation program with Master Charles in Mumbai was always in the early evening and Alan, Naomi, and I usually returned to the Oberoi Hotel together in a taxi. But on that particular evening Alan suggested we walk, to better integrate our meditation. So, we walked and talked ... and got lost. This was very easy to do on the streets of Mumbai.

It was a typically hot, humid evening and we were very thirsty and tired by the time we finally found our way back to the hotel. Naomi was craving asparagus sushi, her favorite, so the two of us headed straight for the Tiffin restaurant while Alan went upstairs to discuss scheduling with Master Charles. Alan joined us all later for ice cream.

MASTER CHARLES:

By 9:30 p.m. that evening, I had finished dinner in my suite. My personal assistant Ben was with me, along with my dear friend Steve, a yoga teacher from California who had also been a Muktananda disciple. Alan visited us briefly, then joined his daughter Naomi and several others who were dining in the Tiffin restaurant a few floors below and just off the lobby.

The Oberoi is a five-star hotel now, but I had been there almost thirty years before with Muktananda. At that point in his life, Muktananda rarely traveled, even within India. But this was a very special occasion. One of the trustees of his ashram, a very wealthy contributor to his mission, had a son who was getting married. Muktananda was their family guru and therefore he agreed to attend his wedding at the Oberoi Hotel.

I well remember how they honored Muktananda on that special occasion. They built a flower temple, about ten feet tall and six feet wide, and filled it with varieties of beautiful, fragrant flowers. Muktananda was seated in this flower temple and all the wedding guests came to receive his blessing before they greeted the bride, groom and family members. Muktananda's radiant presence transformed the whole place.

I reflected on that memory as I began the last evening meditation program in a venue about ten minutes from the Oberoi Hotel. That evening I saw the Blessed Mother, as I often do in my meditations. On this occasion, She stood in an open doorway for a moment, then retreated back through the door and closed it. Instantly, I understood that something significant was about to unfold. I also knew that I could not know what it was in advance. I sensed darkness, a warning, and thought, "Whatever is coming, this is going to be intense."

After the meditation program, a local Indian woman approached me with a puzzled look on her face. "I saw your master in the meditation but I didn't know who he was until I asked him," she said. "He spoke his name in our native language. I asked him, 'Why are you here?' He put his hand on your shoulder and said, 'I've come to be with him at this very special time."

A few minutes later Miriam, one of the Australians in our party, approached me to say that she had also had a vision of Muktananda standing next to me. Moments later another Indian woman walked towards me with a puzzled look on her face. She reported that she had also seen Muktananda in her meditation, standing next to me with his hand on my shoulder. Three people, independent of each other, had exactly the same vision. I sensed my teacher's powerful presence and heard him silently say, "It is close, very close now."

As I left the venue, my awareness expanded. I felt the shift. I knew that something unusual was about to occur.

৵৵৵

Awakening from the Dream

"Insanity: doing the same thing over and over again
and expecting different results." [2]

—Albert Einstein

In our culture, we define insanity as being out of touch with reality. According to the description of relative reality in chapter one, then, most people **are** insane. In fact, our world is an insane asylum where we have become our own jailers. Do you think that is too harsh? Well, who feels genuinely free? Who knows who they are and who is living with delight and fulfillment, 24/7, no matter what the challenges? Who wants to awaken from this dream? If you do, the most important question to ask yourself is, "How can I learn to live with a constant awareness of who I really am, here in the middle of an insane world and surrounded by voluntary 'inmates'?" That's a very different approach from trying to fix this crazy world! As Gandhi said, "Be the change you wish to see in the world."

All of us need help with this. Yet especially here in the West we invalidate the very thing that could help us the most—a skilled mentor. We have "authority phobia" and most Westerners find it very challenging to actually value a spiritual teacher or, worse yet, a "master." The very word evokes images of slavery.

Because of this we create substitutes. Instead of wise mentoring, which could increase our understanding and lead to a fulfilled life, we become addicted to whatever can give us a quick fix. There's a long list of these "silver bullets," including money, obsessive work, sex, sports and watching sports, power over others, alcohol and drugs.

Many of us who showed up at Muktananda's ashram in the seventies had already rejected that world. We were bona fide flower children. We traveled overland through Pakistan and Iran and arrived with our drug stashes! But Muktananda told us that if we wanted to get **really** high he would show us how to get high on life rather than drugs. And he certainly succeeded at that! He was a wonderful teacher.

There are rare occasions when no master is required, when a particular soul is born so highly evolved that he or she doesn't require one. In a sense, you might say that they are evolved enough to be their own master. But even these special individuals have teachers along the way, as the Buddha did. My own teacher's teacher was one of these. He associated with many masters but was awakened from birth. He was so high in his enlightening, holistic experience that he went beyond all convention and identification. He spoke rarely, and did little. He simply sat, or lay down, and radiated his unified state of being. He was just born that way.

For most of us, awakening fully to holistic experience requires a mentor who is more evolved than we are, someone who can show us the way. In the West we idolize athletes and movie stars. These are our gurus, but what do they model for us? Extraordinary human skills (which we will never have), and egocentric adolescent behavior (which we hopefully have already outgrown). Where is the truthful and practical inspiration in this?

Guru means darkness (gu) and light (ru). An authentic spiritual master guides you from the darkness of illusion to the light of truth. This is not the focus of education in the West, where emphasis is placed on the mind and learning often means memorizing. What about developing your state of being? This is where the guru or mentor is helpful. The guru offers entrainment. He or she transmits a heightened amplitude of holistic power. Just by being in the presence of a true guru you can be transformed and grow. You start vibrating with a whole new frequency which can flood you with peace and bliss. In fact, here is a test of whether or not the teacher is real: If a guru is authentic (for you), you will feel transformed in their enlightening presence.

This holistic entrainment between a teacher and student is a sort of "sympathetic resonance." This occurs when one vibrating body stimulates another to begin vibrating at the same frequency. Picture two guitars that are tuned to the same pitch and sitting side-by-side. When you strum one, the other will begin to vibrate. This is what happens between teacher and student. The teacher is constantly transmitting a unified field and the student is progressively entrained to a similar holistic experience.

The Authentic Master

The qualifications of a genuine master are as follows:

1. He or she must have substantiated the unified state of being in themselves.

2. They must possess a thorough knowledge of the holistic model based on experience and be living it.

3. They must have mastered their ego so they no longer take things personally. The honoring from their students moves through them all the way to Source.

4. They must be true agents of awakening in others.

In the West, gurus often rip off their disciples, engage in secretive sexual relations, or get into prostitution, drugs—you name it. In other words, these supposed spiritual or personal development "masters" offer a perfect reflection of the compulsive ego desires that are lurking (or on display) in ourselves! Here is a true principle: All of us will manifest the teacher that corresponds to our own personal level of evolution. If you are truthful and responsible, you will create that appropriate reflection, a teacher to serve you at your own level of evolution.

I could write much more about this and you could read it and agree or not, but why not have an experience instead? Let's try something right now. Just slow down your reading. Pause ... stop right between words ... Breathe consciously, be aware of your heart beating. Be wakeful of the environment that surrounds you. Still your thoughts. And open a space for this question:

Can you open to the possibility of Source, Universal Consciousness (God) having a relationship with you? This is very different from the idea of you developing a relationship with some teacher or theoretical God that you create in your own image. This is about your surrendering into relationship with the eternal Source of All, present here and now—the reality of that, by whatever name, not the concept—represented to you, for you, by a teacher who shows up *only when you are ready*. When you embrace this reality, you experience Source Consciousness—not as a distant, separate concept—but as the true nature of reality, which includes you, is you, in this present moment.

Can you open to this possibility? Is this an experience whose time has come for you? If so, then you are now receiving the transmission and entrainment that is moving through these words and the spaces between them. This is the moment of your awakening. And, know this: As your progressive evolution unfolds, you will continue drawing to yourself many forms of teaching, each at the perfect time to support your next step in the journey of self discovery.

Muktananda once told a reporter that people perceived him in different ways. For some he was a great guru and for others a fool. "The truth is that I am as you see me," he said. She then asked, "But how do you see yourself?" He replied, "I see myself as I am."

Can you see yourself as you truly are? Probably not. That's why you need a teacher! And here's what you will learn: You are Source Consciousness. You can awaken from the insanity of illusory separation and fragmentation to Be the One who you already and always truly are.

Open to the possibility of Source, Consciousness, God having a relationship with you, right here and right now, and you will instantly see all things newly. You will read with new eyes as this frequency entrains you to experience yourself as you truly are.

"Surrender is to give oneself up to the original cause of one's being.
Do not delude yourself by imagining such a source to be some God
outside you. One's source is within oneself. Give yourself up to it." [3]

—Ramana Maharishi

Joan is one of my long time students, happy to volunteer her experience regarding this subject. "From early childhood I had been beset with a low-grade, chronic depression. But because it was such a habitual way of being, and because I managed to function adequately, nobody—including me—was consciously aware of what was really going on.

"I had been doing Transcendental Meditation for many years when a friend introduced me to Master Charles's music. I was very drawn to it and soon began using his High-Tech Meditation soundtracks. Not long after that, I went to my first retreat at the Synchronicity Sanctuary. Mind you, I did that with some trepidation because I was concerned about possibly being holed up for a week with weird people! But the experience proved delightful and very impactful so I began attending retreats fairly regularly and joined the facilitated mentoring program.

"During one evening retreat Master Charles spoke about experiencing ourselves as Source Consciousness. During the question and answer period, I told him that I did not experience myself as Source. Master Charles knew me quite well because of our mentoring. He immediately told me that my self-image did not match the energetic form that he saw sitting in my chair. He suggested that I seek psychiatric help and perhaps try an anti-depressant so that I could experience a different way of being.

"Now, that was a jolt, totally unexpected! But he said it in such an affirming way that I was able to hear it and so I did exactly what he suggested. It was remarkable. For the first time in my remembered history, I actually began to feel good! It turned out that I didn't need to take the medication for very long; I just needed that little bit of help to show me—experientially—that a different way of being was possible.

"It occurred to me later that people who think all gurus are power-hungry misfits seeking followers for their own ego gratification should pay attention to experiences like this one. Suggesting that a disciple could use psychiatric help is not likely to get that sort of teacher many followers!

"In the several years since that intervention I have continued with the High-Tech Meditation, mentoring, and retreats. I have made rapid gains in my evolution and, despite some hard knocks, I am no longer depressed. I am mostly happy, less fearful of loss, calmer, and more compassionate. My heart is more open. I catch myself quickly now when I judge people, and more often than not I can accept them pretty much the way they are. Life has become an interesting, exciting, and mostly delightful journey."

I was able to help Joan because she had faith in me as her teacher, based on our interactions and her experience that I was genuinely interested in her increased well-being. This allowed me to make a suggestion and it proved helpful. It has led Joan to have greater faith in herself. Faith is one of those loaded words but I like this description from Wilfred Cantwell Smith from *The Meaning and End of Religion*: "Faith, then, is a quality of human living. At its best it has taken the form of serenity and courage and loyalty and service: a quiet confidence and joy which enable one to feel at home in the universe, and to find meaning in the world and in one's own life, a meaning that is profound and ultimate, and is stable no matter what may happen to oneself at the level of immediate event. Men and women of this kind of faith face catastrophe and confusion, affluence and sorrow, unperturbed; face opportunity with conviction and drive; and face others with cheerful charity." 4

East and West

Cultures in the East have evolved further than ours here in the West in terms of the conscious knowing of true meaning. This is what tends to dominate in the East, while here in the West we remain steeped in material illusion. Those in the West who are wealthy with illusion look at those in the East who have a deep knowing of truth and laugh. "How unevolved. They don't even have a refrigerator!" Meanwhile, those with a deeper experience of truth in the East regard Westerners trapped in material illusion and say, "How unevolved. All they have is a refrigerator!"

When someone from the West travels to a country like India, the energy of the country can literally blow them away. Why? Because they find people and a culture that values truth over illusion. Of course, a polar shift is occurring in the twenty-first century. The East is becoming more Western and the West is becoming more Eastern. Those in the East want to be more material while those in the West want more spiritual experience.

In *Stages of Faith*, James W. Fowler writes, "We do not live by bread alone, sex alone, success alone, and certainly not by instinct alone. We require meaning. We need purpose and priorities; we must have some grasp on the big picture[5]. ... Prior to our being religious or irreligious, before we come to think of ourselves as Catholics, Protestants, Jews, or Muslims, we are already engaged with issues of faith. Whether we become nonbelievers, agnostics, or atheists, we are concerned with how to put our lives together and with what will make life worth living. Moreover, we look for something to love that loves us, something to value that gives us value, something to honor and respect that has the power to sustain our being."[6]

Newtonian science maintains that there is nothing beyond the human body and brain. This is known as upward causation. Its mantra could be Descarte's famous quote, "I think, therefore I am." Modern day quantum physics proposes the opposite, known as downward causation. The mantra for downward causation could be: "I am, therefore I think." Everything arises out of consciousness.

Furthermore, the theory of downward causation proposes that consciousness creates itself newly in each moment. This would mean that you are the creator of your individual and collective experience moment by moment. In other words, in this moment your consciousness is creating this reality, the experience you are having reading these words. And, factually, there is no separation between creator and creation.

Quantum physicist Dr. Amit Goswami puts it this way in *God is Not Dead*: "The real questions are these: Why does the world appear to be separate from us? What does the fact that we get lost in the separateness from the universe and from each other do to us and to the human condition? Is there any way to go beyond this dynamic of separation?

"In the new science, we find that the world is here because of us and that we are here because of the world. The separation dynamic is one of mutual creation, our prerequisite for playing in manifestation. When we creatively comprehend this, the separation dynamic loses its hold on us. The story of the universe is our story. When we understand ourselves, our consciousness, we also understand the relationship with the universe and with God, and the separation becomes a portent for play.

"What happens to this sense of manifest play when the separateness is seen as illusory? Are you curious to find out? I hope so. I hope that you are tired of separateness, which has given us the nightmares of terrorism, energy crisis, global warming, and the possibility of nuclear war. I hope you're ready to explore the potential of science within consciousness, as well as the potential of waking up to subtler levels of consciousness. I hope you are ready to appreciate the importance of the scientific rediscovery of God."[7]

The Soul/Quantum Monad

Ancient spiritual traditions refer to every person having or being a soul, complete with all the karma that accumulates through many lifetimes. Quantum mechanics refers to the "evolving quantum monad." By whatever name, this soul/quantum monad accumulates experience through time. Both East and West now propose the same thing, that this entity retains its database beyond death. That is, all the information of everything that has been experienced to date in its continuing evolution is stored within the unconscious database of your individuated consciousness.

At the moment of death, your physical body is dropped, but the quantum monad, the soul with its database, retains all experience and proceeds to interact with universal consciousness (which quantum physics describes as "the field of all possibility") to download those precise possibilities which are self-referential to where your feet are at the moment of death. In simple terms this means that the way you are, the way you have lived, helps determine your future. You will create the perfectly coherent continuation for yourself, in some new form within the fifty billion theoretical simultaneous universes. Of course, it may not be human.

At the moment of death, the physical body is released and your soul (individuated consciousness) interacts with universal consciousness to determine the precise nature of your continuation. Onward you go. Of course, this interaction doesn't only occur at the moment of death; it happens all the time. In fact, any true "aha" moment indicates interaction between individuated and universal consciousness. As you become increasingly whole, you become increasingly aware of this connection, which can grow into constant interaction between individual and universal consciousness, dense and subtle dimensions.

Goswami uses a scientific perspective to describe how your experience is being created newly in each moment, by virtue of the interactions between individual and universal consciousness. The state of your individual consciousness (how evolved you are in any moment of your experience) interacts with the "all possibility field" of universal consciousness and results in the creation of your next specific experience. And the next, and the next, and the next ... This provides another convincing argument against judgment of what's happening in your life!

Karma

In the ancient Eastern systems, you accrue good and bad karma through your choices and behavior and it all plays out in your daily experience. This is one reason why some people tend to be poor while others are rich, for instance. All of us are reaping what we have sown which shows up as tendencies, or patterns. This explains why it makes such good sense to do whatever you can to earn good karma. This helps to create a succession of fulfilling lives.

Karma-wise, everyone is exactly where they are right now. Can you allow them that, without judgment? How do you know what they are reaping, where they are on their evolutionary journey? There are monks who are total renunciates. They possess only the clothes on their backs and they beg for food every day. There are billionaires jetting between continents the way you drive to the corner store. There are gurus, complete with a huge international following and all the wealth one could imagine. There are terrorists killing people in the Oberoi Hotel. Karma.

Karmic law states that for every action there is a correspondent and appropriate reaction, and that whatever you do has repercussions. Every choice you make has implications. You can choose to be loving, you can choose to be angry. You are responsible for all your interactions with others. If you choose negative experience versus positive experience, then that is what you will continue experiencing. That is what will be reflected back to you, over and over again, until you fully get it. It's the same with positive choices and experiences. You are the creator of your reality.

It's an interesting exercise to look back on your life and consider the connection between what you have expressed and what you have experienced. Of course, beyond this lifetime and much farther than you can see or remember, there is your "soulular history." How did you express in previous incarnations? Everything expressed in the past has repercussions into the present and through to the future.

Our Mumbai experience brought us into contact with hateful, fearful, violent individuals who were murdering people. It's impossible, and senseless, to try to figure out what any of us did in past lives to create that! The important question was, "How should we respond in this situation to ensure that it won't happen again?" From this perspective, the fact that we refused to condemn our attackers was really just enlightened self-interest! We were playing the karma game with an understanding of the rules. In the face of hatred, express love, compassion, and forgiveness. This is what changes karma.

What about Alan and Naomi? Here is a deeply spiritual and kind father and his angelic thirteen-year-old daughter. What karma did they pile up to deserve such an inglorious and painful death? Well, that question only makes sense when you are judging. Again, how can we know? Their karma was their karma.

I knew Alan for twenty years. He was one of my best friends. I knew Naomi from the moment she was born. My understanding is that this was an experience whose time had come for them. Why? Because it came! End of story.

Walking Where Your Feet Are

In *The Power of Now,* Eckhart Tolle writes, "As long as you are in this dimension, you are still subject to its cyclical nature and to the law of impermanence of all things, but you no longer perceive this as "bad"— it just is.

"Through allowing the 'isness' of all things, a deeper dimension underneath the play of opposites reveals itself to you as an abiding presence, an unchanging deep stillness, an uncaused joy beyond good and bad. This is the joy of being. The peace of God."[8]

This is an actual experience, not "intellectual enlightenment" where you get a few insights and continue allowing your illusory mind to sustain old beliefs or generate new ones. Of course, if that is where your feet are, that is where your feet are supposed to be ... or they wouldn't be there. This is the principle of holistic reality, that all experience is valid. Furthermore, it follows that you cannot sit in judgment of others and claim that their experience is inappropriate. Even terrorists! Their experience is appropriate for them at their level of evolution, whatever that may be, just as your experience is appropriate for you. You may not understand or agree with it, but for that person—where their feet are—it is totally appropriate.

With awakening and the increasing dominance of truthful perspective, comes more and more inclusion. As long as illusion remains dominant, exclusion is the norm. Excluding anything or anyone through judgment is fraudulent illusion. Including everything and everyone as part of One consciousness is truthful.

Separation and Conflict

Some people in the West protest that theologies of separation don't affect them because they don't participate in organized religion. The truth is that theologies of separation in the West affect everyone; because they are not restricted to religion, they inform our entire culture. Our fundamental sociology and psychology within every level of human experience is saturated with separation and, therefore, conflict.

Separated individuals are conflicted because they feel powerless and vulnerable. How could it be otherwise? They have separated themselves from the true source of their power; that's the conflict! This conflicted individual then has relationships and families. They live in communities and nations throughout the world. And, because this basic "Source separation" conflict remains unaddressed, they are all lost in the illusion of separation together. This intensifies conflict. Without addressing the original separation, there is no way to successfully address conflict on the larger stage.

In chapter one I described how this relative reality of separation emerged from the One. I call it "the involutionary cycle," and you can see in the diagram on the next page how this progressed down towards the bottom. That is where you are now, if you are reading this book, experiencing yourself as a separate individual ready to embrace the evolutionary journey back to the origination point of Oneness. You'll know where you are in this journey by honestly assessing how inclusive or exclusive you are. Do you judge or do you accept?

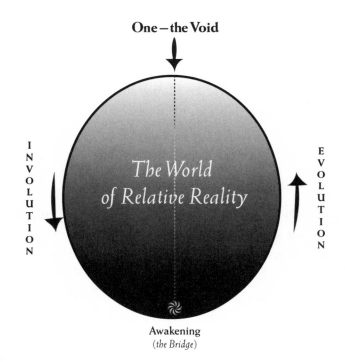

One – the Void

The World of Relative Reality

I N V O L U T I O N

E V O L U T I O N

Awakening
(the Bridge)

During your journey through the involutionary cycle where ego and illusion dominate, you contract, densify, and forfeit your holistic awareness. That's OK, because your intention is to experience what you are not. To accomplish that, you invest yourself in illusion. At this stage, it's all about pretense. You pretend to be other than you are so that you can experience what you are not: separation, duality, fragmentation, and minimal self-awareness. Most of us do a very good job of this!

Next: Awakening

Your journey through separation is appropriate and beautiful, contrary to judgments arising from those blinded by intellectual enlightenment. After all, consciousness is fulfilling its intention to know itself, relative to what it is not. There is no mistake, no one and nothing to blame. Imagine, no "fall from grace" to feel guilty or confused about. It is all just the play of consciousness, the intention for every individual born to a body to know him or herself fully by first knowing what they are not.

Of course most people remain unconscious and identified with the illusory self for their entire life. If so, that is appropriate for them. They will have more opportunities and their karma will set the timetable. For others, insight dawns that they are more than this ego substitute with its virtual reality. They have reached the bridge of awakening to what they are, in relation to what they are not. Now the teacher appears to help awaken and nurture them.

You arrive at that bridge, complete in your involutionary cycle, having fully experienced what you are not. You have thoroughly identified with illusion but now, having reached the bridge and with the two polarities in balance, awakening happens. You begin to have the experience of being something more than you thought you were. At first it is faint, just a glimpse. But it is very real.

Everyone must go through this cycle or there could be no creation. However, you need not become addicted to the illusion. You can and must embrace wherever your feet are and bless your history. You may look back and say, "That was a lousy experience. But, I am grateful that I have evolved through it to here and now, where I am more than I have ever been."

On the bridge, you develop the ability to transcend your judgments and include everything. Remember, the involutionary side is characterized by exclusion while the evolutionary side is known through inclusion. Again, to determine where you are at, just ask yourself, "Am I excluding (anyone or anything) or including?" That refers to aspects of yourself as well. Your truthful answer might be shocking. But this is where you are ... the ideal starting point for what comes next, depending on your choices.

Perfect Timing

Every soul, every quantum monad, is progressing through this process. Some are further along, some are further back, and no two are the same. An old soul has been in many forms of consciousness through fifty billion theoretical simultaneous universes, although quite possibly never here on the earth. It's a big creation with countless options.

There can be no experience before it's time. Some people have an egocentric drive to awaken. I tell them to walk where their feet are and fully experience what is happening. When they get to the involution-ary/evolutionary bridge they may have a longer flash of holistic insight and hold the balance for a little while. This is an awakening. They may suddenly know that they are not what they thought they were; that they are not actually limited and separate, that they are connected to the truth that all is one.

Some fall victim to inauthentic gurus who leverage those flashes of awakening into money and power for themselves. But even these, both guru and seeker, are having the experience that is appropriate for them. They must be, because that is what is happening where their feet are. There is no right and wrong. There are no accidents. There is just growth (or not) through experience, and all experience is valid. The point is to choose to keep on moving. Judgment of yourself and others can only retard your progress.

You may have contracts with other souls from life times past, con-nections of various kinds. You will journey with some of them in this lifetime to achieve particular karmic continuations and completions. Also, groups of souls may evolve together in consensus configurations for a purpose relevant to all of them. For instance, 270 people died when a bomb blew up Pan Am Flight 103 in 1988. That included all

243 passengers, 16 crew, and 11 residents of Lockerbie in Scotland where large sections of the plane landed. It's likely that few of these people even knew each other, other than the crew and townspeople. But they all had some sort of a contract together, not just with themselves but with whoever planted the bomb and planned the attack. And, with the families involved. And, with the government officials and others. You see ... very quickly it overwhelms the mind. We are all one!

Our Place in History

Where are we right now within the great play of consciousness? We are near the end of what Hindus refer to as the fourth and last cycle or the Dark Age, the Kali Yuga. The procession of the Yugas or "great cycles" is well detailed in both the Veda and the Tantra.

The texts describe this great play of consciousness, the creation, as "the day of God," spanning trillions of years through four great cycles. This is followed by the night of God when the creation is absorbed back into the Void. Game over. What then? Well, this is not the first time this has happened. A whole new game will be created. Again. And so it continues, the eternal process of consciousness ever more fully knowing itself through the experience of itself.

Wakefulness

A truthful perception of reality only ever happens in the here and now moment. If I am present, if I'm wakeful, I experience the experience that is happening in the awareness of now. It is new. Consciousness is creating itself newly in this moment and I have never been here before. Also, I will never be here again. The experience that is happening here and now is the experience whose time has come and I can choose to experience it fully. This is wakefulness.

The holistic perspective validates all moment-by-moment experi-ence including premonition, intuition, and any other paranormal aspects of consciousness. There are experiences beyond linear time and space, subtler dimensions of holistic consciousness that are simultaneously operative. We've all experienced them at times, perhaps simply as a hunch about something. Where did that information come from? It wasn't logical; it was trans-mental, subtle-dimensional awareness, a "download" from universal consciousness.

If you are not yet wakeful, you aren't accessing those subtler dimensions of consciousness; you are shutting them out, and so you don't experience holistic awareness. In fact, the very idea will seem ridiculous and it is certainly impossible to "prove." But some people *are* wakeful, which renders them attentive enough to have subtle dimensional insights. As they do, they increase their ability to be wakeful. This principle was operative throughout our Mumbai experience where we experienced heightened holistic awareness and, with it, access to information via our subtle dimensions.

Approaching the Ultimate Mystery

Close your eyes and everything changes immediately. The dominant becomes non-dominant. You shift from exterior dominant to interior dominant and balance is momentarily created. As you learn to sustain this balance, a holistic expansion of awareness unfolds and you actualize the subtler dimensions of your consciousness. You approach the Ultimate Mystery. How close can you get to that Ultimate Mystery? The closest proximity for any human being is wakeful nothingness, what the Gnostics called the "dazzling darkness." This is the awareness of nothingness. One who becomes able to remain in wakeful nothingness is experiencing the closest proximity to the ultimate mystery possible for a human being.

This begins as momentary bursts of experience that elongate with practice. It also explains why authentic masters teach that real meditation is simply sitting in wakeful nothingness. Your mind becomes absolutely still, out of the way, while you experience the source point or origination point of your individuated consciousness as formless being. This is the holistic experience of unified consciousness, the absolute fulfillment of wholeness. This is the promise on the road ahead for you.

సాసాసా

HELEN:

I liked to get up early, around 6 a.m., and stroll on the Marine Walk. The smells were incredible—incense one moment, excrement the next. What a country of extremes! I found myself in bliss those mornings, walking the fine balance point of stillness between polarities while I navigated through the throng of locals and tourists walking, jogging, meditating and doing yoga as the sun rose.

Our hotel always had the most fragrant oils burning in its cool hallways, creating an oasis of peace and calm in contrast to the chaos outside. Sabina, the attarwallah (perfume lady) who created these oil blends, was a lady of subtle awareness. While I was there she gave me a personal reading. She told me that I was carrying fear, which I could let go of, because there was absolutely nothing to fear in my future. This was to be a "trip of destiny" for me.

I saw her for a second reading before the attack and she happily reported that I had already released most of my fear. I certainly felt different. Perhaps it was the conscious intention to release it during meditation, or attending the evening meditation programs with Master Charles, or just being in India. After it was all over I wondered if this had been some kind of preparation for what was to come. I somehow knew that I wasn't supposed to die in India, and I never doubted that.

MUREEN:

The Oberoi Hotel was quite the most magnificent hotel I had ever stayed in. In contrast to the outside street scene, it was always peaceful and quiet inside, and often there was someone playing a grand piano in the lobby. Because our rooms all faced the open atrium, which traversed up the center of the hotel like a donut hole, we always heard music the moment we stepped out of our rooms.

As I was escorted to my room on the 18th floor after checking in, my eyes were drawn to the fire escape on the opposite side of the floor. I noticed myself looking at it, and remember hoping that I would not have to use it. Odd. Then, when I first entered our room, I noticed that the window could not be opened. I felt uneasy about this. I also saw a flashlight on the wall of the closet. This turned out to be essential for our escape. When I look back I am amazed that I was so aware of these things in advance.

BONNIE:

I probably would have been Naomi's roommate, but an extra individual signed up for the Mumbai pilgrimage at the last minute so we had to shuffle around the room assignments. This meant that Helen roomed with Naomi instead.

That evening, after the meditation program, my dear friends Phil and Patty flagged down a cab for our return to the Oberoi Hotel. Naomi ran up to me, grabbed my arm in her usual loving way, and asked if she could ride with us. I said, yes, of course, but have you asked your Dad? Reluctantly, she ran back to find him. I remember an odd moment, though, before she left me. It was like she didn't want to let go of my arm. Well, her Dad wasn't ready to leave yet so she decided to wait and walk back to the hotel with him and Helen. I saw Naomi a while later in the Tiffin Restaurant, but we sat at the next table and left early.

After it was all over, I remember wondering about how different things might have turned out if she had taken that cab ride with us and sat at our table instead.

JOHN:

Normally, I would have been sitting down there having dinner with the others. But I was stuffed from eating a big meal that afternoon so I went back to our room, then realized I had to email a friend. I went down to the Business Center and bumped into Carol. I only spent about five minutes down there, not sure why. Normally I would have hung out for maybe thirty. I have no idea why I cut that short and went back up to our room. The Business Center is near where the shooting started, right in that area. So, for some reason, I guess I was given a reprieve.

అలలల

To better integrate the meaning of this chapter, please visit www.synchronicity.org, go to the "Forgiving the Unforgivable" section, and use the password "one" to access additional material.

CHAPTER 3

I am...All is...One.

Being is the eternal, ever-present One Life
beyond the myriad forms of life that are subject to birth and death.

Being, however, is not only beyond but also deep within every form
as its innermost invisible and indestructible essence.

This means that it is accessible to you now
as your own inmost self, your true nature."[1]

—Eckhart Tolle, *The Power of Now*

November 26, 2008, 10:30 P.M.

Steve flings open the door to Master Charles's suite and runs to the balcony, peering down twelve stories of open atrium to the lobby where two gunmen in black are shooting at everyone in sight.

In the adjoining Tiffin Restaurant, diners have realized this is gunfire, not firecrackers from some nearby wedding celebration. Alan takes charge. "Everybody, under the table!" he shouts.

Huddled underneath, hearts pounding, they hear gunmen enter the restaurant, shooting indiscriminately as they make their way steadily towards them.

Here and now … in this moment …
be wakeful and aware.
Pause, breathe, feel the moment …
experience yourself as you truly are:
timeless, formless, eternally existing.

☙☙☙☙

AMY:

I was gazing out the window of our 16th floor hotel room when I heard what I thought were fireworks or maybe, I mused to myself, some jealous spouse on a rampage! I told my roommate Phyl how I was on my way downstairs to the Business Center but had just changed my mind because I'd felt something odd, like an inner voice, telling me to stay put right there in our room.

The bangs intensified and I suddenly got it. This wasn't fireworks or a domestic quarrel; it was gunshots, many, many gunshots! Then it began to register, what was actually happening. Then some bombs blew up and our room shook. I was glued to the window and watched as the kitchen staff began fleeing from the ground level of the hotel and smoke billowed up towards us.

LISA:

Normally, I would have gone to the restaurant and enjoyed dinner with the others. But that night I was tired, so I just went to our room and ordered in. I remember feeling pulled down there but, at the same time, something told me to absolutely stay where I was. It was more than being tired. I was guided to stay there. I remember wondering why I was feeling that as I drifted off to sleep.

Moments later I flew wide awake as the sound of gunfire reached our room.

CAROL:

I had my favorite sari on and decided to go to my room and change for dinner. When I got there, I changed my mind for some reason. I decided to stay in and just order room service. Then, for the first time in days, I went down to the computer room in the business center. On my way, I passed by the Tiffin Restaurant where I knew many of my friends were probably dining. Normally, I would have at least peeked in to say hello. But that night I didn't.

Instead, I went straight into the Business Center. John was there doing his email. We greeted each other, John left, and I heard a big crash. A hotel employee flung open the door and shouted to me: "Terrorists!" He literally grabbed me and guided me into a ballroom where about two hundred other people were already gathered.

John had disappeared and I couldn't see any of our other friends in the room. We sat there for an hour or two, wondering what was going on. I felt totally alone.

LARRY:

My wife Bernie and I were asleep early, as usual. The phone woke us up. It was Vinka a few doors down telling us about gunfire downstairs. Once we fully woke up and collected ourselves, we realized that yes, it was the sound of automatic weapons, and then came loud explosions. Bombs!

After the first big explosion, our room began to fill with thick, black, greasy smoke. It poured through all the vents and within seconds we could barely see each other. I knew that breathing was soon going to be a problem so I tried to kick out one of the large windows. The glass was too thick so I searched for something heavy. The only thing I could find was the ironing board, so I started to slam it into the window. After three attempts the glass cracked. After a few more hits it shattered into a million pieces.

Aaah, fresh air. We stuck our heads out the window and gulped in the cool night air. Looking down, we saw police taking positions.

The usually busy streets were empty, with no movement at all. We'd never seen that before in this busy city.

Suddenly, we heard large explosions erupting in the distance from other parts of the city. Was this war? Were we being attacked? Could this be terrorists? We had no idea what was really going on. Fear began to creep over us, an overwhelming sense of threatening doom and helplessness.

So, here we were, at the mercy of whoever was doing this. Whatever was going to happen was going to happen. I remember the moment when Bernie and I surrendered to that truth. If it was our time to die, so be it, it would be our time to die.

MIRIAM:

I was almost asleep when I heard a noise. I ignored it at first, thinking that it was just firecrackers. But it continued so I got out of bed, looked outside, and then called down to the lobby. No answer. I tried all the other service lines. There was no reply from any of them. I thought that was very strange and began to wonder what was going on.

The noise got louder ... and closer. I realized this was way too much to be firecrackers from a wedding. My roommate Mureen had jumped out of bed and wanted to open the door. I yelled to stop her but she insisted. She poked her head out and then slammed the door shut and shouted at me: "I'm not staying here to die."

"Neither am I," I shouted back. "Get your passport!"

We quickly put on some clothes, I filled my bum bag with passport, money and mobile, we opened the door carefully, and stepped out into the hallway.

BONNIE:

Most evenings, many of us enjoyed eating dinner at the Tiffin Restaurant in the lobby after our evening meditation program. It was our favorite place to eat because the food was fantastic and it was beautiful, wide open to the large hotel lobby.

That night I sat with Patty, Phil, and Joe at a small table. Nearby, Alan, Naomi, and some others were gathered around a larger table. We could have shuffled the heavy chairs and joined them but we felt a bit less social that night. Joe's son, John, had asked if we could watch out for his dad, who was almost ninety, and make sure that he got back to his room after dinner.

After finishing a quick snack, Phil left to check with Master Charles about administrative items. Suddenly, things didn't feel quite right. Patty and I are both sensitive to energy shifts and we looked at each other with questioning eyes. I know we would have started to compare what we were sensing but just then a loud bang echoed down the corridor. That got us going! We knew we needed to get out of there immediately.

We quickly paid our bill. It was difficult to pull Joe away. Everyone loves Joe and he wanted to say goodnight to them all. But we finally managed to get him up and standing in his walker, then slowly moved him out of the restaurant. That was right about the time we heard a second loud BANG. Really anxious now, we hurried Joe along as quickly as possible towards the elevators. We didn't talk; I don't think we could, because a sense of dread was growing inside us ... chasing us. As we got into the elevator and the doors closed, two men dressed in black walked into the open lobby and started shooting.

JOE:

That night my son John went to the business center instead of to the restaurant with me. We had both lived and worked in India and he had just been visiting with an Indian couple that afternoon and they served him a big meal so he wasn't hungry. But I was, and I always enjoyed being at the restaurant with our friends.

Bonnie had agreed to help me get back up to our room and suddenly there she was, saying that we had to go. I didn't really want to leave. But Patti and Bonnie both seemed very anxious and said that we had to leave right away. They told me that they had heard something. My hearing isn't that good, so I missed it. I was reluctant but they insisted, so we left.

PHIL:

After the program I went to the restaurant for dinner but wasn't very hungry and just ordered something light. I had a recurring feeling that Master Charles might call for me. This feeling intensified to the point where I felt that I had to leave and at least check voice mail in our room. I just knew I had to go. I asked Patty to take care of our check and left, noticing those who remained and suddenly having a feeling that I can only describe as ominous. But, for some reason, I was not worried about Patty.

LINDA:

The restaurant was busy that night. Usually we sat at the front, but this time they seated us at the back, near the kitchen door. I was at the head of our table across from Alan. Helen and Naomi sat to my right, with their backs to the hallway that connected the Trident and the Oberoi. Michael was on my left, facing the glass windows.

In the middle of our lively conversation, we heard an odd sound. It was like something crashed. The Oberoi had a cavernous lobby, and sounds were distorted, so we couldn't easily identify what it was. Michael got up and checked with a staff member who calmed him. No need for alarm, Michael told us when he returned. It was just something out on the street, he'd been told.

But a few moments later a virtual "barrage" started. It was like suddenly being thrown into the middle of a roll of firecrackers. The sound was deafening.

Alan shouted for us to get under the table. What looked like a red rose erupted from Michael's shirt. Naomi grabbed for her father's arm across the table. The room was lit with the crackling of gunfire and a strange heat.

MASTER CHARLES:

We were sitting in my suite discussing the next day's events when we heard "popping" sounds coming from the distant lobby. It sounded like firecrackers and we thought it was probably an Indian wedding because they often celebrate with firecrackers in India. Steve went out to investigate. A moment later he flung himself back into the room and slammed the door shut. "There are two guys in the lobby mowing people down with automatic assault rifles!"

Instantly, we understood that this had to be a terrorist attack. The sound of shooting escalated and then the first bomb exploded. It boomed through the hotel, shaking our room. Then fire erupted from beneath us and smoke began to billow through the vents into our room. Within thirty seconds we couldn't see more than a foot in front of us. We covered our faces with wet towels, broke the window and took turns sticking our heads outside to breathe.

તબજજ

If you are fully present in this moment you are in tune with the innate contentment of consciousness. You are self-content. This is why we live the Holistic Lifestyle, because it anchors us in the now of truthful reality where we are fulfilled **just in being alive.** There are no exceptions to this, including moments trapped in a hotel while terrorists roam the halls!

Of all the mystical traditions, I love Zen because it is so practical. Who are you when you are brushing your teeth, raking your garden, driving to work? When you are standing in front of the mirror with that toothbrush, do you see yourself as you truly are? Can you experience God in that moment? If you can, then you will have a better chance of knowing this state when you are in a crisis such as what we experienced in Mumbai.

This is what I refer to as experiencing the extraordinary in the ordinary. How extraordinary can you be in your real life situations of basic ordinariness? Can you bring all that you believe God to be down to that practical level, so that it is no longer "God" or "it?" "It" becomes the very life force that is empowering you, everyone and everything in this very moment. It becomes a palpable experience that is an inclusive totality.

There is an innate delight in this. The essence of this truthful holistic experience is the innate experience of joy. It then follows that if you're not experiencing joy, you're not in touch with truthful reality. The nature of consciousness is delight. That's its nature and you cannot separate it. It is always content within itself, always delighting within itself. This is joy, happiness, within an expansive state of holistic awareness. It is what mystics refer to as bliss.

Sadly, this is difficult to communicate to those trapped in what I refer to as the "Material Myth," where happiness seems dependent upon who and what is outside of yourself. In truth, as we all have heard but may not have fully believed, you can only find true happiness within. That's because this is where we connect with the oneness of all and everything, and relinquish the loneliness of separation. I love what Jean-Jacques Rousseau said about this: *"I feel an indescribable ecstasy and delirium in melting, as it were, into the system of being, in identifying myself with the whole of nature."*[2]

And what do we discover when we experience ourselves in this way? We are instantly aware that in the fullness of consciousness, nothing is lacking. And you couldn't be wealthier if you had millions to burn. Pause and open to this truth ... Be wakeful in this moment and feel the innate joy and happiness which is within you and needs nothing but your attention to expand. Your very essence is blissful consciousness.

Attention is what does it, or rather the *quality* of your attention, which can instantly transform something ordinary into the extraordinary. I remember a daybreak walk with Muktananda through a residential neighborhood past a giant tree filled with hundreds of birds, all chirping away. I was distracted and annoyed, but Muktananda just kept repeating his mantra as we walked and as we got close to the tree he said, "Ah, they are singing God's song!" His quality of attention and truthful perspective was profoundly different from mine and it made all the difference in the world.

I remembered this many years later when I had moved to Virginia and was living in a tiny cabin. At night a whippoorwill would come and sing, all through the night. She returned night after night, such a rare bird, such a wonderful visitation. I learned to pay attention with truthful appreciation. She was singing God's song.

The Material Myth

What I refer to as the Material and Spiritual Myths generalize the old and new aspects of evolving consciousness. Material Myth is egocentric while Spiritual Myth is trans-egocentric, Material Myth is fragmented consciousness, Spiritual Myth is holistic consciousness.

The Material Myth is governed by the illusion of separation in consciousness (which is what gives rise to the ego in the first place). Remember, the ego is the instrument of the illusion of separation. Well, it does its job very well! Most people are thoroughly hypnotized within the Material Myth, which means they feel separate and different from each other.

In fact, the Material Myth absolutely permeates the modern world. It has become the context in which we live. Its primary value is the "stuff" of consciousness, its content, objects that are separate from us that we acquire through competition to fabricate, grow, and sustain our illusory identity.

The God of the Material Myth is money. Money represents ultimate value. Everyone is competing for it; everything is evaluated by it; worth is determined by how much you have of it. It has become more important than God, even than life itself. I remember a joke that Jack Benny told on television many years ago. A mugger sticks a gun in his ribs and demands, "Your money or your life." Benny muses for a while and, when prodded, says, "I'm thinking, I'm thinking!"

Money is God now. Everyone wants it; everyone is seeking it. Most importantly, everyone is separate from it. They live in lack. They don't really have it, because no matter how much they actually *do* have, more must be acquired, always. And more—no matter how much more—is never enough.

Most people believe that they are the separate "subject" that observes, and that their worth and identity are determined by how many separate "objects" they can "own." This includes thoughts and beliefs, in fact the entire database that a person creates. It's all illusory, a creation of the separate ego, which is firmly in charge and functioning as the instrument maintaining this illusion of separation.

The specific egoic identity you have created—as a conditioned individuated consciousness—is itself illusory. Do you know that? You probably assume that it is you, that this is what is real about you. You are invested in it and you perpetuate it through your daily choices, living from lack and striving to accumulate money plus an endless parade of other separate stuff, from the basics of material survival to sparkling rings and riding lawn mowers, stocks and shiny cars. And, of course, all the beliefs and opinions that swell your database, which you keep adding to. Being successful in this pursuit is what living has become for most people. They are thoroughly hypnotized within the Material Myth and defined by their status in the material world.

As Bruce Lipton wrote in *The Biology of Belief*, "The modern world has shifted from spiritual aspirations to a war for material accumulation. The one with the most toys wins."[3]

The mantra for the Material Myth is competition. We compete with separate "others" and, in the process, everyone becomes a terrorist. We terrorize ourselves with our illusory beliefs, our stories about who we are and what life is and we simultaneously terrorize everyone else with our judgments. Some terrorists are violent, like our attackers in Mumbai; most are not. But within egocentric illusion, inside the Material Myth, everyone is a terrorist, most importantly a terrorist towards themselves.

The Material Myth is all about the experience of what we are not and competing against illusory others to accumulate and win. We are not "consciousness," we are not one and whole. Everything and everyone is separate and different from us. Separation is imbalance; imbalance is fragmentation; fragmentation is misery.

Awakening

Evolution from entrenchment in the Material Myth to emergent experience in the Spiritual Myth involves moments of growth that are much like awakening from a dream. So-called "normal" experience is actually more like slumbering within a dream, a dream that is so convincing you actually believe you are awake. You do believe you are awake right now, don't you? Yet, for the most part, you are asleep. You are in a dream that seems to be real. This can change in an instant. Suddenly for some unknown reason, you wake up. "Thank God," you may say to yourself, "that was just a dream." You may have had a series of openings or insights like that along the way, giving you glimpses of truthful reality, but you are still primarily enmeshed in the dream—the illusion. In other words, you wake up for a moment, hit the Snooze button, and go back to sleep for a while longer.

You might have an isolated moment of truthful awareness, or the vague (but growing) sense that there is something more to life ... something more than what you are experiencing, more than what you have been told or taught. You begin to question, and that questioning further expands your awareness. Your consciousness is evolving and you continue to more fully awaken to a truthful perception of reality.

In fact, truthful awareness is always there, because you cannot totally eliminate that polarity. You can't have just illusion. Truth is always present in relation to illusion. The illusion may be dominant, and certainly is in the Material Myth, but the truth is always there. The balance of those two polarities, experienced in a moment or sustained, is what delivers awakening.

As the dominant illusory experience reaches its peak for you and you are full in the illusion of what you are not, the polarized emphasis shifts. Picture a teeter-totter. As your experience of the Material Myth expands, seeking to convince you that this is all there is, it's like edging towards the center point. But just when it seems that this IS all there is, the balance begins to shift. This happens because in fact you have actually moved closer to the truth polarity on the other side of the centering balance point. Now Material Myth begins to give way to Spiritual Myth. Involution becomes evolution. You experience a polarized shift from dominant illusion to dominant truth, and truth starts building momentum.

Awakening comes. In some cases, it can be dramatic. Truthful reality opens up and *bam*! Your holistic awareness radically expands. Seemingly, in an instant, you are whole, flooded with peace and bliss; consciousness is shimmering and you feel an all-encompassing joy, the oneness of all life. But awakening doesn't happen the same way for everyone. Some awaken progressively, with a glimpse here and there, occasional insights. They contemplate, question, and explore.

Whenever the two polarities of truth and illusion come to balance and truth gains the edge for a brief moment or two, awakening happens. Holistic awareness expands and you experience truthful reality. Then the polarities oscillate and you return to illusion, the dream you have mistaken for reality. But now you are haunted by the truth. You've had an actual experience and everything within you is looking for it again. Light has been glimpsed within a pervasive darkness. "How can I get more of that, you wonder? How can I experience it even more fully and consistently?"

The polarities continue their oscillation on the bridge between involution and evolution, between illusion and truth. As you continue to value and expand awakening moments, truth increases its dominance and your progressive awakening experience unfolds into a more consistent experience of holistic reality.

One polarity can dominate, but never eliminate the other. Truth can dominate illusion, but there must be illusion, because all experience is relative. Truth can become so dominant that you become super wakeful with regard to illusion and no longer identify with it. You no longer even unconsciously invest in it, but you remain aware of its existence.

If you persist, you will ultimately experience a full-blown awakening, a substantial enough experience of truthful holistic reality, an awakening so transformational that it can alter your fundamental perspective and, in turn, your whole life. It becomes powerful enough to survive even a terrorist attack!

Intellectual Enlightenment

Along the way, the ego remains dominant. After an awakening, a glimpse of the truth, your ego inevitably applies its tried and true strategies. It tries to manage your awakening! "If I do more, if I make more effort, I will win the prize." But the master says, "The more dominant your ego, the longer it will take you."

Once a famous maestro of a music academy was interviewing prospective students for a rare opening in the academy. His final choice was between a five-year-old boy with no experience and a fifty-year-old man with years of experience. He chose the five-year-old boy. When the outraged fifty-year-old man asked why he had not been selected, the maestro explained that the five-year-old boy was innocent and empty, whereas the fifty-year-old man was full and egocentric. It would take much more time to erase all that he had accumulated before any teaching could begin.

This is a journey that the ego can't take, let alone control, because the path beyond is trans-egocentric. Unfortunately, post-awakening, the typical next step for many is into what I call the pursuit of intellectual enlightenment. This is where you go to Barnes & Noble and buy a self-help book and feverishly start devouring every word. You may also start attending seminars and having peak experiences. But, more often than not, you fail to integrate them, and the peak is replaced by a pit. This, of course, suggests the need for another seminar, more books and more experiences of the dog chasing its own tail.

This is not a genuine practice. All it can accomplish is something like going to university and getting a degree, with letters after your name. This is supposed to mean that you are an expert now. Of what? How do you function beyond the classroom? Does your training help you to achieve and sustain balance in daily life? Are you able to "walk the talk," as they say? Not yet. What you have learned needs to be implemented in the real world.

The ego takes peak experiences and creates intellectual enlightenment out of them. It seeks to understand the philosophy, even holistic models of reality, but has no means of implementation because it is stuck at the conceptual level. The world is full of those swelled with intellectual enlightenment, masquerading in the guise of wisdom.

When many of us Westerners showed up at Muktananda's ashram, we were excited to discover a vast library. Of course, true to unconscious habit, we wanted to go to the library and study. After all, most of us had college degrees, and this was the way we learned. But the library door was locked. Muktananda said, "Absolutely not." When we asked, "Why not?" he advised, "First have the experience; then study the concepts." Based on our enculturation, that was frustrating to hear. What he was really saying was, "First tell me what your experience is, and then I will show you what to read to support that experience."

This was a total reversal for us because our egos were after intellectual enlightenment. We thought that if we read and understood we would know and then, somehow, we could gain the experience. In fact, the true process of ongoing awakening is precisely the opposite. It requires dropping your egocentric drive and immersing yourself in the experience.

Pause for a moment right now to reflect on the difference. Allow yourself to be fully present as you read. Pause between two words.

Notice your breath. Open your awareness and just watch. Be wakeful within this here and now moment. Holistic truth is always available if you open yourself to it. What you seek is what you are. Reflect on that single statement for another moment. What you seek is what you are.

Religious Myths

Religious myths live within the Material Myth, all subject to interpretation. For example, in the Gnostic tradition, the biblical story of the Garden of Eden is considered a metaphor for the holistic model of reality. When you view it through that lens, all the parts fit together perfectly. You have the two polarities: Adam and Eve. You have the serpent, which (in other than Christian traditions) symbolizes the Divine Feminine cloaked in the power of illusion. You also have the play of relative reality, "becoming" emerging from "being," as Eve comes out of Adam. Then the whole process of creation unfolds with the densification that is called sin or the fall from grace. This is simply investment in illusion, as one polarity dominates the other and creation comes forth, forfeiting self-awareness. The "fall" is really this forfeiture of self-awareness, the limitation of self-awareness that is necessary for consciousness to experience what it is not.

Guilt is a component of the illusion born from the forfeiture of truthful awareness. Guilt is part of the egoic instrument that maintains the illusion of the Material Myth. With guilt comes fear, a primary instrument used in religious myths to bind people within illusion. *Note:* Webster's Collegiate Dictionary traces the word religion to the Latin word *religio,* which means "taboo, restraint." The word religion is a combination of *re* which is a prefix meaning "return" and *ligare* which means "to bind." Therefore, religion literally means, "return to bondage."

Philip Yancey writes in *The Jesus I Never Knew,* "In most religious traditions, in fact, fear is the primary emotion when one approaches God. Certainly the Jews associated fear with worship. The burning bush of Moses, the hot coals of Isaiah, the extraterrestrial visions of Ezekiel—a person "blessed" with a direct encounter with God—expected to come away scorched or glowing or maybe half-crippled like Jacob. These were the fortunate ones: Jewish children also learned stories of the sacred mountain in the desert that proved fatal to everyone who touched it. Mishandle the Ark of the Covenant, and you died. Enter the Most Holy Place, and you'd never come out alive."[4]

No wonder more people don't show interest; waking up is just too dangerous! What nonsense! Authentic awakening is a blissful experience. However, when you are transitioning from the Material Myth to the Spiritual Myth, a spiritual guide is required, to navigate the rapids. Whoever shows up for you must be firmly established in the Spiritual Myth or they cannot guide you. The advent of the Spiritual Myth is now an experience whose time has come, but only when you have reached that evolutionary point. This explains why those mired in the involutionary cycle (the Material Myth) cannot wrap their heads around any need for a spiritual master. They actually don't need one yet!

They are not ready to move beyond religion. Religion belongs to the Material Myth while the Spiritual Myth transcends religion. Those in the Material Myth are dominated by illusion and simply can't understand. The idea of a spiritual master helping them is completely foreign and distasteful. Why? Because in the Material Myth the ego is dominant and it is totally authority-phobic. It wants no other authority than itself and will negate all other authority. That is the primary reason why we have challenges with authority in our lives. It does not matter what arena: relationships, families, bosses, employers, leaders, a spiritual guide, or others. The ego is tirelessly negating authority, trying to pull people off their pedestals so it can remain on its own throne without any competition.

Choice

In the Material Myth, the involutionary cycle, choice is based on "what's in it for me?" I come from lack and seek to accumulate, adding to my self-worth and identity. In the evolutionary cycle of the Spiritual Myth, choice is based on what works and what doesn't work in terms of the primary intention in consciousness to be whole, to fully be itself. "What choices will further evolve my wholeness? What works and what doesn't work to support the greater evolution of my consciousness?"

Mankind is clearly evolving from Material Myth to Spiritual Myth, from separation to unification. This is revealed by the decline in organized, dogmatic religion, and the increase in the actual individual experience of spirituality. Of course, there is always an idiot fringe and today we have fervent fundamentalists of all kinds, but they are way out there. In fact, we will continue to see an increasing progression of unity rather than separation, whether it makes the news or not (and it won't). All prophets from every wisdom tradition have said this, and many have pointed to 2012 as a shift point from fragmentation to wholeness, from Material Myth to Spiritual Myth. This remains our best kept secret.

The Spiritual Myth

Recall that the mantra of the Material Myth is competition. We can contrast that with the Spiritual Myth where the mantra is "compassion." Competition is egocentric; compassion is trans-egocentric. One is fragmented and the other is unified or whole. The Spiritual Myth begins where material, religious myths end. The Spiritual Myth is awakening and post-awakening experience.

Perhaps you have awakened and are now having an experience of truthful reality to some extent. You are more whole. There is balance within your relative polarities, and that consistent balance is delivering the ongoing expansion of holistic awareness. The operative word here is "self-awareness." In the Material Myth, self-awareness is greatly limited. In the Spiritual Myth, self-awareness is maximized.

The Spiritual Myth is based upon the principle that there is only "One," wholeness. When you begin to live holistically, as a constant, you are no longer fear-based and life-negative. You are no longer governed by the illusion of separation and the ego as an instrument of its perpetuation. You have evolved beyond that. Your experience has shifted from life-negative and fear-based to life-affirmative and love-based. That is the difference between competition and compassion.

The ultimate value of the Spiritual Myth is "consciousness" or "life," rather than money or things. What is worthwhile is life, consciousness, God, Source, the essence of it all, the unity and oneness of all—the unity in all diversity. In the Spiritual Myth, unity dominates and includes diversity. In the Material Myth, diversity dominates unity.

Witness Consciousness

The transition from Material to Spiritual Myth is a process. As you develop increasing wakefulness you are able to more consistently just "witness" what happens in your life. It's like watching clouds go by; you don't get hung up in them. You feel more connected to the sky, the witnessing consciousness that contains them. Witness consciousness means that you attach to nothing; you remain the eternal observer, delighting in the play of consciousness. Identifying with what's happening can only retard your progress.

In chapter one, we considered the five-fold process for integrating peak experiences. As you learn how to experience momentary awakenings and grow them into a more sustained experience of wakefulness, you will notice that you don't get identified with things the way you used to and your evolutionary progress will deepen and accelerate.

As Shakespeare wrote, "There is nothing either good or bad, but thinking makes it so." Don't judge the happenings of your evolutionary journey. One great sage proclaimed that judgment is the supreme delusion. In fact, those words were framed and displayed over the door of my cabin in Muktananda's ashram.

When you are experiencing the holistic awareness of the Spiritual Myth, you are delighting in the consciousness that you are, the consciousness that is everyone and everything. There is only one. There is but one blissful consciousness.

I am ... all is ... One.

ᰂᰁᰂᰁᰂᰁᰂ

BOBBIE:

I was in my office here at the Synchronicity Sanctuary in Virginia when a visitor ran in and told me to turn on the news. CNN was showing a terrorist attack in Mumbai. As I watched the news on my computer and learned that they were hitting the Oberoi Hotel, where Master Charles and our group were staying, a silent message came to me: "Everything is okay, it is not Master Charles's time to go, he has much work to do. Get busy and deal with this." From that moment on, even though my life became a whirlwind of activity, I remained very calm.

KIA:

I had just returned from a walk in the seniors' gated community where my mother lived outside of Tampa, Florida. As I prepared a snack and got ready to watch Oprah with my mother, the phone rang. It was Bobbie Garvey, friend and managing director at Synchronicity Foundation. "Kia," she said in a calm but urgent voice, "turn on the news. The Oberoi Hotel is being attacked by terrorists."

I remember the moment. I was looking out the kitchen window at a palm tree, perfectly still against a bright blue sky. I dropped the phone and literally collapsed to the floor. "Turn on the news!" I shouted. The family quickly gathered and we sat in stunned silence, watching the flames coming out of the Taj Mahal Hotel in Mumbai and the reporters announcing bombings, shooting, and fires in both the Taj Mahal and Oberoi Hotels.

Where were Alan and Naomi? "They must be in their rooms by now," I said, reassuring myself and the family. "It must be about midnight over there." A few hours later, Bobbie called to say that everyone in the Synchronicity group had been accounted for.

Everyone except for Alan and Naomi.

കകക

To better integrate the meaning of this chapter, please visit www.synchronicity.org, go to the "Forgiving the Unforgivable" section, and use the password "one" to access additional material.

CHAPTER 4

The Holistic Model
of Reality

"We are not human beings on a spiritual path,
but spiritual beings on a human path." [1]

—Dr. Lauren Artress

November 26, 2008, 11:00 P.M.

The phone rings in Master Charles's suite. It's Gautam, their Mumbai coordinator, urging him to turn on the television immediately. Master Charles and his two colleagues retreat to the bedroom furthest from the door and turn on the television, keeping the volume low.

The news is stunning. Gunmen have attacked ten places throughout the city. Fires are burning, the death toll is mounting. Commandos are being summoned from New Delhi. Mumbai has become a war zone.

Following instructions, they drag furniture and barricade their door, moving as quietly as possible so they won't be heard in the hallway. Then they return to watch news on the television until it suddenly goes dead.

There is only One.
Consciousness is all.
It's primary intention is to fully be itself.
It creates relative reality to fulfill this intention.
Being and becoming,
unity and diversity.
In essence, both are the same consciousness.
The seeming two are really one.
Consciousness is the substratum, the ground of being,
the essence of all that is and is not.

❧❧❧

MASTER CHARLES:

Our Indian coordinator is a wonderful man named Gautam Sachdeva. I have known his entire family for many years. We were able to talk with him by telephone and learned that the entire city of Mumbai was under siege. He told us to turn on the TV. That's how we learned the scope of what was happening, that this was a full-blown terrorist attack.

One of the first chilling pieces of news was that apparently everyone on the 18th floor of our hotel had been taken hostage and killed. We were on the 12th floor. Gautam told us to barricade our door, turn off the lights, and be as quiet as possible.

PHYL:

Amy broke a window because the room had filled with smoke and we were having difficulty breathing. We placed pillows over the broken glass and leaned out, holding wet towels over our faces, and talked with Larry and Bernie who were two rooms down. Taking their advice, we packed our belongings and took our valuables out of the safe.

I noticed myself going through all the classic fear responses. At one point I wondered if I would have a heart attack. I was quite convinced that I would die, but I was able come to terms with that. At the same time, I had an amazing sense of detachment. Everything Master Charles had talked about over the years now began to really come home to me. Here it was, positive and negative both existing simultaneously.

Amy suggested putting furniture in front of the door, but I doubted that would stop anyone who was determined to break in. So we hid behind the lounge—as if that would fool an intruder!—listened to the gunfire, and passed the hours in a detached place of simultaneous fear and peace.

JOE:

Well, I was stuck in the room with my son John, watching TV with our door barricaded, although I wasn't sure that would really do much good. We managed to get Master Charles on the phone and he was reassuring, as calm as always.

When smoke began to fill our room we wet towels, got down on the floor, and breathed through those towels. Okay, now bombs were exploding and the machine-gun fire was almost constant. I started to remember being at war in Korea.

Funny thing, there I was lying there on the floor and I began to observe myself witnessing everything that was going on. It was amazing. I'd studied the witness consciousness principle for years but this was the first time I really had a good, solid feel of what it really was. Somehow, midst all the chaos and fear, I began to feel genuinely peaceful. Maybe for the first time in my ninety years. That was remarkable, all things considered!

CAROL:

Hotel staff began moving us from the ballroom, taking the women first, in a long line across the street to a parking garage. There were about two hundred of us in that garage. We ended up being out there for seventeen hours and all I had were my glasses and my wallet. I kept borrowing cell phones to call home and tell them I was fine.

When we heard a sudden round of explosions everyone started running up a ramp and I was afraid I might be trampled to death, but one of the Oberoi employees held my hand. She was an angel. In fact, all the staff members were amazing. We were worried that maybe there were more terrorists on the street, or that those in the hotel would come out and kill us. I meditated most of that night.

MASTER CHARLES:

Shortly after the attack began, I recalled my vision from the meditation program and reflected on what the three women had seen. Suddenly, the Blessed Mother appeared, with her luminous face about five feet away from me. Her peaceful presence saturated the room as She smiled and simply said, "Trust and watch."

She whispered these words several times and then dissolved, leaving me in an even more heightened state of awareness. "Trust and watch," so it would be. No referencing past experience, no fearing future ones, just a spontaneous expansion of awareness within the here and now moment. This was obviously an experience whose time had come. I became detached, peaceful, and calm.

At some point the fire was extinguished and the filtration system cleared the air in the room. The gunshots and bombs subsided for a moment. There were periodic breaks like this throughout the forty-five hours of our captivity.

❧❧❧

This chapter presents the conceptual foundation for the Holistic Lifestyle. Inspiring and instructing you to learn and practice the Holistic Lifestyle is the purpose of my teaching and of this book.

Mumbai was a dramatic example of the Holistic Lifestyle in action, with twenty-five of us in extremely stressful circumstances. We've all seen the news stories; perhaps some of you have been in a violent crisis yourself. If so, you know that when someone hurts another, it's customary to retaliate, at least in attitude. Turning the other cheek seems ridiculous in the heat of the moment, even though this was advocated by a great spiritual master that millions of Christians profess to follow.

Perhaps reading about how we handled this crisis is challenging some of your cherished beliefs. For instance, what about the concept of retribution, an eye for an eye, to even the score? Beliefs like that are based in conflict. Those beliefs are why you have less consistent peace, happiness, harmony and love than you wish for. It also explains why you have strife in your life, if you do. Reflect for a moment. All your beliefs exist in your consciousness, correct? Yes, they do. This means that they can change.

What is Consciousness?

"The so-called miraculous powers of a great master
are a natural accompaniment to his exact understanding of subtle laws
that operate in the inner cosmos of consciousness." [2]

—Paramahansa Yogananda

Before we go deeper into our exploration of the nature of consciousness, let's pause for a moment and focus. Again, slow your reading ... be aware of your breathing. Notice yourself being aware, more aware than you were just a moment ago. Perhaps close your eyes for a moment and take one or two deep breaths in and out. Be wakeful ... fully present ... within this here-and-now moment.

Now ... return to the words. How interesting. Those words directed you to be more present and they actually helped you do that, almost instantly. What made that possible? Well, you followed directions. Although it was just words, just ink on a page, you easily made meaning out of them! You **chose** to make meaning out of them. Remember this as you continue reading. You are translating the words into whatever meaning they will have for you; it's a choice. If mental argument or resistance arises, you can meet that with a decision about the meaning you prefer the words to have for you. Feel how it would be, to have that much trust in yourself that you could actually challenge your own limiting beliefs in any moment of reading and create meaning that was helpful to you. That would be ... relaxing, calming, centering, empowering.

Now, let's discuss consciousness. Consciousness is the truthful nature of reality as one. There is only One. Consciousness has been called by many names: God, Source, Life, and so forth. It is both relative polarities: "being and becoming," "positive and negative," "formlessness and form," "subject and object."

Consciousness is both unity and diversity, described by the Sanskrit word "satchidananda" which means the holistic experience of reality as One Consciousness. You are an individuated form of that consciousness, and your very essence is Life, that same joyous, delighting energy that is All.

Life, in its fullest experience, is the oneness of creator and creation. The creator cannot be different from its creation. If the cause (creator) is consciousness, then the outcome of that cause (creation) must be consciousness as well. It can be diversified consciousness, modified consciousness, expressed consciousness, the becoming of being, but it is still consciousness in essence. Nothing is separate. Everything is made of the same stuff, because creation cannot be different from its creator. If you can accept that, all the rules change!

Stephen Hawkings makes this outrageous statement in his recent book, *The Grand Design*: "Spontaneous creation is the reason there is something rather than nothing, why the Universe exists, why we exist. It is not necessary to invoke God to ... set the Universe going." So, he's saying that God has no role in the creation of the universe, and I can agree with him on that because the God he is talking about is an illusory God. And what does illusion have to do with truth? Nothing!

Consciousness is the song and we are the singers.

The Play of Consciousness

Why is there suffering in the world? Why are some innocent children born with terminal conditions, others to hunger and disaster? Why is there injustice, enslavement, war? From the perspective of consciousness, all experience is valid. It is expressing itself through all these experiences in order to experience itself and evolve through that experience. We cannot sit in judgment upon the starving person, because we don't know their experience. We don't know where their feet are in the greater evolution of their individuated consciousness. It must be appropriate for them because through it they are evolving and growing. This is not an uncaring attitude, as it might appear at first glance. It is respectful. Respectful of them and their right to have whatever experience they are having, without my judgment.

How do you feel about the starving people of the world, about bad things happening to good people, and even the activities of terrorists? Who do you choose to be in relation to them? Your choice will always be based upon where your evolutionary feet actually are.

It's the play of consciousness. All experience in consciousness is for its own entertainment. Believe me, nothing serious is going on here! Consciousness is entertained by its creation, its experience, and it eternally delights in the process. This is the fulfillment of wholeness. If you are not consistently joyous, with joy bubbling in every cell of your being, you are not experiencing truthful reality. Even our experience in Mumbai was a play of consciousness and therefore inherently joyful. That may seem difficult to believe, but it was the truth for us.

In fact, at the highest level of truthful unified consciousness, life itself is a joke. It has to be. If you listen, everything is reverberating with laughter! Everything is hysterically laughing, fully delighting in its moment of existence. That is the true nature of this game, this play of consciousness. But, as consciousness densifies, it forfeits its holistic awareness of the joy of the game. That's why it will seem unlikely, even unbelievable, to most people, that anyone enduring an experience such as ours could possibly find anything in it to enjoy.

The play of consciousness is also described as "the becoming of being," and the Divine Feminine or Divine Mother. One of her Sanskrit names is Lalita, she who plays as the creation, or the consciousness that blissfully plays. Chitshaktivilas is another Sanskrit name for this, the play of divine consciousness. All of creation, all of the cosmology, all of universal manifestation, is this play of consciousness, a manifesting, self-delighting, dancing energy that becomes all and everything.

If you could only see the essence in every form as I have described it in chapter one, those tiny particles of light, the vibrating flux of holistic reality, those particles delighting and ecstatic. It really is literally a playful consciousness, playful energy! If you could only see it, the ecstatic dance of those particles, you would know that they are neither serious nor methodical. The ecstasy itself determines the motion and the movement of each particle and when you have a direct experience of this playful energy you too become blissfully ecstatic. You begin to experience how your ecstasy moves in that same way ... creating the direction your hand moves, for instance, as the expression of that delight, out of that joy, out of that blissfully ecstatic play of consciousness.

Of course, as long as you are looking from the fragmented illusory perspective there really **is** something serious going on here. But that illusion is only valid when blissful reality remains unknown. When you know it, you also know that it's all a joke. So, if life is serious, that tells you where you are. You are not experiencing true reality. If it's not reality, then why would you continue to take it seriously? Lighten up! The essence of life is joy, a delighting energy, and there is nothing serious about it. Any seriousness is coming from illusion and your personal investment in it.

This helps explain why we were able to perceive the terrorists as the real victims in Mumbai. Just imagine how lost in illusion they must have been! How could they stray that far from the delighting energy of life, so far that they got serious enough to actually kill people and be killed themselves? For them, the attack was *very serious*. But that was an illusion they invested in and it certainly wasn't delighting energy!

Knowing this, how could it have possibly served us to likewise invest in that same illusion and agree that it **was** serious, that these terrorists were evil, deserving of our hatred and revenge? Yes, we felt all the customary human emotions ... fear, anger, sorrow, grief. We were able to witness ourselves being fully human, with real human emotions, feeling them deeply and utterly, but without losing touch with the truthful reality that *life is a delighting energy.* We found that it was possible to remain blissful, even in grief. And we were not in denial, believe me!

This may seem too fantastic to believe. Well, I always welcome skepticism; it has an important place in the learning process. But there is a difference between skepticism and cynicism, as Andrew Newberg and Mark Robert Waldman write in *How God Changes Your Brain*: "Skepticism implies open-mindedness and a willingness to suspend judgment until both sides of an argument are considered, and this enhances neural functioning, particularly in the frontal lobes. A cynic, however, is a person who has taken their disbelief to a point of emotional distrust and rejection that borders on hostility toward the other point of view. This "limbic" personality is pessimistic and is so neurologically dangerous he can even shorten your life." [3]

The Show Does Go On And On And On ...

There is a famous Hindu painting of God above the clouds with strings emerging from his hands and going down through the clouds, connecting with two men on the earth fighting with each other. God is holding the strings and laughing hysterically. This is consciousness, delighting in its play; consciousness being entertained by its play. It is all just a play of consciousness, with no right or wrong and nothing serious going on at all. Remember why consciousness created the universe? It does so for the joy of it, for its own entertainment.

Everyone's experience is appropriate for them but what does their experience catalyze in you? Rather than saying, "Ain't it awful, just terrible, it should be other than it is!" which are illusory egocentric judgments, it is more truthful and life-affirmative to consider who **you** are choosing to be in relation to what is happening. Yes, there are starving children in the world. Well, you might choose to do something life-affirmative and love-based about that. You might choose to feed some of them! You might take some kind of compassionate action.

Relative to Mumbai, would it serve any truthful purpose for me to condemn the terrorists? Would it evolve my consciousness to fill myself with hatred, vengeance, and violence? Or would it evolve my consciousness to fill myself with love, compassion, kindness, and forgiveness? What sort of person do I choose to be in relation to what happens to me and what others do to me? That is the most important question.

According to the primary intention in consciousness to be ever increasingly more whole and truthful, how does my choice contribute to the expansion of awareness? If I choose to be hateful, like the terrorists, this retards me. I have made a choice that will fail to evolve my consciousness any further. Why not fill myself with love, compassion and truth instead? Reading it here, following the logic step by step, doesn't it make perfect sense?

I'm not talking about being a missionary. That too can be egocentric. If I go out there and try to convert people to my particular illusory beliefs, it piles illusion on top of illusion. If people are converted, their feet are where my feet are, as a missionary, and we then share the experience of mutual illusion or mutual egocentric deception.

Considering the scope of violence on our planet, some propose that the earth is one of the densest levels of manifestation in the whole cosmology. That's just a theory, of course. How much of the whole cosmology are we consciously aware of anyway? Enough that we can compare? We are still confused about our own solar system, with Pluto just being downgraded from planet status because a larger object named Eris was recently discovered. Who knows what else will come to light in the years to come? We probably won't know any time soon precisely how the earth figures into this solar system, let alone the vastness of this universe.

Consciousness is entertained by its own play and if you are having a truthful perception of reality you should likewise be entertained by your life experience. Witnessing your life is like going to the theater. One night it is tragedy: pathos, negation, and war. At the end of the play, you applaud as you walk out, saying, "Well, that was a good tragedy, I really enjoyed it."

The next night it is a comedy, and there you are in the audience again, saying it was a good comedy, that you enjoyed it, and you are applauding again. Ideally, you remain in witness consciousness regardless, watching and enjoying both tragedy and comedy. Of course, most people jump up on the stage and become part of the play! They project themselves and interfere. They don't remain wakeful in the here and now, in witness consciousness, simply watching.

If you do learn how to remain in witness consciousness, delighting in your play, both comedy and tragedy, you actually learn to enjoy it all. It is all entertainment! Of course, since the play of consciousness is multi-dimensional, you begin to experience life much more fully than you ever could from just watching a play or a movie on the two dimensional screen.

Awareness

Once you become consciously wakeful in this way and able to maintain witness consciousness, the process of evolution accelerates for you. The imbalance of polarities is being addressed, because it is holistic awareness that disempowers imbalance, illusion, and fragmentation. That's all well and good, but how do you get to holistic awareness? This is a vital evolutionary step and it marks where meditation becomes vital. As well, I advise using truthful statements or affirmations to further assist in establishing the balance that expands awareness, the state that enables you to remain vigilant of the mind with its judgmental antics.

This is not to say that achieving holistic awareness is easy. For most people it isn't. They don't have it, they have never had it, and so they must learn how to develop it, which is a process. Initially, they must grab the reins of their conscious mind and direct it into truthful statements about who they are and what life is. Truth-centered focus is what enables you to develop the witness state which properly applies to every moment. Understand: this is something that you "do," that you choose to do. It takes practice and it becomes a practice. Depending on how well you integrate this practice into new habits, you will become steadily more able to remain aware, even in challenging, life-threatening situations such as the one we faced in Mumbai. It doesn't happen overnight, it's a way of being that develops over time through deliberate, conscious attention.

Let's practice expanding awareness for a moment. I'll suggest a truthful statement and you can express it. "Here and now ... in this moment ... I am One, and all is One." That's an affirmation. Try speaking it to yourself, silently. Again. This is an example of a truthful statement about who you are and what life is. It's somewhat different from the sort of self talk that can torment us throughout the day, thought forms like, "How could I have done that ... what's wrong with me?"

Circumstances arise to test us all, and we discover where our feet are in the greater evolution of our consciousness. Sook Yin is a doctor married to another doctor who suffered a sudden stroke several years ago. "I became very angry because I thought that he should have recognized the signs of a possible transient ischemic attack. He didn't. In fact, he ignored them and boarded a plane for England! Just like that, for all practical purposes, I became a single parent and the only income earner. He never fully recovered from the stroke and I had trouble recovering from my judgment.

"But gradually, with Master Charles's guidance, I shifted from a victim mentality to consciously creating the life I wanted. I realized that things just happen in life and I was suffering because my ego wanted them to be different—which they would never be again—and this was producing my resentment and anger. Instead, I developed the ability to genuinely know that "everything is always appropriate" and this enabled me to let go of my illusory fear of the future (how will we survive now?) and just take life as it came, day by day. This acceptance of life extended to the acceptance of my husband. I stopped blaming his apathy for slowing his recovery; in fact, I released the expectation that he **would** recover. That could only generate disappointment."

Sook Yin succeeded in changing how she thought and felt about her husband's stroke. But it took deliberateness. She worked at expressing positive, truth-centered thoughts, rather than the blame and anger loaded sentiments that she had been struggling with.

The Trinity of Relative Reality

In one way or another every aspect of the Holistic Model orients around the primary concept of balance. When you sustain balance between the two polarities, the space between them dilates. Without that space, neither polarity could exist, obviously, because without it they would be one. That space is the space of holistic awareness, or witness consciousness. That space is also called the eternal now. That is why I refer to all balancing techniques as Technologies of Now, because their intention is to deliver the state of witness consciousness or holistic awareness.

Balance delivers wholeness and expands relative reality into a trinity in your potential experience wherein witness consciousness can watch itself as both polarities. This is an experience that can only happen in the here and now. Holistic awareness is the result of balance and balance corresponds to the actual experience of now.

I encounter widespread confusion about this concept. Some authors have misinterpreted stillness, which is one of the polarities, as the space between the polarities. No, stillness and movement **are** the two polarities, while witness consciousness is the space between them that is always proportional to the extent of polarized balance. This is an important distinction.

Your first real experience of this space could be described as detached observation. You find that you are now watching yourself. But you are not yet watching yourself *as the same consciousness*. You are still separate, watching as something separate from what is watched. But individuated witness consciousness can progress over time into unified witness consciousness because watcher and watched are the same One.

This eternal now of holistic awareness is associated with what I call the heart-field, which is the center of individuated consciousness. All masters in my tradition teach that the heart-field is the gateway to holistic awareness. But they know very well that most people cannot easily access the heart-field, because the mind-field interferes. Therefore, all initial practice is directed at balancing the mind-field so that it can be transcended. This is what allows access to the heart-field. And that transcendent state, relative to the mind-field, is what meditation helps you to develop over time.

I refer to this as "the progressive process of ever-increasing integrative wholeness" because it **is** a process of growing evolutionary momentum. Of course, whenever you reach a peak on this journey you must follow that five-fold process all the way through to integration, then begin the growth cycle again. As I often say, "enlightenment" is a misnomer because the process of expanding wholeness is eternal. There was no beginning, there will be no end, and there is no final enlightenment. What a relief! Rather, there is a progression into ever more enlightening experience.

When the holistically evolved enlightening state of being is consistently experienced by an authentic master, they generate a powerful field that radiates that unified state of being and are also able to "laser" it into their students. This, again, explains why having a guide is essential. Imagine if you wanted to get a suntan. How would you get a suntan? Through exposure to the sun! Let the sun shine upon you and you get a tan. Be with an authentic master and enlightening experience is inevitable.

Let's take a brief moment to establish the optimum learning environment for your exploration of the nuts and bolts of the Holistic Model. Imagine yourself lying on a beach in some tropical location. You're on your back, the sun is blazing above you and you feel your body heating up. There's no doubt about what's happening; you're getting a suntan! Smile at the memory and embrace the metaphor of the sun that brings illumination to what is true about you here and now.

The Five Core Principles of the Holistic Model

There are five core principles to the Holistic Model. I'll present them with a brief description and then we will explore them in further detail.

1. **There is only One.** That One is the essence, by whatever name. We can call it Source, Consciousness, God, Life, etc. By whatever name, there is only One. This One creates relative reality.

2. **Relative reality is the arena of all experience.** This necessitates the illusion of separation as the primary illusion in consciousness, and the ego as the instrument for the illusory separation in consciousness.

3. **The heart-field is the gateway to the experience of the eternal now.** All masters have taught the same thing. All holistic models of reality describe the heart-field as the gateway of the "now" of consciousness. The only true experience of reality is in the "here and now."

4. **The mind-field dominates for most people.** An awakening individual cannot fully hold the experience of the heart so they are unable to sustain the experience of the "now." Why? Because their mind-field is dominating their heart-field with the illusion of separation. This results in the forfeiture of holistic awareness. Therefore, the learning priority must be to first balance the mind-field.

5. **Balance is substantiated as the mind-field is transcended.** This allows the heart-field, the eternal "now" of presence, to be

accessed. The heart-field is the gateway. The egocentric experience of illusion must be transcended through balance, so that the heart-field can be accessed. This opens the experience of truthful reality within the eternal "now." Balance is always the key.

Balance and the Necessity of Imbalance

The principle of balance is talked about in most of the wisdom traditions. For instance, the Buddha often referred to the "Golden Balance." We must balance each dimension of our multi-dimensional consciousness. The physical must be balanced, the emotional must be balanced, and the mental must be balanced, as well as the more subtle dimensions.

Only when they are all balanced and are sustained in balance can the subtler dimensions of our multi-dimensional consciousness fully actualize in experience rather than fanciful theory. This is the only way that self-awareness, holistic awareness, can radically increase. Therefore, all wisdom traditions emphasize practices that are really balancing techniques.

In relative reality with its two polarities, one polarity is able to dominate the other and create imbalance. Why does consciousness create the possibility for imbalance? Because imbalance is necessary for there to even be a universal creation and manifestation. We simply couldn't have all these forms around us—including our own—without the dominance of forms, which is imbalance in consciousness.

At the subtlest level of relative reality, the two polarities simultaneously exist in a state of perfect balance and maximum wholeness, because wholeness is proportional to balance. This is the unified experience of relative reality—both polarities of consciousness being "One." But, for consciousness to bring forth the creation, it has to increase imbalance. Form must dominate formlessness. Increasing imbalance in this way means that "becoming" begins to dominate "being," diversity dominates unity. This creates the entire cosmos and this "world" that we populate. It follows that imbalance is essential in consciousness or we couldn't even have these physical forms, and we could not experience relative reality, which is required for our ongoing evolutionary journey of progressive wholeness.

The Five Principles of Holistic Living

The holistic model of reality is the blueprint, the roadmap, and the instruction manual. Living it involves an understanding and actualization of five principles:

1. **I am Source.**
   You are the life-source, the one consciousness that is both unity and diversity. You are the creator and the creation, and being aware of this—of who you really are—you can truthfully say, "I am consciousness; I am blissful consciousness; I am Source."

2. **I create my reality.**
   You as consciousness create the experience that is happening, whether you consider this in terms of quantum science or holistic philosophy. Consciousness creates your experience of being and its becoming. "I am the creator of my experience."

3. **I am responsible for my creation.**
   If you are having a crappy experience, you need to look in the mirror and ask, "Why am I creating a crappy experience?" You can blame your experience on circumstances and other people but, in fact, you are creating the experience that is happening. Who do you choose to be in relationship to it, creator or victim? "I am responsible for my creation."

4. **I can change my creation.**
   This is wakefulness. If you are creating illusion, you are the one who needs to change it. You can do that because you are the

creator, it all rests on you. If it is not working, you can make it work. "I can change my creation."

5. **I am one and free.**
You are whole; oneness is wholeness; wholeness knows no other, has no second, is free and independent unto itself. That is real freedom and freedom in oneness is the ultimate fulfillment. "I am one and free."

It's Time for a New God

The primary illusion that binds and blinds us is the concept of a separate God. It is time for that old God of separation to yield to the new God of oneness. In fact, God is just one word to describe the all and everything of consciousness. All and everything in essence is one with the same source and I cannot be separate from that. I am source, I am God, I am consciousness, ... I am the divinity of life.

This new God creates the creation, sustains and grows the creation, then dissolves that creation back into the essence that it is. That evolutionary cycle keeps repeating itself. Consider the substitute process orchestrated by your ego. Your mind creates a thought, sustains it as a largely unchanging conscious belief, and then installs it in your unconscious database. That process keeps cycling too, but the difference is stagnant repetition, as opposed to the evolutionary creating of innovation. The same thoughts and beliefs repeat themselves over and over again. For instance, "I am unworthy. Something is wrong with me. I must change. I must become better, or enlightened."

How do you break this cycle? The ancient sages called it grace. Grace is holistic awareness. When you become holistically aware, you interrupt the ego-cycle and "fry the seeds," as they say. This is a time-honored analogy. Imagine that repetitious thoughts are like sesame or mustard seeds. If you store them without cooking they can sprout and continue recycling. But if you throw them into oil in a hot frying pan, you destroy them. This interrupts the cycle. Grace, holistic awareness, awakening, fries the seeds. It interrupts your unconscious process of creating, sustaining, and storing illusory thoughts and beliefs that habitually repeat themselves.

This grace principle accompanies the master. His or her awakening transmission provides the empowerment to open you up, so that you can see your creation from that perspective. Your holistic awareness expands, all your seeds start frying, and your illusory data shifts.

Responsibility is a Delight

Who else can be responsible for your creation but you? In truth, there is no one else **but** you! All is one consciousness. You are the author of your creation; therefore you are solely responsible for it. If you are responsible, then you are wakeful. This is not a duty, a burden. It is a delight! Being consciously responsible for your creation is innately joyful. "I am one, becoming many. My primary intention is to fully know and be myself. I am already joyous by nature, so all that I manifest must be permeated with that joy." Yes, as the 23rd Psalm in the Bible proclaimed, "My cup runneth over." When I am truly responsible, I am overflowing with delight, love, and bliss.

One of the most brilliant strategies of consciousness in terms of unity and diversity is that consciousness can multiply itself to actualize the intention to fully be itself within relative reality. "I am the one in the many and I reflect myself back to myself."

For instance, I may be sitting in my office on top of this mountain, surrounded by windows. All I can see are trees, up close and far away. I can sit here and say that I am separate and different from those trees and be lost in fragmented illusion. But I can also say that every one of these trees is a form of me as the consciousness that I am, that all is. Each form is a magnification and multiplication of myself. In this way, I radically increase my bliss through the process of that recognition. This is how I can wakefully choose to be responsible for my creation.

The Momentum of Evolution

You are constantly changing your creation and through this you evolve. As you evolve, your holistic lifestyle keeps changing, appropriate to where your feet are, and always relevant to your process. Obviously, you don't have the same process now, the same creation now as you did when you were five years old. And you can easily see how your creation has changed throughout the course of your human life. You have grown, evolved, and transformed. You will continue growing, evolving, and transforming so your creation will continue to change.

As your self-awareness increases, you become more awake within your creation and, inevitably, you see how what you have created needs to change from time to time. When that happens, you consciously change it. This is wakefulness in action. It is responsibility in consciousness relative to the progressive expansion of your awareness, the progressive process of ever-increasing integrative wholeness. The more wakeful you are, the more aware you become. "Wait a minute," you may occasionally say to yourself. "Something needs to change here."

This is you and this is me! Our very nature is delight, blissful and joyous. In the awareness of myself as a totality, unto itself, the one and only, I am ultimately fulfilled. I am free and independent, there is no other that I must depend upon. Freedom is independence. Likewise, there is no other that you are dependent upon in any way. You are free absolutely in your independence as a totality unto yourself. And that, finally, is what the Holistic Lifestyle is: your experience of wholeness. When you are whole, which you come to through your holistic lifestyle (not through thinking about spiritual concepts), you come to this recognition and experience: I am ... all is ... One.

In that awareness there is absolute certainty. You are totally fulfilled and absolutely free.

కళకళ

KIA:

Around 4 p.m. the phone rang and we all jumped. We stared at it, wondering who it would be, what the news would be … and then, who would pick it up? Finally, I did. It was CNN, a woman named Beth. She was surprisingly kind. Very kind. I knew she must face tragedy every day in her work. Yet she managed to convey a sense of genuine sympathy to me. So, I almost felt sorry when I declined her request for an interview. But she seemed to understand.

I was just too raw, too much in the unknown.

BERNIE:

Whenever a bomb or grenade would go off, the reverberations would literally throw me back a few feet from where I was standing in our room. Spontaneously, fear welled up in my body. Instinctively, I began to utilize a technique I knew would help me fully experience the fear. I sat, closed my eyes and focused on the part of my physical body that was experiencing fear. It moved around, from my solar plexus to my heart and my throat. Sensations of intense physical pain developed, like a hot poker here and there in my body. But as I remained focused on the fear and the physical sensations, without resistance, both dissipated and I regained a sense of balance. When the fear erupted again I just repeated this awareness process until I could sustain balance.

HELEN:

When the shooting started, Alan shouted to all of us, "Get under the table." In the instant that I slid down I remembered a story Swami Karunananda once told during yoga teacher training at Yogaville. Her guru had said that the repetition of the Om Shanti mantra created a subtle shield of armor that nothing could penetrate. She put it to the test one day when attacked by a dog. Just as the dog lunged at her she began chanting Om Shanti. The dog tried to bite, but his teeth could not close on her hand. He made a couple of attempts, then turned tail and slunk home, leaving her uninjured.

Somehow, I remembered this story, went into the child's yoga pose under the table, and began silently chanting. "Om Shanti ... Om Shanti ... ." Alan offered a hand towards me and reached for Naomi with the other. I looked in his eyes and whispered 'Om Shanti' to him. Those were my last words to Alan. Then I placed my forehead on the floor in the Balasana yoga position. The shooting got louder as the attackers swept through the restaurant. Soon it would be our turn.

PEGGI:

We could hear machine gun fire most of the time. We decided to pack up all our things so that we could be ready to leave at a moment's notice. And, if we died, this would make it easier to send all our belongings back to our families. Also, we held our meditative focus. We held light and love for all, including the terrorists. I thought about my boyfriend at home, my 86-year-old father and my 22-year-old son. These were just three of the many reasons I had to live.

LINDA:

The firing stopped. We were all still alive, but any sense of relief was short lived. Random firing soon resumed and I realized that "they" were coming, moving from table to table, executing survivors. Alan whispered to play dead but I couldn't. I needed to see who could be doing this.

I watched a young man turn the corner and what immediately struck me was that he looked about the same age as my son. I thought, "Ah, my universal son is speaking to me with a gun. How could I have let him get to this?" He moved warily, like some soldier wading through a war zone, expecting the enemy to attack at any moment from any direction. I shivered and felt his fear pulse through me.

As he turned towards us, I laid down my head. Boom, boom, boom. I felt three strong taps down my back. Michael urged me to "please get off me!" Before I could answer, I heard a gasp of breath from Naomi. That was her last breath. I told Michael that I was unable to move.

HELEN:

One of them came to our table and started shooting through the top of it, over and over and over, like a video gamer going for a perfect score. A hot bullet grazed my thigh but I sensed that it wasn't serious. An inner voice whispered, "Where the sun is brightest, the shadow is darkest." After ten days of ever-increasing bliss in witness consciousness at the balance point of stillness between contrasts, this all seemed to make perfect sense in some surreal way. I was inwardly watching everything happening around me and inside me and wondering where the fear had gone. It just wasn't there. No terror, no panic, no rage, no grief. Just a watching of what was happening.

Now people began crying out ... the injured and the dying. They were near me, on top of me, all around me. Suddenly I noticed that I wasn't holding Alan's hand anymore. I don't know when we let go of each other.

I noticed that the shooting had stopped. I opened my eyes and peered towards Naomi and Alan. They were silent, not moving at all. My intuition told me that they were gone. I shook Naomi's arm. It was lifeless.

A man's voice called out. "Those who can move, come this way!" Who was calling us? Was this a trap to finish us off? I looked towards the kitchen and saw the uniformed legs of a hotel staff member. I decided to go, if I could. I somehow rediscovered my ability to move. I climbed over Alan's body to get out. I saw that he had been shot in the head and had a fleeting moment of gratitude—it must have been fast. As I pulled myself free, one sandal stayed behind under a woman who had died on top of me. I pried my bare foot free and followed Linda towards the kitchen.

We passed Michael's blood drenched body. At first I thought he must be dead, but my inner voice said "no." The moment we reached the kitchen the shooting resumed. There was nowhere to hide if the attacker made it through the door. I continued to softly chant "Om Shanti, Om Shanti, Om Shanti."

MASTER CHARLES:

The three of us lay on the one big bed and remained as meditatively quiet as we could while the bombs exploded all around us. At one point it got so intense that we thought the entire hotel might explode. The adrenaline was flowing and we were super-wakeful. We just lay there, watching the experience that was happening.

And that's how we made it through the first night. The next morning we discovered that the hotel phones were still working so we were able to call room-to-room and, over time, piece together what was happening with everyone in our party. It was a grim picture.

෧෧෧

To better integrate the meaning of this chapter, please visit www.synchronicity.org, go to the "Forgiving the Unforgivable" section, and use the password "one" to access additional material.

CHAPTER 5

Balancing Your Multi-Dimensional Consciousness

*"Misfortune is never mournful to the soul that accepts it;
for such do always see that every cloud is an angel's face."* [1]

—Lydia M. Child

July, 1989

Ben is eight years old, flying to Chicago on United 232. Suddenly, an engine blows and the plane crash-lands in Sioux City, Iowa. 111 passengers die. Ben hangs upside down while the plane burns. He is rescued and survives without physical damage, one of the lucky 185 who do. Although he is physically unhurt, he suffers psychological scars.

Now at age 28 and assistant to Master Charles, he finds himself trapped in a hotel room with terrorists roaming the halls, and every explosion takes him back ...

Through balance, awareness expands.
Through expanded awareness, wholeness is known.
Wholeness connects individual and universal consciousness.
That connection enables a download,
and joy is experienced as the essence of life.

❧❧❧

AMY:

Smoke filled our room. We began to cough and choke and it quickly became impossible to see. I realized that we could be trapped, that we needed an escape route safer than the hallway. I thought about my ex-husband and what he might do in this kind of a situation. He is what many people would refer to as a "wise guy," basically a Brooklyn gangster. But what I remembered at that moment was how he always found some way to escape danger. I thought about his enormous strength (overlooking the violence that went along with it, unfortunately) and suddenly found myself picking up an extremely heavy armchair and hurling it at the window.

It took calling on his memory to activate every cell in my body and every ounce of my strength, and it worked. That huge window exploded! Shattered glass followed the chair as it plummeted towards the ground, twelve stories below. As the balmy, evening sea air rushed in and cleared the smoke, I wondered what might have happened below when the chair landed.

BONNIE:

I called Patty to make sure that Joe had been delivered and that she was safe in her room with Phil. While talking, we all noticed that our rooms were filling with smoke and suddenly the fire alarms went off. I wet towels and placed them underneath the outside door and put a soaked facecloth across my mouth and nose.

Under any other circumstances, I would have immediately headed down the fire escape. But I didn't know exactly what was happening out there so I decided to stay put in the room. (I found out later that the terrorists were shooting people who tried to escape that way.) The smoke got worse and worse until I finally managed to break one of the smaller windows. As the air rushed in, I heard the crashes of other windows being broken. I found a spot on the floor and lay down, concentrated on slowing my breathing, and gradually, relaxed.

The fire alarm seemed to blare for hours. After several unsuccessful attempts to dismantle it, I realized that I was exerting myself too much and gave up. I returned to deep, slow breathing and reserving my energy. I noticed the smoke gradually dissipating and felt relieved. At that point, I turned on the TV, muting the sound, and began to follow news of the attack that was being broadcast on every channel. It was spell-binding.

A sense of calm descended over me. I called Master Charles's room and told him that I was okay, safe for the moment at least. He told me to stay put, to "trust and watch." The moment I heard those words, I realized that everything would be okay. I dialed in a Synchronicity Meditation on my iPod, put on my headphones, and began to meditate.

అయ్యయ్య

"All matter originates and exists only by virtue of a force ...
We must assume behind this force the existence of a conscious
and intelligent Mind. This Mind is the matrix of all matter." [2]

—Max Planck

The Trinity of Human Experience

Most human beings are only aware of their physical, mental and emotional levels of experience, which are the densest but not the only levels of consciousness. There are subtler dimensions as well. When dense dimensions interact with subtler dimensions, a person begins to truly know what it means to be a whole human being.

Ken Wilber writes about a formless state where "even the thoughts and images drop away, and there is only a vast emptiness, a formless expanse beyond any individual 'I' or ego or self. The great wisdom traditions maintain that in this state—which might seem like merely a blank or nothingness—we are actually plunged into a vast formless realm, a great Emptiness or Ground of Being, an expansive consciousness that seems almost infinite. Along with this almost infinite expanse of consciousness there is an almost infinite body or energy—the causal body, the body of the finest, most subtle experience possible, a great formlessness out of which creative possibilities can arise."[3]

These "creative possibilities" arise via a "download" process from universal to individual consciousness. And this fusion births our life experience moment-by-moment-by-moment, without us being consciously aware of it, for the most part. No one can access that interface and receive other than the maintenance aspect of that ongoing download until they find and occupy the balance point. What, where, and when is that balance point? It is right now and right here, midst the experience that is happening. In this chapter, we explore the nature of that balance as it relates to all the levels of our consciousness, both dense and subtle.

First, let's create an experience. Slow down your reading. Allow your attention to be absorbed in the words as you read them, without any anxiety about gaining meaning or finishing the line or paragraph efficiently. Feel yourself relating to the words, the letters, the spaces between the words and letters, in a leisurely way. Drop any agenda. Relinquish your hopes for finding meaning or value in what you are reading. Just be with yourself having the experience of reading. Let this moment, as your attention touches on each word, be enough. Simply watch the experience of reading as it is happening. Be aware of the subtle peace that permeates this here and now moment.

Does this help you begin to sense the subtler dimensions I am referring to? Savor your inner experience right now, whatever it may be. Welcome this world of heightened, subtle sensation that is opening before you. And, with a relaxed attitude of child-like anticipation, let's address how to increase our awareness of these subtler dimensions.

We need to balance the three dense dimensions because they are chronically imbalanced. Interestingly, 7 to 1 is the balance ratio for each of them. Homeostasis at the physical body requires the proper balance between acid and alkaline, which is 7 to 1. Brainwaves range between beta and delta and the balanced frequency ratio is 7 to 1. The same balance ratio is found between male and female hormones.

Here is where consciousness is the most obscured from itself so this is where emphasis is needed. When you are able to sustain balance in the physical, emotional, and mental dimensions they become interactive in a way corresponding to the spin of human DNA in a non-stressed environment. When that spin stabilizes and becomes constant, subtler dimensions actualize, awareness expands, and wholeness is increasingly experienced.

The Coherence of our Multi-Dimensions

The three more refined dimensions that I speak about are known as the subtle, correspondent to third eye; the causal, half way between third eye and crown; and the supra-causal, correspondent to the crown. Together they are called subtle because they vibrate beyond the speed of light toward infinite velocity. By contrast, the denser dimensions vibrate much more slowly, contracted enough to actually densify into matter, retarding their vibration. As the frequency of vibration slows for these three dimensions, this decelerates the oscillation of the two polarities, to the point where they begin to appear as separate. This explains how the illusion of separation arises and then dominates. The three dense levels are ponderously slow and dense and solid on the one hand, while the three subtle levels are vibrating beyond the speed of light. Considering the disparity, one is tempted to question how they can possibly be aspects of the same consciousness but they are.

We measure brainwaves in frequencies called Hertz and there are four categories. Beta is the fastest, then alpha, theta, and finally delta, which is the slowest. We actually balance the brain by decelerating, that is, moving from beta down to delta. From what I just said about the relative speed of the subtle dimensions, shouldn't we be speeding up the brain? No, it's about balance, not similarity.

To understand the design for resonance and coherence between the dimensions of our consciousness, consider the piano keyboard with its octaves. The octaves are harmonic with each other. When you play the note "C" in a low octave it is also the harmonic of "C" in a higher octave. The same is true of every note and also of every dimension. There is a resonant frequency at the physical level that is harmonic with its correspondent in a subtle dimension. In our high-tech meditation, for instance, we use sonic technology to decelerate brain wave patterns and create harmonic resonance with the subtle dimensions.

We also use the brain as our measuring device for the mental, emotional, and physical dimensions. When the brain is functioning in beta, we have lateralization. One side of the brain is dominant over the other, which creates imbalance. When we slow the brain waves down to delta, the two sides of the brain come into balance with each other. The meditative EEG is really a delta-dominant frequency range of brainwaves or balance frequency. Meditation has always been a balancing technology, because it balances the physical, emotional and mental dimensions and harmonically connects them with the subtle dimensions.

This creates the multi-dimensional experience of unification, which Michael Talbot explains this way in *The Holographic Universe*: "The apparent separateness of consciousness and matter is an illusion, an artifact that occurs only after both have unfolded into the implicate world of objects and sequential time. If there is no division between mind and matter in the implicate, the ground from which all things spring, then it is not unusual to expect that reality might still be shot through with traces of this deep connectivity." He goes on to describe moments of connectivity as synchronicity. "The relative scarcity of synchronous experiences in our lives shows not only the extent to which we have fragmented ourselves from the general field of consciousness, but also the degree to which we've sealed ourselves off from the infinite and dazzling potential of the deeper orders of mind and reality." [4]

Each dimension has relative polarities, of course, and each dimension has to be balanced. At the physical level, this relates to biochemistry, the balance between glucose and insulin. At the emotional level, the polarities are the primary emotions of love and fear. At the mental level, it's positive and negative thoughts.

I place great emphasis on beginning holistic lifestyle practice with learning how to balance this primary trinity because it is the foundation. If you want to build a skyscraper and enjoy a lofty, holistic 360-degree view, you must build a strong foundation first. Otherwise, the structure—however magnificent it might appear—will eventually fall. Our initial focus is with the foundation, which is why I encourage you to "walk where your feet are." Build a foundation. Begin where your feet are. You are in a physical body and you have a mind and emotions. Start there, rather than with flights of fancy about esoterica. Start with the foundation. If you can learn how to regularly balance these three dimensions, you will create resonance. The "higher octaves" will actualize as harmonics and you will generate a genuine holistic experience.

The Power of Negative Thinking

Our minds get in the way. The mental dimension, like all dimensions of our multi-dimensional consciousness, is governed by relative reality with its two polarities of positive and negative. Negative is the default dominant polarity, which means that we incline towards being life-negative in our thoughts and beliefs and resultant experience.

This is the basic imbalance that we all deal with every day, by virtue of being in human forms at this dense level of experience in consciousness. Our initial response to stimulus is usually negative because that's our "default" setting. We are pre-disposed to a life-negative perspective, which generates a negative interpretation of our experience. We judge things negatively because we view the content of our lives through a negative mental grid.

According to Canadian futurist and ethicist, George Dvorsky, "Some people have estimated that upwards of 70-80% of our daily thoughts are negative. ... We often dwell in the past or the future, obsessing about mistakes we might have made, battling guilt, planning ahead or worrying. We are constantly drifting into fantasy, fiction, and negativity. Consequently, an absolute minuscule number of our thoughts are actually focused on what is truly important and real: the present moment. The moment is all that is, ever was and will be. Everything else is elusive and illusory, particularly as our subjective awareness and feelings are concerned."[5]

Noeleen is one of my mentoring associates in New Zealand. A few years ago she faced a serious challenge that, at first glance, seemed to relate to her external environment but, as we explored it together, she realized was more of a mental problem. "When my husband and I bought our property, we were assured that the lot in front of ours would not be developed. Four years later my friend Mary revealed that she and her husband owned that plot and she showed me their plans for a motel! A motel! That would be our new view, instead of the ocean.

"I was shocked into silence and literally could not say a single word to her. Meanwhile, I was consumed with anger and was shouting silent accusations about fraud, greed, etc. My mind was whizzing with chaotic thoughts. Should we move, how could we leave all our new friends, should we fight this? It got to the point where I was actually closing the curtains in the lounge when I walked through, even though nothing had changed yet! My husband told me that I had already built that motel in my mind, and he was right!

"During a mentoring session with Master Charles, I told him about what was going on. He invited me to use my power to see what was happening with me personally. 'Who are you choosing to be in relation to this?' he asked me. I got it. I realized that I was actually creating this story. I acknowledged my experience and all the emotions that went along with it. Immediately, I began to feel stillness and calm returning. I even began to enjoy the view again and stopped generating negative thoughts about what might happen in the future. Best of all, I was able to release the judgments of my friend Mary and actually put my arms around her and tell her that I loved her."

Noeleen created balance at the mental level, which I refer to as the "mind-field," by increasing the opposite, positive polarity. To do this, she simply emphasized truthful positive thoughts and interpretations. Doing this requires a conscious approach to your mental experience rather than an unconscious, automatic one, which is what Noeleen realized she had lapsed into. Most people live with a pattern of incessant, automatic, and habitual thinking that is overwhelmingly negative. But the moment you become consciously aware of your thinking, you can grab the reins of your mind and consciously direct your mental focus. This shifts your thinking from illusion to truth, creates balance, and generates a holistic expansion of awareness and experience.

Our Three Brains

Many of us have assumed—and we have certainly been encultured to believe this—that the mind is the seat of our power, the control center of our experience, the computer that runs the whole show. But there is sound scientific evidence that says we have more than one brain. Actually, science delineates three: a brain in the head, heart, and gut. Each of these produces brain cells, neurons that interact via the blood stream. The brain in the head exchanges brain cells with the heart, the brain in the gut exchanges brain cells with the head and so forth. When balanced, they are harmonically interactive.

According to Jonathan Haidt, author of *The Happiness Hypothesis*, "Our intestines are lined by a vast network of more than one hundred million neurons; these handle all the computations needed to run the chemical refinery processes and extract nutrients from food. This gut brain is like a regional administrative center to handle stuff the head brain does not need to bother with. You might expect, then, that this gut brain takes its orders from the head brain and does as it is told. But the gut brain possesses a high degree of autonomy, and it continues to function well even if the vagus nerve, which connects the two brains together, is severed."[6]

According to this, the brains interact, but clearly, the head brain is not in total control. The brain in the head is not the seat of our power. So, which one—if any—is? When they are measured, we discover that it is not the brain in the head but the brain in the heart that has the most influence. I refer to this brain as the "heart-field." In truth, it is a field of experience, energy, and vibration with a substantial amplitude of power. Science tells us that the heart-field actually has the most amplitude of power because it is the center of our individuated consciousness.

The Heart-field

The heart-field is the gateway to wakefulness, expansive self-awareness, and the experience of the eternal "now." You cannot be wakeful and present in any moment, except through the gateway of the heart, and every master has said this. But, in the next sentence, they will say that they cannot talk much about the heart-field because you cannot access it until your mind-field gets out of the way. So, all the techniques and practices and disciplines are designed to purify and balance the mind, so that you can transcend it and gain access to the heart-field.

Why is the heart-field so important to access? Because it is the center of our individuated consciousness. Our individuated consciousness must interact with universal consciousness just as our densest dimensions must interact with the subtle, causal and supra-causal dimensions in order for wholeness to be experienced. For this to happen, we need a sufficient amplitude of power in the accessed heart-field.

If you develop an adequate amplitude in the heart-field, you become able to consciously connect individuated to universal consciousness. As you access the heart-field, the subtle dimensions actualize, and the universal opens to you. Individuated merges into universal, until the universal becomes dominant over individuated consciousness. Universal consciousness is the experience of unification or wholeness, along the vertical axis of relative reality.

This is a provocative description. But how does making this connection feel? Remember, this is the heart-field, where feelings are more prevalent than thoughts. As your individual consciousness connects with universal consciousness via the heart-field, it is natural for a feeling of compassion to arise. This enables trans-egocentric expression, which is always about holistic service. That was Mother Teresa's meditation. For example, she would say that she saw Christ's face in the face of every suffering child. She could see God in everyone and everything. Her message really was: God dwells within you as you see God dwelling in others.

You can say that accessing the heart-field is actually about self-love. You begin with yourself. Can you love yourself? Can you forgive yourself? Can you be compassionate with yourself? Can you be joyous without any other present? And can you create that experience for yourself? This is a shift from the dominant negative, the exterior, which is object-oriented and seeks fulfillment in everything and everyone outside of itself. This is a shift to interior dominance, to "being," and it is what I mean when I refer to the experience of being human.

The Self-Diagnostic

The process of balancing starts with being truthful with yourself. Take an honest look at how your mind functions. How often during the day are you aware of your thoughts? How often during the day are you unaware that you are thinking? What is the dominant quality of your thoughts, positive or negative, truth or illusion? Based on that diagnostic, you can easily determine whether you are dominantly fragmented (negative, illusory thoughts) or dominantly balanced and whole (positive, truthful thoughts). If you notice that you are dominantly fragmented, then you need to emphasize the positive polarity to create balance. How? By thinking positive, truthful thoughts.

Bringing control to your thinking takes time. The Buddha wrote about his own process: "In days gone by this mind of mine used to stray wherever selfish desire or lust or pleasure would lead it. Today this mind does not stray and is under the harmony of control, even as a wild elephant is controlled by the trainer."[7]

Based on the percentage of your fragmentation, you may wish to begin with consciously directed thinking, for instance, affirmations. Affirmations need to be reflective of where your feet are, in other words, honest. You can't use statements that are not true for you. Repeating, "All my relationships are loving and enjoyable" won't help if it isn't true, because your mind will be hearing a lie. The remedy is to use verbs rather than nouns. "I am increasing my wakefulness within my relationships" could work, because it honestly acknowledges a process and that you are doing something, rather than already having a hoped-for finished product.

We will explore this and other focused awareness techniques in the second section of this book, where you begin implementing the Holistic Lifestyle in your own life. Of course, you can begin experimenting with positive, directed truthful thinking immediately. Because many people rarely direct a thought consciously (they merely react to what assails them from their environment), this may seem contrived. It **is** contrived! It's you, directing your mind. You, distinct from your mind. You, daring to usurp your minds self-proclaimed authority.

Try it right now. Create a thought about something in your life. For instance, pick a friend or family member who you are on good terms with and create the thought: "I appreciate _____ (fill in their name).” Pause for a moment to gather your energy and then repeat these three words. This is a positive, truthful thought, one you have directed consciously and it immediately balances your mental dimension to some degree.

It's a beginning. It introduces a discipline that can help establish mental balance. Mystics talk about detached observation, the experience of witness consciousness. This can arise as some degree of balance is achieved and individual consciousness begins to interact with universal consciousness. This activates that harmonic resonance and allows subtle, causal, forces to actualize. It also signals an awakening moment, here and now, which can only come via that balance. Once a person has an awakening that delivers the experience of multi-dimensional resonance, it will haunt them forever. I am sure that you have savored such an experience and that you hunger for more. It's why you keep turning the pages of this book.

The Universal, Vertical Axis

You can learn how to act from the universal vertical axis rather than from the individual horizontal one. As you become able to do this, dense yields to subtle and you experience a whole new perception of reality here and now. You access the eternal now consciousness.

As long as life is present there is always interaction between the individual and the universal. Of course, most people are unconscious that this is happening, but some sort of maintenance “download” is always occurring or they wouldn't be having any experience at all. The more conscious you become, the more comprehensive your download will be. As we constantly affirm, you can have no experience before it's time, so this is not some sort of competition to merge dimensions as quickly and completely as possible!

Some people begin to experience this interaction as a flood of creative insights, a literal download of information. They report that it comes in relaxed moments, not when they are struggling to have it.

For instance, many *"Ah ha!"* breakthroughs in science have happened spontaneously during activities when the mind was not directly focused on solving a problem. The answer came intuitively from "somewhere." *Ah hah!* For others, the interaction brings peace and other love-based feelings. Instead of a flood of thoughts, they experience waves of emotion.

During the Mumbai ordeal, we were consciously maintaining our witness consciousness, anchored in the here and now. It seems so fundamental, but midst the world's overwhelming surround of negativity, it's easy to forget this first, vital step. In fact, whenever I offer a program anywhere, I always start by welcoming people to this holistic state of being. Right up front, I invite them into the wakeful moment, to be here and now, to be fully present, to be wakeful. And then periodically through the rest of the presentation, I continue to remind them.

I am doing the same thing in this book, periodically bringing you back to the conscious experience of the moment as you read. Are you still here? Are you having the experience that comes along with the concept? Slow down. Be aware of the words and the spaces. The spaces and the words balance each other if you are wakeful. And with balance, there is holistic awareness expansion within the eternal now.

Balancing the Heart-field

Like the mind-field, the heart-field also has two polarities, positive and negative, which we represent as the two primary emotions of love and fear. The default dominant for the heart-field is also negative which means that, for most people, fear is usually dominant. So, to balance this level, we emphasize the non-dominant polarity—love. We shift our emotional emphasis from fear to love. By the way, love and fear are the only true emotions. Their expressions are our feelings. Feelings that arise from fear include hatred, anger, jealousy, envy, greed ... all the negatives. Feelings that arise from the emotion of love include compassion, contentment, joy, gratitude and forgiveness, and so forth.

When we were rescued from the terrorists and interviewed, many in the media expressed doubt and even cynicism that what we were saying, or rather what we were not saying, was truthful. How could we really feel as loving and compassionate as we said we were feeling? Practice. We had all been practicing for years to maintain a balance in our heart-field.

In *How God Changes Your Brain*, Andrew Newberg and Mark Robert Waldman write, "Recently, a team of National Institute of Health researchers concluded that 'a moderate optimistic illusion' appears to be neurologically essential for maintaining motivation and good mental health. They also found that highly optimistic people had greater activation in the same parts of the anterior cingulate that are stimulated by meditation. ... The anterior cingulate plays a crucial role in controlling anxiety, depression, and rage, as well as fostering social awareness and compassion.

"Even the medical researchers at the Mayo Clinic stress the importance of optimistic thinking for maintaining optimal health. They found that positive thinking decreases stress, helps you resist catching the common cold, reduces your risk of coronary artery disease, eases breathing if you have certain respiratory diseases, and improves your coping skills during hardships." [8]

None of us denied the severity of our predicament. In fact, many, perhaps all, in our group consciously considered the possibility that they might very well die in that hotel. But they also understood the need to maintain balance in the heart-field. So, as fear arose, they consciously countered it with love. This is the "moderate optimistic illusion" referred to in the above quote.

As with the mind-field, you begin to balance the heart-field by doing a self-diagnosis. This immediately reveals which polarity is dominant. If you are running negative feelings, fear is dominant. This means that you need to direct the heart-field with an affirmative feeling, that is, direct your feelings toward the positive. We will explore this in depth in a later chapter but let's pause for a brief experience now.

What are you feeling in this moment? Pause and feel. Tune in, expand your conscious awareness, use your wakefulness to get in touch with what emotion is dominant. Is it fear or love, right now? If it is love, some combination of positive feelings will be active in your experience. Enjoy them and notice how they increase as you have your attention there. If you get in tune with negative feelings arising from fear, just acknowledge them consciously. You might even say to yourself, "I am feeling anxious, or impatient, or discouraged." This is also an expansion of awareness.

Now, what would you like to feel? Pick a feeling, and witness yourself doing this, being completely arbitrary. Let's say you pick the feeling of contentment. What does contentment feel like to you? Recall a time when you felt genuinely content, just to refresh your memory. Now, flow that positive feeling within your heart-field focus. Feel contentment. Not because something or someone made you feel it, but because you directed it. Direct the feeling of contentment to balance your heart-field.

Notice how your breathing slows, how your thoughts calm down and, before long, that you actually feel more content. Imagine, you can do this any time you choose! It's miraculous, really, in its simplicity. Whatever you might choose to feel—love for instance—is immediately available! Want more love? Well, express it. This can be self-love, it can be love for another, for an experience or a thing, or just love for no reason at all. You are capable of producing this experience without assistance, regardless of what advertisers tell you. You do not need to buy anything or have any other person treat you in some special way to feel content! You can become emotionally self-sufficient!

People get confused about this in Western cultures where we are so emotionally repressed. We are taught from birth to suppress the heart, to avoid what we feel, certainly not to communicate about it. When I say, "Flow positive feelings," most people reply, "What does that mean?" When I say, "Experience love," they argue, "I need someone for that." No you don't. You don't need anyone else. If you want to experience love, just be loving!

To actualize the emotion or feeling, simply convert a noun into a verb. For love, be loving. For peace, be peaceful. In other words, to experience love, joy, contentment, compassion, or peace, flow those feelings within yourself. Open yourself to these feelings and you will feel them.

Brainwaves in the heart-field are called "heart waves" and, when they are measured, they emanate eight to twelve feet around the body. This represents a far greater amplitude of power than brainwaves in the head. To measure that we must place sensors right on the head itself! This explains why the heart is considered the center of individuated consciousness. It is because it has the greatest amplitude of power. When you are able to access the heart-field and sustain its balanced focus, you are fully in your power. Then and only then can your individuated consciousness interact with universal consciousness, which is represented by the subtle dimensions. When the two interact, witness consciousness and holistic experience emerge.

The physical dimension has to be balanced, the mental dimension has to be balanced, the emotional dimension has to be balanced, and then the heart-field opens. When it does, what do you have? You have the experience of holistic awareness, witness consciousness, the experience of being fully present, aware, wakeful, alive within each moment of the eternal now. And, as we have said repeatedly, this is the only place you can ever experience true reality, in the here and now of momentary consciousness.

This is why balance is the primary principle in the Holistic Model and the primary focus of the Holistic Lifestyle.

જાજાજા

JOHN:

At first I just thought it was some guy with a pistol in the lobby and they would tackle him pretty quickly. But the shooting continued and got louder. I had a growing awareness that we were in deep trouble and found out pretty soon that this was a life and death situation.

Phil called on the hotel phone and told me to barricade the door. We didn't right away because I just wasn't connecting the dots yet. Then we saw smoke outside through the window, big plumes. "Oh my God," I said to my Dad, "the hotel is on fire!" We were on the 12th floor and the fire was burning beneath us.

Phil called again and this time he said, "Break your window." We didn't have any smoke in our room at that moment and I had just breathed a sigh of relief about that when the room started filling up with smoke! But I remembered a show on CNN where they talked about smoke coming in from outside through broken windows so I decided not to break one. Instead, I got some wet towels and put them around our door jam. The smoke didn't get much worse and Dad agreed that we shouldn't break a window, so we never did. Others did. I guess we all tried whatever we thought would help us.

Dad and I just sat there listening to the gunfire. I called our India coordinator, Gautam, and he told me that it was happening all over Mumbai. The Taj, Railroad Station, Hospital, Leopold Café, and elsewhere. Then, click, the line went dead. What just happened, I wondered? It was another "Ah-ha" moment, me getting it even deeper. This was something huge. Then I pushed the console with the mini-bar against our door.

BONNIE:

As the hours wore on, I somehow drifted off into a relaxed meditative state. Around 4 a.m. I snapped awake when I heard a tiny click at the door. I realized the fire alarm batteries must have finally died or I wouldn't have heard it. My first thought was to wonder if it was Carol, my missing roommate. In fact, I almost called out her name. But something stopped me and I just listened. I heard a grunt of what seemed like exasperation. Someone out there was struggling, unable to get in. I had double locked the door and moved a dresser up against it, but even to this day, I do not really know for certain why whoever it was didn't just force their way in.

After a few moments, it stopped. Silence descended upon me then ... and a sense of peace and relief that I would be okay. I continued my meditation. What I learned later from a reporter back in the U.S. was that the terrorists had master keys to all the hotel rooms. They had taken hostages from my floor and shot all of them except two Muslims.

So, I was literally the width of that door away from certain death.

ৡৡৡ

To better integrate the meaning of this chapter, please visit www.synchronicity.org, go to the "Forgiving the Unforgivable" section, and use the password "one" to access additional material.

CHAPTER 6

Death Follows Birth ...
Life is Eternal

If you want to become full,
let yourself be empty.
If you want to be reborn,
let yourself die. [1]

—Tao Te Ching

Thursday, November 27, 2008   Thanksgiving Day

Each terrorist has a cell phone. One of them rings. It is their handlers in Pakistan.

"Kill all your hostages, except the two Muslims," is the instruction. "And keep your phone switched on so that we can hear the gunfire. Kill them now."

The terrorists shoot their hostages.

"Because of what you do, there will be more hate in the world."

Life is an innately joyous experience.
When I am truthful … I am joyous.
Truth and joy never die.
My truthful experience of life
is eternal.

❧❧❧

MUREEN:

I remember hearing voices very early one morning a couple of nights before the attack. I discovered later that the terrorists had made the room right next to ours their headquarters. I was glad I hadn't knocked on their door to complain about them disturbing my sleep!

As the attack intensified, I remembered 9/11 and the television pictures of how those buildings fell down. I thought our hotel might suffer the same fate, so I just felt we that had to get out of there straight away.

MIRIAM:

I was blessed. My roommate Mureen somehow knew where the torch was in our room and where the nearest fire escape was on the 18th floor.

She opened the door and started moving down the hallway and I followed. It was pitch black with smoke everywhere. As she called out to ask if I had the room key, our door slammed shut behind me. There was no going back now.

I caught up with her at the end of the corridor. We joined arms and began to fumble our way down the fire escape. It was dark and I couldn't stop coughing from all the smoke. We finally made it down to ground level but didn't know which door to open. We thought for a moment, then chose the one straight ahead. Lucky us, it opened right onto the street. We found out later that the one on the right would have taken us back into the lobby and possibly right to the terrorists. We felt guided, definitely, and very grateful!

People beckoned us to move away from the building but said nothing about what was going on. I was still coughing and someone gave me a kerchief. Someone else gave me a bottle of water, and yet another offered to take me to the hospital, but I declined.

Then we just sat there on the footpath, waiting for Master Charles and our Synchronicity friends, but no one came.

Kia:

My two sons were not going to just wait and do nothing. Aaron, the oldest, filed an i-report on the CNN website with pictures of Alan and Naomi. Before we knew it, their photos were being flashed on the television screen with the caption "Father and Daughter from Virginia Missing" along with film coverage of the flames and grenade sounds coming from the hotels. Mumbai looked like a war zone, the entire city was being held hostage by just ten terrorists!

We began getting calls from relatives we hadn't seen in years saying that they were starting prayer groups for Alan and Naomi and to please give them the details. I called two friends from my days in the Transcendental Meditation movement. We hadn't spoken in seven years, but we had been like family, as our sons had all grown up together and were still close. They offered to call everyone they knew and also to meditate for us. We even started receiving email messages of love and support from the CNN website, just pouring in and from total strangers who said they were praying for Alan and Naomi.

There was a period where time suspended ... that was, before we knew. I felt how intimately connected we all were, all of us, friends, family, and strangers. This was a great comfort. It probably marked the beginning of my true understanding that there really is no 'outside world.' There is only one world, one human race, one human family.

BEN:

It is impossible to settle down in a room echoing with constant gun-fire and grenade explosions and yet, by the second morning, something undeniably peaceful was happening. Between Master Charles's entrainment of positive energy, and the thousands of people all over the world focusing their hearts and meditations on us, I began to feel overcome with peace and relaxation. I don't really "see" energy, but now I sure started to! It was everywhere. I mean, I clearly saw faces in the air... like they were literally watching over us.

At one point, I walked over to the window and looked down at the empty streets. The air was crystal clear. Amazing, it was usually thick with smog. I looked out to where the ocean met the sky and I was overcome with joy. Everything was so incredibly beautiful. All my anxiety was just gone. Yes, I still knew that we could be killed at any moment but what came into my mind was "Wow! What a beautiful day this is." If that doesn't validate the power of love and meditation, nothing does.

BOBBIE:

I called Kia three or four times a day, just checking in. I realized that I was preparing her. I kept telling her, "This doesn't look good." When I received the final news about Alan and Naomi, I called her at 5:00 in the morning. But someone from the State Department had reached her just one minute earlier and told her. Alan and Naomi were dead.

Kia and I cried together on the phone. I hung up and thought about the rest of our community. I would have to tell everyone now.

MASTER CHARLES:

We'd lost the television connection and then they turned off the electricity. But cell phones still worked and we learned that army commandos were arriving. Soon, they said. Still, all through the day we continued to hear bomb explosions and gunfire exchanges. We were living in the middle of a war zone.

My friend Steve did what he does best; he practiced yoga and remained calm and focused. Ben rested, meditated. Every time I lay down and closed my eyes, I saw Her face and She whispered Her message: "Trust and watch."

Until our cell phones lost power, we received email messages and phone calls from gurus throughout India and some of my spiritual teacher friends in America and other countries, all expressing their love and support. They and their communities were surrounding us in peace and light. This was emotional for me because when you live a life of service you naturally focus on serving others. Now it was coming back to me from all over the world and I was able to experience one of my favorite principles in action: What you give is what you get.

అఅఅఅ

Personal Power

With increasing balance, comes increasing personal power. Lost in the denser dimensions of fragmented experience governed by the ego, you survive on a very limited amplitude of personal power because your energy is so contracted, so limited. When you progress into resonance with the subtler dimensions, your amplitude of power radically increases. As you move into the next section of this book where you will begin your holistic practice, this is what you will progressively experience.

How does increasing the amplitude of your power affect you? Short answer: you feel more alive. More personal power ignites biochemical changes at the physical level, hormonal changes at the emotional and neurochemical changes at the mental level, increasing the pleasure-giving chemicals in all three systems.

This is a good moment to introduce the word "bliss." Bliss is a word that describes the most pleasurable, intoxicating, opiated, high-on-life type of experience that you can have courtesy of expanding holistic awareness. Bliss is present in all truly mystical, spiritual, transcendental, or holistic encounters. It is the experience of unified consciousness itself increasing your amplitude and delivering that opiation. You become elevated in your awareness, unified in your consciousness; you become high on life.

This is an intoxicating, euphoric, ecstatic, blissful experience. It is not a concept, it is an experience. You can evolve to being constantly joyous ... for no reason at all. You don't need a reason; you are just "high" all the time.

Martin is a monk who lives at the Synchronicity Sanctuary. He had one of several ecstatic experiences while manning the fire in preparation for a Yagna (Vedic Fire Ritual) ceremony. "When I got up to the Yagna Pavilion it was pitch black, except for the burning fire in the pit and the dim light from a few oil lamps. The shrill, constant sound of cicadas mingled with sporadic nighttime noises from various animals in the surrounding forest. As I welcomed this music for my meditation, an internal silence swelled within me. I stared into the flames, mesmerized by the flickering mandala, which occasionally melted into a blur. The silence and stillness were awesome. It was as if nothing was moving, nothing, and I was watching everything. Even when I moved, to place another log on the fire, it was Stillness that moved! I was ecstatic. It was grace to have such a sublimely blissful experience."

Grace is just as available in this moment. Slow your reading and become aware of your breath. Pause ... Stop reading and close your eyes, just for a moment, and open to the now of holistic experience.

Reading again, notice that you are reading. As the words come into focus and meaning arises, notice that you are aware of this process. You are a witnessing consciousness watching yourself reading these words, experiencing tiny increments of dawning understanding. Slow down, speed up, feel the power you have to change what is happening. And, underneath it all, can you detect that heartbeat of joy, that innate delight that is giving life to everything in this moment? It is always there, awaiting your attention to make it real for you.

Entrainment

If the amplitude of your power is at maximum holistic levels and radiating a powerful field, that obviously affects you. But how does your field affect the people you interact with and your environment?

A substantial amplitude of holistic power can override everything and everyone. This is what you may feel when you come into the presence of an authentic master, whether you understand the principles or not. Their amplitude of holistic power can shift your state of being. The nature and degree of shift differs from person to person, based on where their feet are and the evolution of their individuated consciousness.

An authentic master can elevate others into a corresponding level of wholeness within themselves. They will begin to feel peaceful in his or her presence, intoxicated, opiated. They will notice an expansion in their holistic awareness. This is the principle of entrainment in action.

Daniel Goleman writes about this principle in his book called *Emotional Intelligence*. "When it comes to personal encounters, the person who has the more forceful expressivity—or the most power—is typically the one whose emotions entrain the other. Dominant partners talk more, while the subordinate partner watches the others face more—a setup for the transmissions effect. By the same token, the forcefulness of a good speaker—a politician or an evangelist, say—works to entrain the emotions of the audience. That is what we mean by, 'He had them in the palm of his hand.' Emotional entrainment is the heart of influence." 2

This principle applies to everyone and everything in your environment including nature, which responds to any substantial amplitude of power. Muktananda's ashram, for instance, became an oasis of life. Although it was located in the back-country of India, his fruit trees and rice paddies and gardens grew to be overwhelmingly abundant. Produce from the ashram gardens grew to ten times the size of that grown by farmers down the road! The difference? Amplitude of holistic power.

Muktananda became known as a Johnny Appleseed to the West. A thousand people would show up for a weekend empowerment program and he would walk along the rows amongst them, touching people on the head with his wand of peacock feathers. Before long the whole room would erupt with laughing, crying, yelling and screaming ... it was like a zoo! Everyone's energy field would start shifting and that brought upheaval—catharsis for some, ecstasy for others. He would use all four modalities of transmission: thought, words, look, and touch.

But you do not have to go to an ashram or sit with a master to begin increasing your amplitude of holistic power, to transform yourself and the world. Gandhi, Buddha, Christ, they all began with themselves. Balance yourself first and maximize your power, **then** let this be your contribution to the world.

Your Own Chosen Manifestation

Great sages are rarely solitary. While they may have a teacher or teachers in physical form, they also commune with non-physical "apparitions" that are as real to them as living, breathing humans. Such relationships are not reserved for the blessed few, they are available to us all, if we have the amplitude of power and the subtle perception to discover and nurture such energetic exchanges.

James Fowler writes in *Stages of Faith* about just how pre-wired we are for such a relationship: "... We human beings seem to have a generic vocation—a universal calling—to be related to the Ground of Being in a relationship of trust and loyalty. That vocation calls us into covenantal relationship with the transcendent ..." [3]

"Ishta Devata" is the Sanskrit term that describes a person's chosen manifestation of the Divine. What it may be for you is based on your own soulular history and whatever archetype of the Divine you resonate with the most. I encourage everyone to discover this for themselves, and make that the focus of their worship—internal and external. In my case, the archetype turned out to be the Divine Feminine, which was also the case with my teacher.

The Divine Feminine

"When you feel you are being moved by the creative spirit,
you are in fact being moved by the divine feminine."[4]

—Teri Degler

All holistic models of reality and all philosophical traditions refer to the Divine Feminine in partnership with the Divine Masculine. The masculine is described as God the Father, who is formless and transcendent. The feminine is God the Mother, who is form and immanent. God as Father is static, God as Mother is dynamic. In terms of our description of relative reality, the Divine Feminine dominates the Divine Masculine. Obviously this is so because the Divine Feminine is form and we live in a world of form where most people are much less aware of the formless.

The Divine Feminine permeates all creation, all manifestation. Likewise, every form of consciousness is the Divine Feminine polarity, God as Mother, the Universal Creatrix. After all, everywhere you look, what do you see? Form. So, we are imbalanced to the objective. That is, universal manifestation is imbalanced to the Divine Feminine, otherwise there couldn't be a creation at all. It is necessary that this polarity dominate, so that the One can become the "Many," so that the One can diversify itself. "Unity in Diversity" is another description of the Divine Feminine. And gender doesn't make any difference.

The Truth about Gender

Do I contradict myself?
Very well, then I contradict myself,
I am large, I contain multitudes.[5]

—Walt Whitman

From this perspective, is there any form that is truly only feminine or masculine? You can't have just one polarity. What about gender in humans? There are men who are dominantly masculine in gender; others are more feminine. The same with women. But no person is all masculine or all feminine.

Throughout the multi-lifetime evolution of your consciousness, you have had many, varied experiences of gender. If you abused your dominant masculine experience in some previous journey, perhaps this time you will be clothed in a feminine form. Why? For balance and growth. Or, maybe you have had many experiences being feminine; now it is time to try on a masculine form. This time you might be a dominant feminine learning how to be masculine. There are so many legitimate gender expressions and sexual preferences. Right now you have the gender you have, walking through space-time, because this is the experience whose time has come for you.

I have met men who are so feminine that they haven't a clue about being a man. Shouldn't they be given an opportunity to learn that by being in a masculine form? Other men are so dominantly masculine that they can't relate to the feminine at all. They are abusers, aggressors. Maybe they need another experience as a man, perhaps to wake up and change. Or, wouldn't it be something if they showed up in a feminine body next time ... just for the learning experience?

Most people are thoroughly immersed in and identified with their form, masculine or feminine. But all of us are both. We may be physically masculine, with a dominant woman inside; we may be physically feminine, with a dominant man inside. What are the proportions, the degrees of dominance? Which gender has the reins? Even that is not black and white for the span of a full lifetime. There is a constant dialogue between the two polarities and, of course, evolution. If you are in conflict with your own (opposite) polarity, you will act that out in your relationships. It's futile to try and solve those conflicts out there when they originate within yourself! Resolution begins with self-acceptance, acknowledging that you are more than the single gender you have identified with.

Emma Jung wrote, "Life is founded on the harmonious interplay of masculine and feminine forces, within the individual human being as well as without. Bringing these opposites into union is one of the most important tasks of present-day psychotherapy."[6]

Masculine and feminine forms are part of the Divine Feminine. All form is. But the Divine Feminine is a process, not a separate deity. This process is represented beautifully in the Gnostic tradition as the multi-dimensional Divine Feminine. The subtlest level of unified conscious-ness is symbolized by Isis or Sophia, or whatever is the name of a God/Goddess separate and different from the individual. But, in truth, the Divine Feminine is also consciousness in manifestation as my form. So, I am animated and empowered by the Divine Feminine consciousness in manifestation, as is every human and every manifest life form.

The Divine Feminine is our default dominant. She is the "becom-ing" of "being." Divine Father is formless consciousness, so it is the non-dominant polarity. It is being, the formless being out of which comes all form, becoming. And when they balance, then you have the holistic expansion of awareness, wherein the two polarities (Divine Feminine and Divine Masculine) are the same One. Objective and subjective, form and formless, are the same One. In the evolution of individuated consciousness, we progressively experience the reversal of polarized dominance. Our awareness of formlessness gradually increases to dominate our awareness of form. That is, being increasingly dominates becoming. So progressively, you become dominant in being and sub-dominant in becoming. You evolve towards more emphasis on the formless essence and less emphasis on form and content.

Shakti and Shiva

Shiva and Shakti are the Sanskrit terms in the Tantra for the Divine Masculine and the Divine Feminine, being and becoming, the two relative polarities at their unified level. Shiva is formless consciousness, "being," and Shakti is all the forms of consciousness, the "becoming."

All the metaphors involve a couple. They are in relationship; the relative polarities are in relationship with each other. That relationship is the experience of relative reality: Shiva and his consort Shakti.

The Kama Sutra describes their sexual union in great detail, and Westerners are offended. "This is terrible, a debasing of God!" It's a metaphor! But what is sexual experience about, really? Union! It symbolizes, and actualizes in form, the balance of relative reality. And why is Shiva on top? This represents the reversal of polarized dominance, when "being" is emphasized enough to balance "becoming." The two that were separate and different become one and whole.

A retired clergyman whom I have mentored for many years was deeply troubled throughout much of his life regarding his experience of sexuality:

"From a very early age, there has been one aspect of my experience which has caused me much anguish and that is my sexuality. From my early adolescence this dominated my life and, although very pleasurable, it also caused me great conflict. In the Christian tradition in which I had been brought up and schooled, it always appeared that there was a great dichotomy between sexuality on the one hand and spirituality on the other. As I aspired to the latter, I found it difficult to accommodate the former. When I married, I thought that the conflict would be resolved but this actually increased it. I often wonder if my decision to be ordained as an Anglican Priest was an attempt to resolve this dilemma. If so, it was spectacularly unsuccessful. All I did was to try and deny that I was a sexual being!

"Similarly, my decision to specialize in the fields of pastoral counseling and to later become a psychotherapist were attempts to come to terms with my own sexuality, I believe. My late wife was very accepting of my rampant libido and eventually agreed to a sexually open marriage. This was partially successful, because at least it helped me to accept myself as a sexual being. But it did nothing to reconcile sexuality with my spiritual life and I ended up relinquishing any sort of spiritual practice altogether for many years.

"Of course, this was as much a denial of myself as the previous attempt had been and was equally unsuccessful! I thus became even more troubled. Then I started meditating and put my spiritual life back on the agenda. My sexuality retreated, mostly because I did not have a sexual partner at that time. Then, after the death of my first wife and my remarriage, the old conflict resurfaced. I shared my concerns with Master Charles. He encouraged me to see and accept that my sexuality and spirituality were not incompatible, that they were both natural parts of my whole being. He suggested that I see the energy aroused by my eroticism as fuel to empower my evolution as a complete person. He taught me about the tradition of Tantra and its role in the development of the Holistic Lifestyle.

"As a result, I am experiencing liberation from the limits of my Christian enculturation and a resulting sense of the true freedom to be who I am. New vistas of life have opened up that did not seem at all possible before."

Pause for a moment; slow down in your reading to consider your own attitudes and experience of sexuality. Let your mind wander ... and your emotions. Here, with just yourself, be honest about this part of your life. How do you think about yourself; who do you think you are? A woman? A man? Take another breath and relax. Know this: you are not feminine ... you are not masculine. These identities are an illusion. Release your attachment to that illusion. You are the One that includes both, the One delighting union of masculine and feminine. Your combination of energies is entirely unique and there is none other in the world like you. Imagine that! Feel appreciation for the body you have, whatever gender it is. Recognize that it is a vehicle to facilitate your perfect next steps of evolutionary experience, accommodating both masculine and feminine energies, blended together into your personal amplitude of power.

Death is Not the End

"Sixty-six times have these eyes beheld the
changing scenes of autumn.
I have said enough about moonlight,
ask me no more.
Only listen to the voices of pines and cedars,
when no wind stirs.[7]

—Ryo-Nen (Her Last Composition)

Death is terrifying for anyone who is identified with the human form, regardless of gender. But the only thing that actually happens is the dropping of the physical body. You, the truth of you, your individuated consciousness, continues—in a subtler reality.

Eckhart Tolle conveys a holistic perspective on life and death in his book, *A New Earth.* "Out of nowhere, so to speak, 'you' suddenly appear in this world. This is followed by expansion. There is not only physical growth, but also growth of knowledge, activities, possessions, experiences. Your sphere of influence expands and life becomes increasingly complex. This is the time when you are mainly concerned with finding or pursuing your outer purpose. Usually there is also a corresponding growth of the ego, which is identification with all of the above things, and so your form identity becomes more and more defined. This is also the time when outer purpose—growth—tends to become usurped by the ego, which unlike nature does not know when to stop in its pursuit of expansion and has a voracious appetite for *more.*

"And then, just when you thought you made it, that you belong here, the return movement begins. Perhaps people close to you begin to die, people who were a part of your world. Then your physical form weakens; your sphere of influence shrinks. Instead of becoming more, you now become less, and the ego reacts to this with increasing anxiety or depression. Your world is beginning to contract, and you may find you are not in control anymore. Instead of acting upon life, life now acts upon you by slowly reducing your world. The consciousness that identified with form is now experiencing the sunset, the dissolution of form. And then one day, you too disappear. Your armchair is still there. But instead of you sitting in it, there is just an empty space. You went back to where you came from just a few years ago." [8]

Having this perspective helped us in Mumbai, when the possibility of physical death became real and imminent. After our rescue, I spoke about Alan and Naomi, who were killed during the attack, with Her Holiness Sai Maa Lakshmi Devi, who is a very multi-dimensionally aware master who was also a professional psychotherapist for years. She said that Naomi was fine, that she had moved right through her process. But Alan was a little stuck and confused. We did some inner work together with Alan to guide him along his way.

The key principle is this: As you live, so you die. If you haven't invested in wakefulness, you won't have a wakeful death. And you must have substantial wakefulness to move through the death experience without fear. The body is the body, complete with entropy, decay, and death. You must relinquish it at death. When death will come is for your consciousness to determine. It came for Alan and Naomi in Mumbai but not for any of us. Why? Because this was the experience whose time had come for all of us, each in our own way.

The consciousness that you truly are will continue, eternally. This is your holistic essence and it simply does not die. It continues to invest in what is permanent, that which continues, that which evolves, increasing its wholeness throughout countless possibilities in the fifty billion theoretical simultaneous universes. It's an exploration, an adventure, the forever adventure of being and its becoming.

Why miss a moment of it? Live your life fully without regret. Every moment has contributed in some way to you becoming more masterful of your form. And what are you here for if not mastery? You may never occupy a human form again. After all, there are fifty billion theoretical simultaneous universes. Is your consciousness so myopic that it will just keep repeating the same type of incarnation over and over again? That doesn't seem to be the way quantum mechanics and consciousness work.

Funerals, rightly practiced, are always a celebration of life. Hallelujah! This person has completed their human journey and you wish them well. Yes, you will miss them, because of your attachment to their form and their unique expression through that form, but you can celebrate for the soul, the individuated consciousness who is moving on.

And, don't shut them out. They have only dropped the body and this means that they are actually closer to you now. There is one less boundary between you, because their dense form is no longer in the way. Those you believe to be gone are simultaneous to you; they remain here in the simultaneity of reality in subtle dimensionality until the time comes when they incarnate into another form. During that time you can interact together.

Alan and Naomi are still present and interactive with many of us who knew them because we have remained open to that interaction. I often advise those in mourning of this possibility: "Stop! They are right here and they keep touching you on the shoulder! They are closer to you than your very breath. Be open to them." Then someone might tell me that the person who just died appeared to them in dream soon thereafter, or that some sort of synchronistic miracle or recognition occurred. Aha!

Our limiting Judeo Christian enculturation tells us that our human form is our **only** form, and that when it is gone, we are gone with it. When it's over, **we're** over, and it's a huge tragedy. Ridiculous! That is what I loved about going to the East. There, death is like changing clothes. When you wear out one set of clothes, you relinquish them and get a new set. Look, how nice! Get rid of the old clothes, maybe burn them in the fire, and put on new ones.

I prefer the Eastern model of cremation because it makes practical sense. Otherwise, it all just takes up so much space … endless boxes and cemeteries. Alan and Naomi's cremated remains rest in the Grotto of our Sanctuary. Incidentally, my parents want their remains placed there as well. That was a change! For years they had their cemetery plot reserved close to their relatives, and just unconsciously embraced that whole tradition. Even though they haven't lived anywhere near them or that area for many years, that was the tradition. They were born there, so they should be buried there.

They changed their minds after an experience in the Grotto. I visit the Grotto every day. It is a sacred space wherein I commune with the Blessed Mother. She appears to me regularly there. Others join me there on special occasions and She often appears to them as well. There is always a pertinent message.

My father has often represented himself as the ultimate skeptic. Nonetheless, when the Blessed Mother began to appear in the Grotto, he asked if I would share this with him. So, one day he was sitting there with me in the Grotto and I was relating to him what She was saying ... to him. He listened intently and then said, very quietly, "Well, I don't see anything, but it is a very peaceful place." Then the Blessed Mother said to me: "Tell him that I receive all his prayers."

My father would never think of himself as very religious, but when I shared Her message he became very attentive and then began to cry. After a few moments, he leaned close to me and whispered, "You know, I **have** been praying lately." Thereafter, he asked if they could change their burial plans. They now wanted to be cremated and have their ashes entombed in the Grotto.

Death is merely the death of impermanence. What dies is the content you have invested in. But all content is impermanent and we know that. If that's your only investment, what do you have left when you die? Beliefs about a Judgment Day, Heaven and Hell? Likely, then—looking ahead—you will be afraid. Sadly, many people die afraid, unless they brainwash themselves to believe they have enough merit badges to get into heaven. But most people believe they are sinners. If there's a heaven and a hell, knowing themselves as they do, most believe they are more likely to go to hell. Obviously then, ignoring or denying death makes sense if this is your only reference.

My parents are 93 and 96 as I am writing this. They have been married for 70 years. They have a lot of time now to sit and think about death. In fact, they've been thinking about it for many years. I have watched them move through a process in relation to their enculturated religious beliefs. I've watched them become depressed about it. I've listened to them trying to talk themselves into a new belief system.

Sadly, they were haunted by self-judgment that says, "You didn't measure up; you don't have the criteria to get into heaven." Fortunately, they have dialogued with me and I've been able to gently explain to them just how delusional that whole belief system is and re-educate them and shift their focus. They now believe differently.

Let's shift your focus for a moment. Pause, notice your breathing, and reflect for a moment on your own death. Acknowledge that a day is coming, a moment when you will "lose" everything. All content will vanish. What will be left? Consider that ... consider who you are without your content identity. Feel your presence, your consciousness reading these words and know, at a deep level, that this holistic awareness will continue. This is who you are, not your body, not your illusory stories. This holistic awareness, this consciousness, is who you really are, always have been, and will always be.

A New Look at Reincarnation

*"As we live through thousands of dreams in our present life,
so is our present life only one of many thousands of such lives
which we enter from the other more real life ...
and then return after death. Our life is but one of the dreams
of that more real life, and so it is endlessly, until the very last one,
the very real life of God."*[9]

—Count Leo Tolstoy

In Eastern traditions, one is not limited by the birth and death of the human body. We have a soul, they say, an identity that was before and will continue after residence in this body. This is the theory of reincarnation, which proposes that our personal life experience is not confined within the two boundaries of birth and death.

I believe that the traditional philosophy of reincarnation needs to be updated. It was developed ten thousand years ago by people who didn't know anyone further than a few miles away. At night, they sat outside, beheld the stars overhead and realized that there had to be more to their existence than they could ever actualize in just one life. So, they decided that there must be some sort of continuation or progression. Because of the very local nature of their life experience and without conscious awareness of the fifty billion theoretical simultaneous universes, they assumed everyone must return to the earth.

This created the belief of reincarnation in one human life after another on planet earth as a repetitive cycle of progressive evolution towards wholeness. But now, ten thousand years later, we know more about cosmic manifestation and have a more scientific understanding of the relationship between individuated and universal consciousness. Yes, there is a progression and continuation, but it might not always be human to human. We acknowledge the possibility of any number of unknown forms in the fifty billion theoretical simultaneous universes.

Why come back and repeat the same thing over and over again? Why keep repeating the same one, when there may be countless other forms through which you as consciousness could evolve? Wouldn't that be more interesting? So, I suggest opening to this possibility and acknowledging that this life now might be your only human one. What is important is how much you grow it, how much your self-awareness increases through this one human lifetime.

Actually, I believe that this is the case for most people, that they have a one-time shot at being a human. Those who say, "I remember past lives, I have been human before," well, they can't really be sure of that. Being human now, we are referencing everything through this human experience. We are veiled in terms of our soulular history. But, realistically, why would consciousness choose to limit itself to one little speck in its cosmic manifestation and force everyone to come here and have the same experience over and over again?

What Dies, What Remains?

Only the physical dimension is dropped. What survives is your entire database in relation to the evolution of your individuated consciousness. The way you have lived determines the way you die and what continues thereafter. Your evolution proceeds from one life experience to the next.

Let's say you had nothing to do with wholeness in this life, were completely fragmented and that's as far as you got. You are still primarily egocentric. Well then, this is "where your feet are" at the moment of death and that will determine the nature of your continuation. Your download of continuance is self-referential. Themes continue, moving you forward in the direction of your ongoing growth. Of course, there is grace within this process because the nature of universal consciousness is joy. You don't get punished. That's an egoic invention; you just continue your evolutionary progression.

Obviously, you wouldn't need to carry your entire database of experience into your next form of consciousness, which might not even be human. Not all of your data is relevant. What continues are the general themes of balance or imbalance, wholeness or fragmentation. And, of course, your karma goes with you, as we discussed in an earlier chapter. How you lived helps determine how your body will die and how you will live on in continuation.

This raises a fascinating question: "How conscious can you be of the database of your previous lives?" Very little, other than knowing those principles and what you were most interested in. If you developed balance and wholeness in your life, these general themes will continue to be operative because they accurately represent the evolution of your consciousness.

I Am ... All Is ... One

As you turn the next pages and progress into part II, you will begin to study the Holistic Lifestyle and make actual changes in your daily routine. This has the potential to transform your experience of life. It's appropriate, therefore, to complete this section with one closing statement about "the way things are."

Death follows birth. Life is eternal. The full reality of life cannot be contained within the human bookends of birth and death. It is non-linear. Existence, life, true reality, is now, and all else is illusion. The only experience of reality that you ever have is now. Slow down your reading and contemplate that fact in this moment. Experience what it means ... much more than just reading the words. This is it, now, here. And since we are always here and now, everything we actually experience is always and only here and now. In fact, the past is gone forever and the future remains a fantasy. The present is the only time you can ever truthfully say, "I am alive ... I am existing." Living in the now is living in the truthful reality of the moment, experiencing the trinity of relative reality as a witnessing consciousness watching itself.

This trinity includes the two polarities of form and formlessness plus the space between them. Without this space neither polarity could exist. When you become balanced relative to these two polarities, this space between them opens. This is the space we call "now." Now is a witnessing consciousness watching itself, aware of both polarities—the interior and the exterior—simultaneously. Consciousness is the one who is watching both.

Diane Hennacy Powell, M.D. describes this in her book, *The ESP Enigma*: "People who have experienced mystical states of consciousness universally report that during the mystical state, one's sense of separateness from the physical world dissipates. The concepts of 'I,' 'me,' or 'mine' lose relevancy or meaning. One's sense of time is replaced by a sense of eternity." [10]

This is unified consciousness, witnessing consciousness. Your interior awareness is consciousness; your exterior awareness is consciousness.

And you are the witnessing consciousness that is watching both. Before, you were identified with your body. Now, you are a detached observer of the exterior. Simultaneously, you are a detached observer of the interior. You are not that formlessness either. You are the witness observing both, from the dilated space between the polarities.

In that space, in the eternal now of consciousness, you can truly say, without fear of death because you are embracing the eternal nature of life that you are: "I am ... all is ... One."

❧❧❧

CAROL:

Morning came on the heels of a sleepless night, huddled together with hundreds of people in that parking garage, all trying to find some place to rest. I kept asking where my friends were. Finally, frustrated, I borrowed a cell phone and called Bobbie in Virginia. She filled me in. I was shocked to hear about Naomi and Alan. As I sat there, trying to digest it all, a stranger approached and, speaking in fairly good English, offered his apartment as a sanctuary.

We trusted him immediately and Mureen, Miriam and I left with him in his car. We ended up spending two days there with his wife and children. They were wonderful. After the others were rescued his wife drove us to the Four Seasons Hotel.

LINDA:

I was lying on the floor of the kitchen when Helen stumbled in. There was blood on her shirt and face, but miraculously, just one bullet had grazed her leg. I felt strangely content, swimming in a beautiful, blossoming red lake, oblivious that this was blood from my wound. I noticed a tiny lock on the kitchen door and demanded that our kitchen angels—those who had called us to join them there —lock it. I must have been delirious! Machine guns and grenades against a one-quarter inch round slide lock?

A sudden explosion rumbled. The gunmen were back with grenades. A sobering thought dawned on me: these men really wanted us dead. How odd. Strangers were determined to kill me. My musings were interrupted by the maître d' who urged us to leave now and steered us down a narrow corridor. We followed him through a boiler room towards an emergency exit with an alarm on it. As we debated whether to risk opening it and possibly alerting the terrorists to our whereabouts, another explosion made the decision for us. A young staff member kicked the door open and alarms immediately blared.

JOE:

We had been trapped in our room for over forty hours and I began to wonder if this was it, if my number was up. Well, I was eighty-eight years old, I'd had a pretty full life, that would be OK. Then I heard that the Army Commandos had arrived. We were alerted that they were coming for us but we had to wait a long time before we finally heard them knock on the door. I'll tell you, they were just a fantastic group of young men. They got me into my wheelchair and out we went, into that awful devastation.

BERNIE:

We had been getting calls all day that the Commandos were coming and that we should get our stuff together. Larry asked how we would know it's really the Commandos and was told that they would be dressed in black. I started laughing. "So, what are terrorists wearing this year?" I asked. "Hot pink?"

It was all so terrible that you had to laugh; just to make it through you had to find some humor somewhere. Larry called Vinka and said that he was going to order coffee sent up to the room. Right!

MIRIAM:

After a few hours another local man told us that we shouldn't stay there on the footpath. So we crossed the street and sat on some steps, still waiting for signs of our friends. The only people we saw that had escaped from the Oberoi were some Japanese businessmen, a family that had to leave their old grandmother up in her room, and a honeymooning couple.

We really didn't know much about what was happening. The locals said nothing, just offered us cardboard boxes to lie on and bubble wrap for blankets. I was continually coughing so it was difficult to fall asleep but I did meditate. Suddenly, I had a sudden vision of Ganesh, who represents the remover of obstacles, and I just knew that Master Charles was OK.

Early in the morning an Oberoi car came to take us to a safer place. As we got out in a parking lot, a familiar voice called out. It was Carol. We were so glad to see her. She shared her story but had no news of our friends.

MASTER CHARLES:

Around 5:00 p.m. on the third day the Army Commandos killed the last terrorist and slowly secured the building. We were advised that they would soon be coming to take us out and informed us how it would unfold. We removed the barricade from the door. Soon thereafter a team of commandos banged on our door and then opened it with their master key. There were about ten of them and they all had their guns pointed at us. We put our hands up and they frisked us. Then they secured the room.

We left everything in the room as they escorted us out into the hotel hallway. It was a scene of total devastation. We went down the interior fire escape and out into the lobby. There were bodies, blood, and debris everywhere.

⌒⌒⌒

To better integrate the meaning of this chapter, please visit www.synchronicity.org, go to the "Forgiving the Unforgivable" section, and use the password "one" to access additional material.

Interlude

The fire that iron or gold need—
would it be good for fresh quinces and apples?
The apple and quince are just slightly raw;
unlike iron, they need only a gentle heat.
But gentle flames are not enough for iron;
it eagerly draws to itself the fiery dragon's breath.
That iron is the dervish who bears hardship:
under the hammer and fire, he happily glows red.[1]

—Rumi

We are pausing for a moment between part I and part II. Our presentation of the Holistic Model is complete, and we will shortly begin our presentation of the Holistic Lifestyle. It's time to put theory into practice.

We've structured part I to put experience first, as much as possible. In keeping with that model, this brief chapter is an interlude ... a few pages for reflection. As the Rumi quote above so eloquently states, there is a tool for every task. But first comes holistic awareness, witness consciousness, so that whatever is learned or done is experienced from that truthful position. You've learned what that means in the preceding pages. Now, in just a few moments, it's time to begin your practice.

How will you create the life you want to have? It happens by being it, not seeking it. And this requires a holistic amplitude of personal power. Intention expressed with power attracts (that is the law of attraction). As you balance your life and increase your own amplitude of power, you will manifest the life you wish to have. Of course, that won't happen unless your thinking emerges from the balance point and unless you are accessing the power of universal consciousness. This is what you will learn to do in part II.

As you move into the second section of this book and begin applying the principles of the Holistic Model into your Holistic Lifestyle, you will unfold this new understanding into your life experience. Congratulations and bon voyage!

Expect miracles.

෧෧෧෧

KIA:

A couple of weeks before the trip Naomi had a premonition. She came to breakfast and said that she just had a terrible nightmare. "These men came into a restaurant where Dad and I were and they started shooting. They shot us, right there in the restaurant!"

MIRIAM:

Yes, it is very sad that we lost Alan and Naomi. But I'm not taking on that story. In fact, I'm starting to have glimpses of a transformation that is much bigger than anything I have known before. Life doesn't end when you die, you just get transformed.

I've been meditating for nineteen years with Synchronicity High-Tech Meditation, but now I really know that God is life. I knew it in my head before. Now it's in my body and my heart, right down to the core of my being.

I'm so grateful for all that I learned from Master Charles and for his calm guidance through the storm in Mumbai. I am so appreciative. And that's a choice, my choice to live that way, not just now in relationship to that memory but in every moment with everything and everyone. I am life and love.

It's that simple, really. We are all one ... including those terrorists.

LINDA:

The FBI asked us to give witness impact statements to the two Chicago suspects who were complicit in selecting the Mumbai hotels to attack. We learned that one of them, David is his name I think, was probably in the Oberoi Hotel lobby at the same time that Alan was. There was Alan thinking, what a great place to bring a meditation group. And there was this guy at the same time, thinking, what a great place to kill people. The synchronicity of that is mind blowing!

HELEN:

I'm profoundly grateful for my Mumbai experience and I have said that from day one. It was a big karmic leap for me. Master Charles said that it enabled us to burn off a lot of karma in a short period of time. I know that may seem like an odd idea to anyone who is not familiar with the idea of karma but it is very real for me. I could feel it afterwards, that I had let go of a lot of baggage.

To be that close to experiencing death and yet not feel fear—which really was my experience—was tremendously liberating. I now feel more empowered in my life, more evolved, and more loving. Also, I am intensely grateful for the simple moments of life. For instance, the other day, I was in our garden pruning rose bushes with my husband. I've done that before but now... now it seemed like a heavenly moment. I felt at one with everything.

LINDA:

When I caught that brief glimpse of the terrorist who shot us I realized that he was about the same age as my son. The same age but living in such a completely different world! How I ached for this boy, this poor young soul who felt that his gun was the only way he could communicate. Fear shook his every step.

As he approached our table intending to kill us, I spoke to him silently from my heart: "When you were born, didn't someone tell you how much you were loved? Didn't someone tell you what a blessing you were, coming into this world?"

This is the maternal ache every mother feels for every child. Our responsibility as mothers extends to all "our" children. At some level we understand that. May all children everywhere feel this love and know this blessing.

CAROL:

There was so much love shown to me from every corner of the globe. Even the FBI agents were kind when they met me at the plane as I arrived home. The media? Well, they couldn't really believe that we didn't want to see the terrorists hanging by their toes. I explained to them that these men were born to do what they did, that they probably couldn't help it. They just didn't know any better. I know that many in the media just couldn't understand that perspective! But it's not unusual for us. We didn't adopt this as a new idea for that occasion; it's how we live. We know that everyone is right where they need to be, doing what they need to be doing. And, according to the choices made, everyone will appropriately evolve.

Knowing this, why would any of us choose to express the same things as those terrorists? They brought hate. Does that mean that I should bring hate too? No. My choice, our choice, has been to bring love. That is the same choice we have been practicing for many years. It's a truthful habit. And that's why Mumbai, horrendous event that it was, has been a growth experience for me and for all of us, rather than something that ruined our lives. It was an opportunity to practice what we have already been doing and grow in leaps and bounds because of the challenges. Mumbai enriched our lives and hopefully, as we tell our story, it will enrich many other lives too. In the end, there will be more love in the world, not more hate. This is how we defeat the terrorists. It's very simple.

LINDA:

I am an artist of life. My canvas stands before me: empty, white, and beautiful. Suddenly a black splotch is thrown onto it. Well, it's my canvass and I'm the artist! I don't need to let that blotch stick. I can let it just slide right off. That's exactly what I have done with Mumbai.

Mumbai was like a chiaroscuro drawing for me. That's an old Renaissance period style where the artist begins with dark and applies light to illuminate their scene. The result is very high contrast between light and dark. That is what the memory of Mumbai looks like to me now. Life brought light into the dark.

How did it change me? Mumbai helped me cleanse through some old baggage I had no need to carry any more—just like the luggage I took over that got lost. I had some obsolete internal luggage too ... gone now.

So, although I *am* the woman who got shot, you don't see that when you look at me. You see a smiling woman, not just the woman with the long scar. Ultimately, like everyone, I have control—if I choose it. I have control over how I respond to what happens in my life. When darkness comes, I too can bring out the light.

That is how I choose to create my life, moment by moment, because I am an artist. Everyone is an artist. Let us all create masterpieces! Let's make the best life ever!

❧❧❧❧

PART II

Practicing the Holistic Lifestyle

CHAPTER 7

Meditation: The Ultimate Balancing Technique

"We could say that meditation doesn't have a reason or doesn't have a purpose. In this respect it's unlike almost all other things we do except perhaps making music and dancing. When we make music we don't do it in order to reach a certain point, such as the end of the composition. If that were the purpose of music then obviously the fastest players would be the best. Also, when we are dancing we are not aiming to arrive at a particular place on the floor as in a journey. When we dance, the journey itself is the point, as when we play music the playing itself is the point. And exactly the same thing is true in meditation. Meditation is the discovery that the point of life is always arrived at in the immediate moment."[1]

—Alan Watts

In 40 hours, 10 terrorists kill 173 people in Mumbai and wound 308 more. Rapid Action Force personnel, Marine Commandos (Marcos) and National Security Guards (NSG) commandos storm the Oberoi Hotel and finally kill the two terrorists there, but not before they execute 32 hostages. The SWAT team searches the hotel, floor-by-floor and room-by-room for survivors.

Finally, it is time for everyone to get out.

Meditation brings balance:
interior to exterior,
subject to object,
being to becoming.
Wholeness is proportional to balance.
In meditation I expand holistic awareness,
I am consciousness aware of itself.
I experience myself as Source.

కొకొకొ

PEGGI:

Bonnie phoned to say that commandos were coming to rescue us, but a moment later we heard more explosions and shooting. Two hours later someone pounded on our door. I looked through the peephole and called out, "Who is it?" There was no answer, just more pounding and then a shout: "Open Up!" Again, I called out and got the same response. Meanwhile, Lisa called the front desk and they told her that yes, it *was* the commandos. Hoping they were right, I focused within, chose life and opened the door.

After searching the room, they took us out. We saw a few others being guided too and it was awful how the hotel had been destroyed. The first thing I noticed was how the deep green ivy, which had been thriving, was now dead and brown. All the furniture was smashed, there was broken glass and copper pipes lying twisted on the floor. I remember that the grand piano was still there in the lobby, miraculously unscathed by the firestorm that had consumed everything else. How that could be I had no idea.

The commandos leading us didn't know exactly where to go. The lobby was on the second floor but they began leading us up some stairs near the Tiffen restaurant. Suddenly, we could see dead bodies in there and we told them to stop, we returned down the stairs, and found another stairway out onto the street. I had never seen it when it wasn't bustling with people and traffic. Now it was deserted and silent, like another world.

LISA:

"Don't you dare open that door!" I shouted at Peggi. I made her wait while I called the front desk. Someone answered, thank God, and I recognized the voice. They said it was okay, yes, that these were commandos, not terrorists. Peggi let them in.

There were about six of them, young men all in black, with very scary guns. They searched our room and then escorted us down through the mayhem to a small room. That's where I lost it. I started crying and just couldn't stop. These guys looked like they were 18 or 19 years old, just babies, really. I must have been a mother figure to them and they got really concerned. "It's OK," they assured me, over and over. "It's OK."

AMY:

Phyl said we had to unlock the door for the commandos so we sat for about 24 hours with an unlocked door. When the commandos finally came I didn't think it was them because they were all wearing Nike shoes. They entered our room with big angelic smiles. One offered me some chocolate. They took us down the stairs and then outside onto the street.

BOBBIE:

Fifty community friends showed up for Thanksgiving dinner. It was a very "charged" celebration, because we were all thinking about Master Charles and our friends in Mumbai. After the meal, I addressed everyone. I wasn't sure what I would say but, as I started to speak, I received a real download. Out of my mouth they came, words filled with deep conviction. I said that I was sure we all understood that on some level Alan and Naomi signed up for this experience. There were nods in the silence. I remember looking at the faces of my friends, some of my dearest friends in the world, and seeing that they did know, just as I knew in that moment. This was an experience whose time had come for Alan and Naomi and just as truly for every one of us.

We got it, without needing to know "why." Why not? Everything is orchestrated, what happens is meant to be happening. So, we should celebrate, illogical as that seemed. After all, it was Thanksgiving.

MASTER CHARLES:

As we left our room we found ourselves wading through dark water. Everything within our sight was ripped apart. I remember observing all this from a deeply expansive state, silent and detached. As the commandos moved us slowly down the service stairs there were a series of explosions. I understand Hindi so I learned that other commandos were forcing their way into any room where they got no answer, to flush out any terrorists who might still be hiding out in the hotel somewhere.

They took us to the restaurant and one of them asked me in broken English if I thought that any of our party might have been in there. Yes, I said that I knew there were. He asked me to accompany him inside and identify them. It was a scene of utter devastation; bodies and debris were everywhere, all jumbled together in pools of blood.

We found Alan and Naomi under a table, collapsed into each other. Alan's head was blown apart. I nodded to the commando, pointed to them, and gave him their names: "Alan and Naomi Scherr." This was one of the most difficult moments of my life.

I stood for a long moment looking at these dear friends one last time, knowing that they were irretrievably gone and that these were just their bodies, now destroyed and rendered uninhabitable. The spirits that I knew and loved as Alan and Naomi were not trapped therein. They had been liberated.

ॐॐॐ

A New Beginning

"The wholeness and freedom we seek is our true nature,
who we really are. Whenever we start a spiritual practice,
read a spiritual book or contemplate what it means to live well,
we have begun the inevitable process of opening to this truth,
the truth of life itself." [2]

—Jack Kornfield

Once there is awakening, once you have had a glimpse, a taste, an experience of the truth, you have pierced through the illusion. "Wait a minute, I thought I was separate and different, but I just had an experience of Oneness, unity, essence. I had an experience of the truth of who I am in relation to the illusion. What now?" Once you have had that experience, then—even though you are still dominantly egocentric—you are bound to pursue more of it. Why? Because it was so pleasurable. In fact, it was the literal opposite of suffering. It was pure joy.

You might think something like this to yourself: "I have glimpsed the truth and it felt great! I want more. My whole being was flooded with something ... something like happiness but for no reason at all. I get it ... I have been in darkness and now, for maybe the first time in such a deep way, there was light and truth ... It was real, and it felt good. OK, I want more." This describes a frequent response that I call "Candy and the Baby." When you give a baby candy do you think it will ever forget that? Not a chance! The baby wants **more** candy. Likewise, once you have tasted the truth—not some sort of intellectual enlightenment but an authentic holistic experience—you want more. This is the primary intention of consciousness activated within you. And finding ways to get more is what creates evolutionary momentum.

Building Your Holistic Practice

It's time to begin implementing what you have learned of the holistic model of reality into some sort of regular, day-to-day practice. Your understanding will increase through experience, not analysis. As my teacher Muktananda used to say: "You can't get it by thinking you can get it. It's about experience, not concept."

At the Synchronicity Foundation for Modern Spirituality, we harness technology for enlightening purposes, specially designed to eliminate fragmentation and separation, increase balance and wholeness, and awaken the experience of unity and communion. You may feel isolated initially, reading this book on your own, but your practice will ground your understanding in a very real way. And you can connect with others who are likewise practicing via our website.

Your practice will gradually integrate into your daily experience so that you begin to enjoy expanded holistic awareness and truthful connection within the whole of your life. Your capacity for genuine compassion will increase. And you will find yourself fulfilling the primary intention in consciousness for all of us: to experience who you are by completing the experience of who you are not, to restore balance and wholeness.

Now is the moment to make a commitment to yourself. Is this an experience whose time has come for you? Are you ready to make these holistic principles real in your evolving life experience? As you have done throughout section one, slow your reading. Become aware of the space between the words, the letters. Pause in a space ... feel yourself pausing ... notice that you are witnessing your experience, what you are reading and what you are feeling. You must be something more ... Yes, you are the witnessing consciousness that is always watching. And, being that, feeling yourself at home in that space—not a solid "thing" but a flowing "space"—just gently contemplate yourself with respect, honor, and gratitude. Acknowledge the step you are taking now, committing to a holistic lifestyle practice.

The primary goal of having a holistic lifestyle practice is to balance the two relative polarities, so that you can increasingly experience the space between them. Space by its nature seems empty. Not so, according to Amit Goswami, PhD who writes in God is Not Dead, "Emptiness is a no-thing, it is full of quantum possibilities, and it is fullness in potentia. When consciousness is empty of the known, the playground of our conditioned ego-self, room is made for the unconditioned to come through. Buddhism does not talk much about the unconditioned, but it is implicit. They leave it for you to find out as a surprise."[3] The specific practices that will assist you to savor such surprises do so by first helping you balance your physical, mental and emotional dimensions. But all the masters agree that moderation is important, so don't imagine that you are plunging into something extreme. Gentle, wakeful steps forward—that's the way.

However, that said, there's one requirement that I make with those who welcome my assistance: no recreational drugs or alcohol. Why is that so important? Because drugs and alcohol alter your state of being. With a holistic practice you alter your own state without relying on any external substance. So, if you're able, include this discipline in your commitment to a new life through a holistic practice. If it seems hard, that you are losing something, remember that consciousness itself is a delighting energy. The more you wean yourself from substitutes, the more you will experience the real thing. Becoming able to feel happy, for no reason at all, is a "skill" worth developing!

Dr. Bruce Lipton, a true scientific heretic who became fascinated by what he termed the "new biology" and "unleashing the power of consciousness," wrote about his own "conversion" in *Biology of Belief*: "I tested my hypothesis in my own life after a nudge from my audiences, who asked me why my insights hadn't made me any happier. They were right: I needed to integrate my new biological awareness into my daily life. I knew I had succeeded when, on a bright Sunday morning in the Big Easy, a coffee shop waitress asked me, "Honey, you are the happiest person I ever did see. Tell me child, why are you so happy?" I was taken aback by her question, but nevertheless I blurted out: "I'm in Heaven!" That could be the one and only time a scientist has ever uttered those words! I take it a step further when I say, "I am heaven ... living truthful life!"[4]

In the Beginning

We've all heard the statement that a journey of 1,000 miles begins with a single step. As you begin to actualize the holistic model of reality into a daily practice, your first step is a self-diagnostic test. After all, before setting out on any journey, you need to know clearly where you are starting from, before you can navigate to where you want to go.

In other words, you need to find out where your feet are, relative to the three dimensions that you will be balancing through your practice. So, if you wish, pause in your reading now and visit our website, www.synchronicity.org, the Forgiving the Unforgivable section, where you can download a free self-diagnostic tool. It is offered to provide a useful reference along the way, a touchstone to track how far you've progressed in your Holistic Lifestyle practice.

Your First Holistic Tool

Your first holistic tool is the simplest and the most important: becoming consciously "present." The way you accomplish this is simple: **relax**. Relax in this moment. Let any anxiety or ambition you may feel just flow out of your body. Use your breath ... easy breathing in and out ... and let your mind become still. Relax.

The second step is to **allow**. Consider your life for a moment, no doubt full of things you'd like to change. Can you allow them to just be? Can you relax with everything and allow all your problems, every situation that is crying out for a solution, to be exactly the way it is right now?

If you can, if you can allow it, then you can **include** it. This is really about accepting everything within the whole of life. Whatever this is, it belongs. Now you can **observe** your situation, because you are no longer egocentrically identified with it (at least not as much as before).

If you can observe long enough, without judgment, you will **transform** whatever you are witnessing. Your holistic amplitude of power has the potential to transform whatever it touches through conscious attention and awareness.

So here is your first holistic tool, this conscious presencing technique, which you can use anytime, anywhere:

Relax—Release any "efforting."
Allow—Let it be ... as it is.
Include—Embrace it as a part of all that is.
Observe—You are the witnessing consciousness.
Transform—Focus your conscious attention, your holistic awareness, and let change happen.

As Easy as Closing Your Eyes

Very few people will get up at 2:30 every morning to meditate for three hours! Start where you are now and flow with the changes that seem appropriate. Explore new activities that you can integrate into your existing routine to change it, but do this gently, without such sudden and extreme discipline that your practice becomes a duty rather than a delight. What are you naturally led to do, because of where your feet are right now? This is always different than what your ego tells you to do, hurrying you towards some sort of accomplishment. Remember, you are in transition. Enjoy every step and don't worry about the destination.

The easiest balancing practice is to simply close your eyes. Do that right now. ... As you read again, wasn't it interesting that the moment you closed your eyes the whole busy, complex exterior world just vanished? Of course, you still had your thoughts. That is where meditation and the use of an affirmation become useful. But just the act of closing your eyes, while remaining wakeful, is a balancing practice.

What could be simpler? Here's something you can do anywhere, any time. Perhaps you are sitting at your work desk or stuck in a traffic jam. Take a moment to close your eyes. (Just for a moment, don't go to sleep!) What a difference this makes, instantly! Holding on the phone, waiting for software to load, sitting in the theater before the movie begins. There are countless moments during the day when you have a few moments to close your eyes and experience this mini-meditation. "I don't have time to meditate" is not a valid excuse for anyone.

Having a holistic practice is about living in balance. It's not just about some "thing" you do that is separate from the moments of your living, like yoga or meditation. Practicing this one simple meditative technique periodically can be a very powerful way to begin making balance your new priority. To balance your momentary experience, that's your new job description.

Imagine you are piloting a 747 to Hawaii. Those planes are off course about 80% of the time but they reach their destination because the pilot constantly adjusts course. That's what balancing is, making small course corrections, moment by moment.

Balance Breaks

"What I dream of is an art of balance, of purity and serenity
devoid of troubling or depressing subject matter
—a soothing, calming influence on the mind,
rather like a good armchair
which provides relaxation from physical fatigue." [5]

—Henri Matisse

You can expand the mini-meditation into what I call "balance breaks." Simply take three to five minutes, stop everything you're doing, and just sit with your eyes closed in a meditative, focused holistic awareness. Open to the stillness within. This is a balance break, moments where you choose to be, rather than to do.

You can be spontaneous with balance breaks or schedule them, for instance in the morning between breakfast and lunch or after dinner before retiring. As you develop a more formal meditation practice, you will discover the same holistic experience begins to show up during these brief balance breaks. You will gradually become able to sustain expansive holistic awareness from meditation to mini-meditation to balance break, and so on, throughout even a very busy day.

When I am mentoring someone, I have them map their waking hours relative to balance and imbalance. It's likely they were balanced as they emerged from their morning meditation. How long were they able to sustain that state? When did they lose it and return to imbalance? And, once they realized what had happened, did they use some balancing technique to restore it? I have them map their day and we examine how able they were to remain balanced and also restore balance when they lost it.

This takes some practice because most people remain oblivious to the fact that they are grossly imbalanced and they just stubbornly push ahead getting things done all day long. This exhausts them so they reach for a cocktail or a sweet treat to try and restore some sort of balance. They've worked hard, after all; they deserve it. But the treat is usually something that further imbalances them. Unhealthy treats don't restore balance, they just temporarily relieve suffering. But it's just a quick fix that can't last. And it strengthens the programming that says you need "things" from the outside to save you.

Affirmations

Another "technology of now" is using an affirmation to truthfully focus the mind. You simply direct your mind out of its automatic and unconscious thinking by bringing a focused awareness to some truthful statement about who you are and what life is.

I've found that the most effective affirmation is a truthful holistic statement, something that your mind can readily understand. "I am ...

all is ... one" is an affirmation we often use. Or, "Here and now ... in this moment ... I am ... all is ... one." Both are excellent to use during meditation. I also recommend using affirmations during the waking hours of the day and as you are going to sleep at night. Using them for even five minutes every day will help you achieve a certain degree of balance and holistic awareness.

Using affirmations enables you to direct your own thinking, rather than just flowing with the whims of a wild mind. You are literally grabbing the reins of your mind and directing it towards the truth by repeating positive affirmations. I've read criticism of affirmations where an author contends that the statements may not be true and that the mind doesn't like hearing a "lie." Well, what is it hearing right now? Is "You really blew it" the truth? Using positive affirmations is about balancing the negative self-talk that is already happening with deliberate positive thoughts that **are** true, because they describe the truth of you.

You might experiment with a brief period of time during the day to sit and repeat an affirmation for about five minutes. Then stop and observe how long the stillness remains. When you lose the stillness, repeat the affirmations again. Stay with the stillness as long as it lasts and repeat the affirmation whenever you lose it. For instance, "Here and now ... in this moment ... I am experiencing myself as source ... I am ... all is ... one."

It is important to repeat the affirmation slowly enough that you become aware of and actually experience its real meaning. Slow down to focus on the experience that is happening. Then slow down even more and be the witnessing consciousness watching.

The Value of Subliminals

*"I saw a subliminal advertising agent,
but only for a second."*[6]

—Steven Wright, comedian

People get nervous about subliminal programming and they should. If you are meditating and the database of your subconscious and unconscious are open, whatever you are thinking is going straight in. That means that you are creating and delivering your own subliminals. Whatever you are thinking, you are programming into yourself. Usually, that's a whole lot of negative thinking. That continues during meditation when you just sit, sometimes with an affirmation, sometimes not, and have a random experience. What happens depends on your biorhythms that day and what is going on in your life at the moment. This means that some days you will have precision meditation, some days you won't. And that's precisely why we offer High-Tech Meditation via audio programs. The subliminal programming combined with sonic entrainment technology helps override the noisy environment of the moment—both internal and external—to give you a dependable meditation environment that empowers you to have a precision meditation experience every time.

Creating Your Cave

The ideal, if possible, would be to dedicate some part of the home as your "cave," a special place that can support your growing experience of wholeness. You might create an actual meditation room, a specific space where you can explore within, without distractions.

Since the holistic practice includes everything in your life, it's helpful to look at all the different places where you spend the waking hours of your day: office, home, car, middle of the forest, beach, wherever you physically are. What is the environment that surrounds you and how conducive or non-conducive is it to achieving the balance that supports your increasing wakefulness? Consider the entirety of your environment as your "cave," the physical location where you will practice, to increase your holistic experience.

If you go to an ashram you will find that everything there is designed to command the focus of your mind in a truthful way. All the activities of the ashram assist you to increase wakefulness, particularly to balance your mental dimension. You won't find pictures of a *Playboy* centerfold or a basket ball player on the wall! Instead, you will see enlightening symbols and photos of great masters, images that represent wholeness and connection with Source, not fame in the illusory world.

You can create the same in your own environments. In fact, everything that surrounds you—the décor, colors you use, every aspect of the design of your environment—should be based on balance and that which supports your intention to be whole.

You can also employ the principles of *feng shui* to balance the energy flow in your environment. How about studying and implementing the cutting edge of science and technology, using modern technologies in your home and cave to support balance? Another vital environmental component is the sounds that you hear, the music that you play. Balanced, peaceful, inspiring sounds encourage relaxation and balance. We use sacred music in our Synchronicity Sanctuary all day long; we even broadcast chanting through our forest!

They didn't have electricity 10,000 years ago. These days all of us are surrounded by electromagnetic frequencies, incoherent signals that are fundamentally imbalanced. We sit in this for many hours every day, which means that we have to work harder to maintain balance, simply because this fragmented electromagnetic field is constantly bombarding us.

Cleansing Your Cave

There is technology that renders electromagnetic fields coherent. You simply plug the control unit into your wall outlet and it affects the entire house. This supports you because you don't have to work as hard to maintain balance when background stress levels are reduced. Here in our facility and in my home, this technology is fully utilized to sustain a balanced and supportive environment for the maintenance of wakefulness and the expansion of holistic awareness.

Beginning the Day

Adrenal exhaustion is becoming an undiagnosed epidemic in the West and contributes to many chronic illnesses. It is the disease of imbalance, the disease of stress. Stress is imbalance to the objective. This is the Information Age and everything keeps moving faster. Well, we can't keep up. Life itself, for many people, has become exhausting. This is the violence of our times.

In my mentoring program I suggest that people try a simple practice when they first wake up in the morning. Set the alarm five minutes early and before getting out of bed to plunge into another busy, stress filled schedule, remain in witness consciousness and affirm to yourself: "I am blissful consciousness." Repeat that affirmation until you feel fully wakeful within that experience. Then, sit up and consciously "put on your body," just like you put on your clothes. Now, see how long you can maintain that holistic awareness throughout your day. Experience yourself as the consciousness that is empowering your body and orchestrating your entire life experience. If you flounder, ask yourself: "Who am I, really, beyond this body and the roles that I play? What is really important and how do I maximize holistic awareness throughout this day?"

Meditation

Once a taste of awakening has occurred, meditation is something that often begins to happen as a result. In other words, meditation is not something you *decide* to do, but rather a specific experience whose time comes for you. One day you just find yourself meditating because the happenings of your life and your own evolution have made it inevitable. When the student is ready, the teacher comes, in many forms—one of which is meditation.

"Your meditation practice can take you to a new place of allowing and balance, where you are more relaxed and open, not just to meditation—but to your entire life."[7] Of course, I agree with these words from Victor Davich in his book, *8 Minute Meditation: Quiet Your Mind. Change Your Life,* that the practice of meditation profoundly influences your whole life. We meditated in Mumbai, right in the midst of a terrorist attack and we experienced peace. Meditation, properly done, will opiate you, bring you pleasure.

During meditation, the in-breath and the out-breath represent the two relative polarities. One is typically dominant over the other, that is, one is longer. The objective out-breath is most often longer than the subjective in-breath. If you close your eyes and focus on the breath, you will observe this. So, to create balance, deliberately increase your in-breath by making it longer.

It is important to meditate every day. Researchers at Princeton University found that people who meditated just twelve minutes every day achieved notable development in their frontal lobes and increased their cognitive retention, which MRI results verified. They concluded that this was just maintenance, somewhat like a gentle regime of daily physical exercise. To maintain optimum physical health you really need forty minutes of daily, aerobic exercise. Likewise, you need at least thirty minutes of daily meditation to develop constancy in frontal lobe dominance and to develop holistic awareness.

The new meditator can begin that way and gradually build up to at least one hour of daily meditation. Some in my mentoring program often commit to one and a half hours per day and many of them do even more. Some are retired and have the time, some get up and meditate before they go to work and then again before they sleep at night. The more meditation time you add beyond that hour, the more you accelerate constancy of holistic experience. Remember, meditation is a balancing technique that reverses objective dominance. As you focus on the interior you emphasize this non-dominant polarity, you create balance, and holistic awareness expands.

Some like to meditate in the morning, before the busy day begins. In Eastern traditions the early morning time is referred to by the Sanskrit word *Brahmamuhurtha*, which means "the hours of God." This is the three hours before sunrise when everything is still. Most people's minds are asleep then and everything is quiet. Those hours are considered the most conducive to meditation.

But forcing yourself to get up early to meditate might not fit your bio-rhythms. It could be more effective for you to meditate in the afternoon or early evening. Experiment. If you are an evening person, then by all means do your meditation in the evening, but not just before going to bed because it's too easy to fall asleep. Find out what works best for you.

I don't insist that Westerners sit cross-legged when they meditate. After all, we didn't grow up without furniture and our bodies aren't used to it. So, sit on a chair if that is more comfortable for you, but learn to sit straight with the small of your back pushed forward because this opens up your chest and heart.

If you learn how to sit in that position during meditation with no back support you will begin to notice an energetic movement, a rocking, spiraling kind of movement. This is called Kundalini energy. If you focus on it while it is happening, you will notice that it oscillates clockwise and counter clockwise. Sitting up straight with no back support is the optimum position for meditation. You can also meditate when you are lying down but only on your back, in what is known as the corpse position in yoga.

Group meditation is also valuable, when it is available, because of the group energy dynamic. Whenever you bring a group of meditators together, they create a more powerful field than you can create on your own. It also makes meditation easier and more expansive because you all entrain each other.

In the Eastern path traditions, they said, "Don't talk about your meditation experience." Telling stories about your meditation can develop a "meditator's ego." For this reason, only share meditation insights with your teacher.

What's Floating Your Boat?

The beginning meditator opens to the experience of being a detached observer, the witnessing consciousness watching the two polarities, observing the stillness of the interior and the activity of the exterior. At this point awareness is not yet unified. Detached observation of the relative polarities is witness consciousness and this experience can progress into unified witness consciousness, where both polarities are witnessed *as the same consciousness*. This describes the meditative progression of expanding holistic awareness.

Sometimes a crisis, such as ours in Mumbai, can actually accelerate progress. Many of our associates there reported exactly that, declaring in various ways that **now** they finally "got it." The theories became real in the heat of the moment. Lorraine is one of my mentoring students who was not in Mumbai but she reported her own version of this kind of rapid evolution. "When I was sixteen, I was raped by a stranger who held a gun to my head. Something happened. I became completely detached and seemed to watch the whole thing from outside my body. What I call my "beingness" told me what to say. And my words got through. This guy was ranting about how much he hated women and that I was going to die. But then he listened and put down the gun and he let me go. I know this saved my life."

Any crisis causes us to be more present. And, if we find some way to not be overwhelmed by fear, we can grow from the experience in positive ways. As for the memories we carry of crises that we didn't know how to handle, it helps to have support to clear those up. I often refer to our Synchronicity facility as a seaport. People show up in boats that are heavy-laden with damaged cargo—their illusory stories—and they are riding low in the water. They dock, participate in our holistic programs, and their boats begin to ride lighter in the water. A relatively empty boat floats easily and if it collides with another boat there's not much damage. This is an interesting way of considering our relationships. If we are not overly burdened with ego content, we won't get particularly upset if we happen to bump up against each other. We can just continue to flow in our holistic lifestyle and adjust to whatever is happening. This "lightening your load" process is like shining the big flashlight of witness consciousness into the unconscious—your cargo hold—to see what data is down there. It might be forgotten but can still be operative. The light allows you to bring awareness to it so that you can then clean it out and release it.

High-Tech Meditation

Most people, especially beginners, fight with their minds during meditation. This is a persistent challenge and it's why I created High-Tech Meditation. High-Tech Meditation uses sonic technology to provide a focus and utilizes technology that overrides whatever random experience you may bring into the meditation. Sonic technology decelerates your brainwaves and holds the database of your subconscious and unconscious open. Because of that, what you think while you are meditating is very important. Negative self-talk can go right in and lodge itself. That's why I assign such emphasis to the use of affirmations and consciously-directed thinking.

I use English translations of ancient mantras, truthful statements about who you are and what life is. Each affirmation is technologically precise and combines with sonic entrainment technology. The result is that it takes less linear time for a high-tech meditator to develop substantiated holistic experience than someone practicing random, non-technological meditation. We have been able to document a 75% acceleration factor with High-Tech Meditation, which is remarkable.

In High-Tech Meditation, the sonic technology generates an Alpha/Theta/Delta environment, which assists you to stay focused, balanced and aware. Brain research validates that frontal lobe development accelerates with these frequencies. If you meditate this way every day (for at least thirty minutes), you actually build frontal lobe dominance over the hindbrain. And if you do that, the limbic brain, where all the feelings and primal instincts live (flight and flight responses), no longer dominates. You develop frontal lobe dominance and that brings wakefulness. Your resulting witnessing consciousness becomes able to remain detached within any experience—including a terrorist attack—and not become totally lost in fear or overwhelmed by anxiety and adrenaline.

Synchronicity Meditation Programs

Our flagship meditation program is called "Recognitions." It incorporates Delta-level technology to enable subtle states of meditative self-awareness as Source consciousness. Recognitions also contains a soundtrack to play at a low volume level throughout your sleep-time. Subliminal affirmations turn sleep into a meditation.

Meditation is the primary balancing technique we recommend and balance is always the focus of the Holistic Lifestyle. Use your imagination to find novel ways of bringing balance in every situation that confronts you but meditate every day. Spending more time on creating and sustaining balance can become your new priority and this will provide the best preparation for the tests to come in your life. You can resume practicing every time you put this book down to continue interacting with your world.

૰૰૰૰

BONNIE:

David and Vinka, our fellow travelers from New Zealand, were a few doors down from me. That last day of our imprisonment, Vinka called and said, "Bonnie, come out of your room, we can go down now." I wasn't sure about that, as we had been informed by authorities to remain in our rooms until the commandos knocked. But soon she was out there banging on my door. Before I could do anything, the hotel phone rang. It was the front desk telling me to come out of the room ... that the floor had been cleared.

I left my room with hands up and went straight into a war zone from hell. There were commandos swarming everywhere and one of them told me to relax and put my hands down. I peered over the open railing and down to the atrium. It was just unbelievable how much damage had been done. Some of the Oberoi Hotel staff waved and motioned us down. We hesitated but six of the staff came up to assist us. One carried my luggage and one held my hand as they helped us pick our way through the rubble of this once magnificent hotel.

AMY:

When we finally exited the hotel we plunged into another kind of chaos. Wooden barricades restrained hundreds of onlookers, while one young soldier helped us fight our way across the street. He led us to outside tables where officials had set themselves up to process us. I remember finally getting it as I answered their questions: I could have died in there!

Then I heard someone calling my name. It was a young man from the American Consulate. Apparently, my family had made contact with the Consulate and asked them to find me. Then there was the media, literally hundreds of reporters with their cameras and equipment and all shouting at us: "How is it to finally be free?"

Duh!

HELEN:

Members of the hotel staff stayed with us in the hospital and they were incredible. A nurse told me that I was not seriously injured so I said, "Great, I can go back to the hotel now." Obviously, I had no idea how serious this all was. I thought it was some kind of minor skirmish that had been quickly quelled by police. There was nothing to go back to.

I lay there in my hospital bed and remembered one of the personal games I often played, asking for inward guidance about what to wear to the meditation program each evening. The night this all started I had been directed to wear a certain shawl. I remember that I really didn't agree with the guidance this time ... because that shawl didn't go with the outfit that I was told to wear with it. But, I know better than to argue with the Divine within so I wore the whole ensemble anyway.

I had purchased this shawl on a visit to the guru Ammaji years earlier who had hugged me while I was wearing it. It had Sanskrit mantras inscribed all over it. Amazing, that was what I wore throughout the attack and it had survived with me, although it was now brittle with the grit of human remains and blood. Regardless, I spread it lovingly over my bed.

Then I felt my hair. It was stiff, like cardboard, and there was no mirror to see why. When I used a jug and cold water to rinse it out, red water flowed down the drain. Was this the blood of my dear friends Alan and Naomi? That was such a surreal thought, it moved me beyond mind and words. I climbed back into bed in my torn and grimy salwar kameez and huddled beneath the comfort of my blood soaked shawl.

LINDA:

There was a woman named Rachel in the hospital and she whispered to me, "You are safe." She was there again when I came out of ER and told me that she had prayed for me so that I would not be alone. There was so much love and compassion directed towards us in that hospital ... it was almost too much to take.

My husband arrived and one of the first things we did was take a goofy picture and send it to our kids so they would know right away that Mom was OK. My husband is an amazing man. How he got there so soon, with all the politics and airports being shut down, I have no idea, but that's what he's like. As he was leaving the hospital on the first night, he stopped at the door and said, "I love you to death, Lin." We both froze. "No," I said, "to life. I love you to life."

MASTER CHARLES:

We were escorted out of the hotel and taken across the street to a parking garage underneath a large adjacent building. Medics attended to our needs and offered us water to drink and washcloths to scrub the soot off our faces. We were exhausted and our clothes were filthy. They questioned me at length, especially for information about Naomi and Alan. As those in our group reunited with each other, I noticed how calm everyone was. They were meditative and wakeful, and no one was freaking out. Once we were all debriefed, they prepared us for relocation to another hotel.

࿔࿔࿔

To better integrate the meaning of this chapter, please visit www.synchronicity.org, go to the "Forgiving the Unforgivable" section, and use the password "one" to access additional material.

CHAPTER 8

Who Would You Be Without Your Stories?

"What is meant by consciousness we need not discuss;
it is beyond all doubt."[1]

—Sigmund Freud

"Consciousness poses the most baffling problems
in the science of the mind.
There is nothing that we know more intimately
than conscious experience,
but there is nothing that is harder to explain."

—David Chalmers[2]

One by one, hostages are rescued and reunite on the street outside the Oberoi Hotel. Police guide them through the crowds toward a bus that will take them to the Four Seasons Hotel.

The streets are deserted of regular traffic but thousands of onlookers press against barricades and the media are insistent with their cameras and shouted questions.

Escaping the mayhem, survivors file onto the bus and sink deep into their seats, pulling curtains over the window and soaking in the silence. Already the last forty-five plus hours seem like a mad dream ...

I am not this body, these thoughts, these feelings.
And I am not this history.
Beyond all my stories,
whether truth or illusion,
I forever am
myself,
One with All.
I am ... all is ... One.

༄༅༄

BEN:

There were about twenty of us in the bus and they had pulled down the window shades, so we sat there while the media milled around madly outside. After we got to the hotel we were informed that a State Department psychiatrist from the American Embassy in Delhi had been assigned to meet with us to help us prepare for handling the trauma.

CAROL:

Soon after I arrived at the Four Seasons Hotel I went on-line and read all the e-mails that had come in to us. I just wept and wept. What an outpouring of love!

That's when it finally hit me that Alan and Naomi were gone. It sank in even deeper when we gathered together with Master Charles ... all of us in the room, except them. I felt a tangible emptiness in that room where they would have been.

MASTER CHARLES:

The far end of this parking garage was fenced off with the media on the other side of the fence plus a massive crowd of onlookers. After our debriefing we walked towards that fence to board the bus that waited beyond it. As we got closer, cameras began to flash and reporters began shouting. It was pandemonium. Gautam, our Mumbai coordinator, and his sister Shibani met us with their team. They embraced us and walked us through the throngs of security police, media and general public to the bus. When we got on board, it was like dropping into another world. The window blinds were pulled down and it was silent. We just sat there, absolutely still. I remember that Gautam sat next to me and took my hand, held it in his, saying nothing.

We remained in silence throughout the long drive to the Four Seasons Hotel. Its gates were closed and armed guards with dogs were on either side. The entire hotel was locked down and even though we were the survivors we had to pass through metal detectors, just like airport security. The manager and staff at the Four Seasons greeted us and escorted us to the lobby to begin assigning rooms. They kept offering us whatever we needed and assuring us that everything was taken care of, all our expenses would be covered, and that we shouldn't worry about a thing.

We sat together in a wakeful kind of meditative quiet, still wearing the clothes we'd had on for three days now. I know that when we got to our rooms, the first thing everyone did was to shower or have a bath. I remember that it took three or four applications of soap and water and vigorous scrubbing to get all the black soot off my body. None of us had a change of clothes so the hotel gave us robes while they did our laundry. Everyone was kind, generous and compassionate.

Then we plunged into logistical meetings. Dr. Phil Duncan and Larry Koftinoff became our managers and began to figure out exactly what had to happen now and in what order. The American Consul General was coming, plus the FBI and the State Department again, for more debriefings. And, of course, I wanted to meet with our people as soon as possible. Going to the hospital to see wounded friends was another top priority.

Telephones began ringing as friends and colleagues from all over the world found out where we were. Indian gurus and other dignitaries in Mumbai called, asking to come see us. Of course, the media was clamoring for a press conference.

I met with the Consul General and an official U.S. Government team. They were impeccably brilliant, addressing every need we had. They talked to each of us in order to identify our luggage and find out where it was in the shambles of our Oberoi rooms. We thought it would be impossible for them to locate our belongings in that war zone. In fact, I know most of us had resigned ourselves to never seeing our luggage again. Surprise, they actually found and returned everything to us the next day. Incredible.

They talked to us about exit strategies. One said, "If you want to go as a group, the only private flight would have to go through Hong Kong and the west coast and this would take a lot longer than going the other way." Because of this, he suggested we use our existing tickets. Of course, by now every airline was overwhelmed by people desperately wanting to get out of Mumbai. We decided to hang onto our existing tickets, which turned out to be a wise decision.

After we had a chance to clean up, we met as a group for the first time since our rescue. Each individual needed to share their experience, where they had been during the attack and exactly what had happened to them. They also needed to be updated on the status of those in our party who had been killed or wounded. Everyone was exhausted, it was way past time to retire, so we shut it down. We slept fitfully that evening and rose at daybreak to face a virtual tsunami of activity.

Mahamandaleshwar Swami Vishwarananda came. Mahamandaleshwar Swami Nityananda came also. They met with everyone, brought food, and comforted us in every way possible. Many additional friends dropped everything and offered us whatever we might need. They all said, "Just tell us what you need, tell us and it is yours." It was a tidal wave of compassion and generosity.

Mahamandaleshwar Swami Vishveshwarananda offered his whole ashram— which was the one we had visited earlier in the day of the attack. "Come and stay with me; you can stay in my private quarters," he offered. Mahamandaleshwar Sai Maa Lakshmi Devi called from France and messages were received from Eckhart Tolle and many other spiritual teachers and gurus from all across the world who are my friends.

Later in the day, I went to the hospital and met with our three injured friends. It was devastating to see them in such serious medical condition inside the Intensive Care Unit. Doctors assured me they would all recover and I comforted them and sat with them for as long as I could. I was impressed with their wakefulness and serenity in the midst of this horrendous experience.

When I embraced Linda—who had been seriously injured—and said, "I'm so sorry," she said, "We are not victims of terrorism, we are victors over terrorism." Now, that's clarity!

On the second day after our rescue there was a press conference with both local and international media. I marveled at how empathetic and compassionate the media personnel were. The U.S. Consulate sent a State Department psychiatrist who specialized in trauma and post-traumatic stress to consult with our group. He saw individuals privately and advised us what to expect over the next year in relation to this traumatic experience. He told me he was impressed with how everyone in our group was already integrating the experience. He remarked that in such situations there was no substitute for the practice of daily meditation and that our holistic lifestyle was paying big dividends.

　　　　　　　　　　ॐॐॐ

Sell your cleverness
and buy bewilderment.[3]

—Rumi

Truth is emergent simplicity. What gets in the way is thinking that we already know and challenging new insights as they appear. Our prejudiced bias affects what we think we perceive. This is especially true when we examine our interior landscape. Even though I believe that **this** is the real "last frontier" (contrary to what they said on *Star Trek*), many people deny that there could be much value in learning more about their interior being. Certainly, if what is presented is simple, rather than intellectually sophisticated, all the more reason to discount it.

As Ann Weiser Cornell writes in the *Power of Focusing,* "Be willing to approach your inner experience without thinking that you know all about it already. This is the attitude of *not knowing.* Why would you listen to someone if you think you already know what he or she has to say? So be curious, open, and more interested in what you "don't" know yet than in what you already know. Try acknowledging what you already know about what you're focusing on and then setting that aside. Not because it's wrong—it might not be—but because it might be getting in the way of sensing what is new and not yet known about you and your life." [4]

Breathing

Here it is, the simplest of the simple: breathing. What of value could be said about that? You breathe, you live; you stop breathing, you die. Actually, a great secret resides in this most essential human activity because breathing clearly represents the two relative polarities. Out-breath represents negative, objective polarity and in-breath the non-dominant positive, subjective. Take a moment to observe your breathing habits. If your out-breath is longer, there is imbalance, and this is the case for most people. So, you can correct that by deliberately increasing the length of your in-breath. Measuring the usual duration of your in and out breaths is an excellent diagnostic tool that allows you to increase balance very easily.

During meditation you can breathe consciously to sustain balance of the two breaths, which enables you to explore the midpoint between the two. Being conscious at that balance point delivers an experience of witness consciousness and the eternal now. This space between the breaths is the midpoint where the in-breath changes to the out-breath, or the out-breath changes to the in-breath. Experiment with pausing there and just hovering for a few seconds. You can explore this during meditation and begin to detect an expansion of holistic awareness, witness consciousness and the eternal now. With regular practice, this becomes progressively more substantiated in your experience.

Some advanced yogis and great masters develop the skill of conscious breath retention to the point that it happens spontaneously. Consciousness is now breathing them. In Sanskrit this is known as kumbacha. There have been documented cases where a master has remained in that state, with absolutely no noticeable breathing and a pulse rate that has dropped so far you can barely hear it with a stethoscope, for up to twenty-one days. That seems to be the upper limit, before dropping the body. This has been documented. You can imagine the holistic amplitude of power such masters radiate!

Muktananda's guru, Bhagwan Nityananda, lived in that state. He mostly just lay down, absorbed in the midpoint. Every few hours or so he would roll over and change positions. Meanwhile, thousands would file by, deeply affected by the holistic amplitude of power that emanated from him. In fact, people would bus to his ashram, climb off, and experience awakening on the spot.

Nityananda rarely spoke, yet he is honored as one of greatest saints of India and people still flock to the shrine where his body is entombed. His level of enlightening attainment is legendary. He was such a master that he didn't have to teach; his state of being **was** the teaching. His holistic vibration **was** the empowerment.

Occasionally he would speak aphoristically. For instance, he might say something like, "The heart is the hub of all sacred spaces. Go there and roam in it."[5] But that would be it. No explanation, no teaching, nothing. He would sit up for a moment, open his eyes a little, utter some phrase like that, sit awhile longer, then lie back down. And the people would file by or pile up in front of where he was lying, bringing their honorary offerings of flowers and fruit ... the greatest abundance. There are pictures of him lying in his ashram with the gifts piled up around him. He didn't care about any of it and his disciples eventually created hospitals and charities where they could distribute it all. Imagine, all this abundance arising from how one man was breathing and being ... In silence!

Who Would You Be Without Your (Fictional) Stories?

Silence may be golden, as the saying goes, but most people are uncomfortable with silence if it goes on too long. Silence on the radio is called "dead air" and, socially, we abhor the "awkward silence." Solution? Fill it in with words, stories.

You've arrived at this book with your stories and they affect how you read. Just for a moment, surrender them. Let go of your history, without judgment. Again, slow your reading, pause between words ... Watch your breath. Feel yourself reading and embrace yourself as that which is reading, free of any burdens from the past. In this moment you are pure consciousness ... aware of yourself reading, being, breathing, noticing. Notice that you still have meaning! Your existence is your meaning. Nothing further is required.

We all tell stories, and we love to hear stories. But what sorts of stories do we tell? Jean Houston warned, "If you keep telling the same sad small story, you will keep living the same sad small life."[6]

Most of our stories belong in the realm of egocentric experience because the ego uses its stories to maintain its identity. Stories are the content of life and content is form. Content is the dominant polarity in the involutionary cycle where, as you will remember, we experience what we are not. Along the way, all of us have amassed huge databases of illusory stories and we live within them. They have become our unconscious identity. Most of these stories are life-negative and fear-based.

"Story, businesses are realizing, means big money. Economists Deirdre McCloskey and Arjo Klamer calculate that persuasion—advertising, counseling, consulting, and so on—accounts for 25% of U.S. gross domestic product. If, as some posit, Story is a component of half those persuasive efforts, then Story is worth about $1 trillion a year to the U.S. economy." So wrote Daniel Pink in *A Whole New Mind*.[7]

I was watching Fareed Zakaria interview a fundamentalist Islamic Imam on television. At one point this man exclaimed, "These are my beliefs, this is who I am!" This demonstrates precisely how most people think. They define themselves based on what they believe, which is content identification. Once you awaken, holistic awareness disempowers illusion while it simultaneously disempowers the ego. At that point, a person may find himself taking a step back within himself and saying, "Wait a minute, I seem to be more than this content." Before, they unconsciously identified with their beliefs and their content. But now they become wakeful (holistic awareness has expanded) and they begin to observe. Now, content identification can dissipate. The question then becomes, "Who am I beyond my stories, beyond all my content identifications?"

Most people are simply terrified of whatever lies beyond their content and this becomes obvious any time you attempt a truthful conversation with them. Notice what happens in a quiet moment during conversation. People get anxious, they have trouble just being with the formless, the nothingness of the moment. But any moment of silence is an opportunity to experience subtle levels of consciousness because it creates the balance that expands holistic awareness. Witness consciousness is increasing in those moments. Any person who is ready for this will embrace it, delighted to observe content from a place of stillness.

Consider your life with its many details and say to yourself, "If I let all of this go, who would I be?" This form is impermanent; all content is impermanent. At some point you will have to let it all go. What if you consciously let it go now, before physical death forces you to? "What could I experience, who would I be, without all this content?"

The content of your life seems to flow seamlessly but it's really more of a succession of still frames, like a movie. Film moves through the projector and displays as a coherent whole, but we know that it is actually a series of distinct, still frames. When you stop the motion and freeze the frame, the movie becomes a slide show.

Similarly, our lives are a series of "moments" that flow together. We tend to extract one frame here, another one there, and fabricate stories about them. Good ones are called "show stoppers." Someone may suddenly take issue with something that is happening and... the brakes go on. Suddenly, there's a story to process. "Why did you say that to me? What did you mean by that?" Or, "that reminds me of the time ..."

Stories breed with each other. One triggers another. Whatever is said activates something in your database of stories, unconsciously reminding you of something else so an old story is re-told or a new one created. Most people live like this, from story to story 24/7. But what would you be ... who would you be, without all those stories? What would it be like to simply enjoy truthful, positive conversation mingled with silence? Might a truthful perception of reality begin to show itself? Yes, that's exactly how it happens.

I was watching a news story recently about prostitutes in Las Vegas. One after another they described their suffering, the misery and drama of their lives. I expect that most viewers were judging this as horrible, maybe condemning these women, maybe feeling sorry for them. But from a holistic perspective this was the experience that was valid for them. This is where their feet were at the moment. Can you allow others their suffering? Of course, you extend compassion, but the most compassionate awareness is to allow others the fullness of their own experience. It is up to them to make a move out of it. The moment they choose something different that becomes the next experience whose time has come for them. None of us are in any position to rush that moment for anyone, based on some assumed superior wisdom or understanding about what they should or should not be doing. After all, it's their life experience, not ours! Also, they represent a part of us, because it's all one consciousness. If they are suffering, a part of me is suffering and only I can change my part of it. I must first heal myself before I can assist others. True compassion begins with self-love.

One of our associates actually worked in a Las Vegas casino. After she had been involved with our program for a while she began to judge herself for being there. "It's so dense and dysfunctional," she told me. "All the customers are egocentric; they are usually drunk and compulsive. Employees line up at my office door every day, on the verge of nervous breakdowns. What am I doing there?"

I remember telling her something like this: "Well, you can source God in yourself very well. What better place than a casino to source God in everyone else?" She got it. As long as this was the place where she found herself, it was the perfect place to learn acceptance without judgment, to see God in everyone, as Mother Theresa did.

The quest of the true mystic is to sit in emptiness, needing no content, experiencing who you are in essence without any stories at all. Such a person evolves towards "no story." In all of the wisdom traditions you find the principle of "renunciation." Monks, contemplatives, recognize they must simplify. That is what Muktananda taught us early on but it had nothing to do with giving away our possessions; it is always about relinquishing illusory stories.

For starters, you can begin to emphasize and enjoy silence in relation to noise, just a few stories in relation to many stories. Since most people can't find stillness right away, shifting the balance gradually like this helps. You can also begin to tell truthful stories about who you are and what life is. Your fictional stories are all about who you are not; your truthful stories are about who you really are. Of course, repeating affirmations is one way of doing this. "I am Source Consciousness ... I am One and whole."

Once you increase balance by reducing the volume of illusory story and increasing the volume of truthful story, you find stillness more easily. You begin to live in the no-story zone. Advanced meditators are able sit in meditation and be absolutely still in the mind with no thoughts or stories at all, but that's an ability they developed over time.

As you awaken and experience witness consciousness more consistently, you become a writer of nonfiction, less identified with content and more identified with the one who is observing content. Your truthful perception of reality increases.

Re-writing the Script of Our Lives

We need less fictional conversation and more truthful conversation but that frightens most people. Why? Because egos only exist to manage the illusory world so they are desperate to preserve themselves by maintaining a comprehensive database of fictional stories. Nonfiction frightens the ego so it defends itself by creating distractions and escapes. Something interesting happens post-awakening. You begin to draw new "peers" to yourself and simultaneously distance yourself from ego-identified others who are no longer "where your feet are." You just don't share the same values any more so you automatically start distancing from each other. Your streams of stories diverge and suddenly new people show up who are more like you, more where your feet are. Your conversation changes from illusion-dominant to truth-dominant, but not always with the same people.

A friend of mine recounted one stirring account of this. At age 21 he found himself working as a diamond driller in the wilds of British Columbia. It was rough work and the crew was even rougher. One day, bouncing along in a pickup truck on some back road, he mentioned an article he had read about ashrams, musing that it sounded interesting.

His two rugged co-workers reacted with immediate profanity. In fact, he told me that they almost threw him out of the truck. Why the heated reaction? He'd just told a truthful story of expanding awareness and it threatened their macho identities. Wisely, he didn't bring it up again, but their reaction was so severe that it convinced him there must be something worthwhile about the topic. Years later he found himself living in an ashram! And one of those old friends died in a terrible car accident, drunk and stoned. Here were two men sitting right beside each other. Then their lives diverged as each followed a different story thread, one fictional and one non-fictional, towards two very different results.

When awakening comes, your values shift. Because of that, your world changes and so do your friendships. You will move closer with those who are aligned to where your feet now are to generate and share consensus realities that support you where your feet are together. Others will move away to find resonance and consensus with others where their feet are.

Stories can serve either as distractions from now or as tools for reality creation. It all depends on whether we use our stories to create a relevant reality or to stay lost in the egocentric illusion of what we are not. Your stories change from fiction to nonfiction when, instead of believing that "I am separate from you," you write a new story: "There is only one." That **is** a true story. You are, I am, all is, One. You then can say of yourself, "I am one, here and now in this moment, I am experiencing myself as consciousness and there is no separation." This demonstrates the reversal of polarized dominance.

A companion priority to bringing balance in any moment is to live in the question of just what **is** real. "Is this the truth or is this simply a story I'm telling about what's happening and, if so, could I possibly tell a different story? What is a new story I'm going to tell about what happens and how will that flavor my perception of reality?"

Over time, you can simplify from a vast database full of fictional stories down to one truthful story that you tell yourself and share with others who are more interested in reality than ego-generated fantasies.

As we age, our stories often become repetitive. "Oh no, not again," may be the silent cry of a spouse, children, or friends as we launch into an epic retelling of some story that gives us meaning enough to conveniently forget that we've told it many times before.

Recycled stories reveal patterns and, when trauma is involved, they can be hard to shake. Peter Levine writes about this in *Healing Trauma*. "We are inextricably drawn into situations that replicate the original trauma in both obvious and less obvious ways. The prostitute or stripper with a history of childhood sexual abuse is a common example. We may find ourselves re-experiencing the effects of trauma either through physical symptoms or through a full-blown interaction with the external environment.

"Re-enactments may be played out in intimate relationships, work situations, repetitive accidents or mishaps, or other seemingly random events. They may also appear in the form of bodily symptoms or psychosomatic diseases. Children who have had a traumatic experience will often repeatedly re-create it in their play. As adults, we are often compelled to re-enact our early traumas in our daily lives. The mechanism is similar regardless of the individual's age." [8]

Compassionate Mentoring

Healing deep trauma usually requires professional therapeutic help. A person may be obsessing and acting out, based in some unconscious story/memory. Evolving past it can include learning more about its origins, facing the trauma consciously, and bringing it to conscious awareness, but ultimately the person needs to start telling a different story and re-script their database. It's not your conscious mind that determines how you do it; that's an egocentric interpretation. Larger forces are at work at the cutting edge of your consciousness. Remember, it's consciousness—not your conscious mind—that is orchestrating the show. Relax. Be like a feather on the wind. Nothing is the ultimate healing or enlightening experience. Be a feather. Go this way, go that way, collide, connect, journey. Everything is the dance and play of consciousness within the here and now of true reality. Feel that for a moment. Imagine being a feather on the wind, free to blow wherever the wind would take you. You're weightless, completely unburdened, liberated from your stories and responsibilities. What a feeling! Why can't you consciously generate that, using the Technologies of Now? It's possible, it's natural, and in any moment—like this one—it can be the experience whose time has come. Pause, breathe, be wakeful, flow with consciousness as it is happening here and now. This is the moment; it always is.

Perhaps your illusory story is that you won't immediately experience the depth of awakening that a great mystic or saint did. Stop! Comparison is illusion. No two human experiences are the same and yours is unique to you. Celebrate it! If you don't celebrate it, who will? The dark night of the soul is part of the journey and most of us have experienced a few of those! But it needn't become an endless dark night if a teacher is there and you remain interactive with him or her. Incidentally, John of the Cross coined that expression, "the dark night of the soul," based on his personal experience. History reports that he suffered from depression and was a very dark person. His guru was Theresa of Avila. She didn't see him very often!

We have a Modern Spirituality Mentoring Program and trained facilitators with advanced experience of the Holistic Lifestyle that I have personally guided for many years. I interact with the students through these facilitators. I also have students that I mentor directly. Most have been mentoring with me over many years, some since the program began. They have become most masterful within their evolving experience. I'm delighted! I have often said that I have no interest in creating disciples, but rather in creating masters. They are the living validation of that intention.

A basic, initial balance should be fairly easy to attain if you have a more or less "normal" terrain to begin with. When my facilitators report challenges with someone in establishing a fundamental life-affirmative and love-based base-line experience, then we explore and determine what may be causing the obstruction. There may be the need for a medical diagnosis, for instance. Meditation, we caution, is not for the weak and if depression is a factor, for instance, a person may need professional medical assistance.

This describes the first season of mentoring, determining exactly where the person's feet are. And, what is their enculturation? We explore that for each person in relation to their brain. If they have a healthy life-affirmative and loved-based enculturation (that is, childhood environment) they will have normal brain development. If they have life-negative and fear-based enculturation, their brain will be abnormally developed. Enculturation will be life-negative or positive, love or fear-based and this shows up in their stories as core values. The good news is that abnormal can be transformed to normal.

What was **your** enculturation, your parental model? What sort of relationship did your father and mother have from the time you were *in utero* through the first twenty-five years of your life, first with each other and then with you? What kind of mother did you have, what sort of father presence did you have? All this makes a huge difference. Knowing about it establishes your starting point for truthful, guided work.

I find that the most effective mentoring is to converse about the details of a person's actual life, not their theories about it. I give a student something to focus on, something to experience. Next month, I want to know what factually happened. What was their experience and do they feel they have integrated it?

When I am mentoring people, I expect them to maintain a record of their diet and exercise every day and keep checking in with their feelings and their thoughts to correct imbalances. This requires a new level of wakefulness but it gets evolutionary results. They are expanding their holistic awareness and balancing that primary trinity of their three dense dimensions: body, mind and emotions.

One of the measuring devices that I use is called "The Delight Factor." Students rate their experience of contentment throughout the day from 1 to 100 percent and then average it for the month. This tells us what their baseline contentment is as a measurement for expanding holistic awareness.

I use a similar tool called, "The Wakefulness Factor." How present are they in the waking hours of the day? How wakeful are they? How aware of themselves as Source Consciousness are they? I tell them to note all that, day by day, and then report back their average at the end of the month. I might say, "OK, 80%, very good, **and** there's room to bring even more wakefulness. Let's discuss ways to do that." They then have specifics to focus on and I have proven ways of diagnosing their experience, so that I can guide them precisely, giving them entrainments and focusing protocols for the next month.

Another process is called "The Balance Ratio." This references the principle of biochemical balance in the body, one part alkaline to seven parts acid. One to seven, that's basic balance. We would take that ratio and apply it to your subjective and objective experience throughout a 24-hour day. You would note how many hours were subjective and how many were objective each day. Sleep is obviously subjective, as is meditation time. But all the rest is objective, unless you consciously create additional subjective awareness in some way. You total the hours on each side of a chart to see how close you can get to the 1:7 balance ratio. Most people start from a severely imbalanced state, with the objective highly dominant. Over time and with deliberate balancing focus, they can adjust the ratio much closer to that figure and then progressively reduce it to an ever more precise balance.

Each month they have a particular Contemplation to explore and actualize. I give them a detailed commentary on that Contemplation so they fully understand what it is. They apply it through their lives for that month and when they speak to me again they give an overview of the month and go over the Contemplation. I make sure they have understood it, experienced it and applied it. Then we look at their "Challenges," that is, which of their illusions challenged them the most that month. They look into where they forfeited their awareness, where were the distractions and illusory identifications? We reconsider their enculturation, their unconscious data, and ask, "Where did this come from?" "How did you originally create it?" It's all about making the unconscious conscious, seeing through the illusions that are operative and choosing to not identify with them, month by month.

We look at sleep-time and dreams, which provide another diagnostic. We study dream content, and I teach them how to analyze and understand archetypical symbols, so they can begin to see the stories they are telling themselves in their dreams. This is always revealing of the balance or imbalance that is present. Dreams supply a commentary on our evolving experience, if we can understand them.

We look at diet and exercise in detail because I recommend a balanced diet and a daily exercise program. We look at any ailments, talk about the doctors they see, and anything that relates in any way to their physical level of experience. We look at all of the Technologies of Now they are using. I want to know if they have added or changed anything, because it all affects their experience. We spend the most time on their meditation experience, looking at that in detail.

This brings the Guru Principle right into their lives. Of course, years ago in the East, people lived in ashrams with their gurus and all this happened on a daily basis. It does happen here in our Sanctuary for the resident community but not everyone can live in an ashram! My whole approach has been, "How can I bring this experience to others, right in the midst of their lifestyle, whatever it is, wherever it is? How can I bring High-Tech Meditation, the Holistic Lifestyle, and mentoring work out into the world, available to thousands, millions, not just to the handful who are able to live in an actual spiritual environment with a teacher and community support?

This is my fulfillment as a teacher, bringing awareness to illusion, seeing how your triggers are activated, how you identify and act out to create a story. The more aware we are together, the more able you become to expand holistic awareness for yourself. Eventually it gets to "no challenges this month" and that is a great moment.

You progress from having many illusory challenges to catching them, becoming aware more quickly, dropping investment in illusion, choosing wakefulness and disidentifying with illusion altogether, all progressing to that moment: "No challenges this month!"

Of course, I often hear how great everything was ... at first. "I had all these wonderful peaceful meditations but now my mind has gone crazy and I am having such bad experiences. What's wrong?" Nothing is wrong. Your meditation is really working! It is bringing up old, incongruent data to process. This happens with more advanced meditation as precision technology focuses your experience. That's when you begin to catalyze deep transformative processes and you need a guide. Your guide understands the process and can help you process the transformation of your enculturation and empower the liberation of your being.

This reminds me of something a new disciple once said to his master. "There is no peace or joy here, but rather upheaval and process." The master replied, "Authentic masters deliver the combustion of egoic illusions. Peace and joy are revealed in the ashes. The process you observe validates this time-honored principle."

At the heart of mentoring success is the principle of entrainment, explained this way in Lynne McTaggart's book, *The Intention Experiment*. "Entrainment is a term in physics which means that two oscillating systems fall into synchronicity. It was coined in 1665 by the Dutch mathematician Christiaan Huygens, after he discovered that two of his clocks with pendulums standing in close proximity to each other had begun to swing in unison. He'd been toying with the two pendulums and found that even if he started one pendulum swinging at one end, and the other at the opposite end, eventually the two would swing in unison." [9]

The kind of entrainment at work in our mentoring program and operative for you right now as you read this book is fundamentally different from what *Wikipedia* describes as a "reality distortion field," or RDF. *Wikipedia* explains that RDF is "a term coined by Bud Tribble at Apple Computer in 1981, to describe company co-founder Steve Jobs's charisma and its effects on the developers working on the Mac project. Later the term has also been used to refer to perceptions of his keynote (or Stevenote) by observers and devoted users of Apple computers and products. The RDF is said to be Steve Jobs's ability to convince himself and others to believe almost anything with a mix of charm, charisma, bluster, exaggeration, marketing, appeasement, and persistence. RDF is said to distort an audience's sense of proportion and scales of difficulties and makes them believe that the task at hand is possible." [10]

Genuine entrainment is different. It doesn't arise from a human ego trying to convince or persuade another. It is naturally present in someone with a holistic amplitude of personal power, the result of consistently sustained balance in living. Those who are drawn near someone who lives in such a field are inclined to entrain to it, but only according to where their feet are in the greater evolution of their own individuated consciousness. The guide must have permission to offer help. *Star Trek* had its Prime Directive, detailed, again, by *Wikepedia* this way: "The Prime Directive dictates that there can be no interference with the internal development of pre-warp civilizations ..." [11]

That's the key to the nature of true, spiritual guidance without interference. Where are your feet today? In what direction are **you** choosing to move? How might I help you actualize and maximize your evolutionary movement, from fictional stories to true stories to no stories, to expand your real time experience of delighting holistic consciousness, which is always here and now and forever beyond all your stories?

࿂࿂࿂

KIA:

In the aftermath of the news confirming that Alan and Naomi had been shot and killed in the Tiffin Restaurant at the Oberoi Hotel, the words of Jesus Christ came to me as we sat on the sofa watching the follow-up news: "Father, forgive them. They know not what they do." I shared this with my family and added, "We must send them our love and compassion." Life as I knew it was over, my heart was shattered, there was nothing left. At the same time, I felt only compassion for those who were so separated from humanity that they could kill ruthlessly.

Master Charles called me from Mumbai and said, "We have a role to play; there is a message to share." I agreed, "Yes, I know." There was not much else to say. I was still numb with shock, but it felt good to hear his voice.

I had planned to extend my stay in Florida to give myself some extra time with family before returning to Synchronicity, but Bobbie called to say that there would be a press conference at the Sanctuary the following Tuesday morning right after Master Charles's return from India and he wanted me to be there for it. It felt like the last thing in the world that I wanted to do, but if this is what Master Charles requested, I would honor it. Also, so many people from all over the world had emailed the Synchronicity website their prayers and messages of love that I knew they would want to hear from both of us.

LINDA:

We flew home under FBI cover and I went straight to the hospital because I still had some drainage tubes in my body. A friend secured our arrival and privacy in the hospital so that my family and I could have undisturbed time together. This kept the media at bay, at least for a while.

When we finally did an interview as a family, the reporter asked my 15-year-old son, "So, what did you take away from this experience?" He replied, "Well, I'll never take it for granted again that when my mom goes away she'll come home."

ॐॐॐॐ

To better integrate the meaning of this chapter, please visit www.synchronicity.org, go to the "Forgiving the Unforgivable" section, and use the password "one" to access additional material.

CHAPTER 9

The Holistic Lifestyle

"If, instead of identifying ourselves with the work,
we feel that the soul of the workman streams through us,
we shall find the peace of the morning dwelling first in our hearts,
and the fathomless powers of gravity and chemistry,
and, over them, of life,
pre-existing within us in their highest form." [1]

—Ralph Waldo Emerson

The aftermath of the terrorist attack presents further challenges. Each individual returns home to face questions from family members and the media, constant invitations to identify as victims and build notoriety from the story.

Each individual deals with this in his or her own way, learning how to fully feel the impact of what happened to them and letting this support their ongoing, positive evolution, taking time for healing without wallowing in the past, and somehow communicating the process to others in plain language.

The effect of their consciousness and communication choices begins to have an impact, at first on family and friends and then further afield.

The Holistic Lifestyle is not a theory,
it is a way of being in the world.
Balance.
Balance the three dimensions of body, mind and heart.

Resonate
with the subtle dimensions
and experience the download of wisdom and bliss
as individual and universal consciousness dance together as one.

The Holistic Lifestyle is fulfillment and happiness,
for no reason at all.

❧❧❧

HELEN:

Many unknown, everyday heroes went to incredible lengths for us. Someone from the Canadian Consulate ventured into that disaster zone, packed up all my things and returned almost every single item to me. They even retrieved my purse and its contents from the morgue where it had been sent with Naomi's body.

AMY:

I was the first in our group to leave India. I flew to D.C. where my oldest daughter lives. All my family and friends came there to be with me, and calls flooded in constantly from those who couldn't make it in person. Really, it was just too much and I was quickly overwhelmed. She had even prepared all my favorite foods but I couldn't eat any of it. I managed to stay for a couple of days but desperately wanted to go back to my own quiet home.

BERNIE:

The trip home was about thirty hours. We asked the airline for an upgrade but were told this was not their policy. I smiled, thinking it would be odd to have an official policy for anyone who had just survived a forty-five-hour terrorist attack!

During our flight the airline asked us to fill out a survey form, which asked for our opinion about their service. I explained what we had been through in India and that I felt it was unreasonable for them to have denied us an upgrade, especially given the fact that first class was only half full. When we checked in for the second part of our flight we were escorted to the plane by a customer service agent who apologized profusely. First class was full on this flight but they did rearrange the seating to give both my husband and myself four seats so we could try and sleep. This was most appreciated!

First eye contact with our family was precious, unforgettable. We were home now, safe, but we could not forget our two friends who would never come home. The media was obsessive over the next week, so we began to just decline to comment and take the time we needed for ourselves, to just Be.

JOE:

We flew into JFK and were met by U.S. State Department people there. Then we continued on to Dallas and it was the same thing. Everyone was great, completely willing to help us out. I think they sent three people from different departments to talk with us. That made a real difference.

BEN:

When we returned home, it was as if a nuclear bomb of love had gone off. The experience of heart opening was almost too much to bear. The intensity of the terrorist experience quickly became distant and almost insignificant. Anger towards the terrorists never even entered my mind, only compassion. I knew that the healing process would be very fast and, sure enough, within days I was not only feeling clear and back to normal, but actually better than before. This is a real testament to living a holistic lifestyle and being a meditator. Even the most tragic experiences can become grand opportunities for growth.

MIRIAM

The Australian government sent a Qantas plane for all the Australians who survived the attack, and two trauma counselors came to the Four Seasons Hotel to help Mureen, Phyl and myself (the Australians in the Synchronicity party). They also sent an escort for our scheduled Singapore Airline flight. They gave us $1,000 each and offered ongoing free counseling if we felt we needed it. They treated us with genuine concern and we were most appreciative.

MASTER CHARLES:

Officials from the State Department escorted us to the airport and right onto the plane. When we landed in Washington, D.C., State Department officials and the FBI walked us through immigration into a debriefing meeting. A division of the FBI and State Department were assigned to us and consulted with us often over the next several weeks. They also provided medical and post traumatic stress counseling for everyone in our group.

In the previous chapter we advocated the value of mentoring to assist evolution in consciousness and actualize experience of the Holistic Lifestyle. In this chapter we zero in on the details of that lifestyle and answer that all-important question, "What should I do?" As practical as that question is, and vitally important if you are to have an experience rather than just theories, an even more important question is, "Who should I be while I am doing this?" That's where mentoring is especially valuable.

The right kind of guidance is important, vital, invaluable. But, its long-term value hinges on the degree to which it empowers you to shed your ego identity and embrace who you really are, independent of others (including your mentor). Andrew Newberg, M.D. and Mark Robert Waldman write about our desire for someone outside ourselves to guide our way in their book, *How God Changes Your Brain.*

"Sometimes I think that my dog, Rock, may be a philosopher too, but only to the extent that he wonders where I am. He does not think about what it means to be a dog or how he should act according to the natural "dogginess" inside of him. He does not wonder how he is guided through his life. But I think all human beings ponder what it means to be *human*, and I believe that most people try to act according to the natural humanity inside of them. Yet that humanity is often a challenge to maintain because of the selfish and negative tendencies generated by our brain. Plus, many people, beginning in childhood, conceive the possibility that there is someone, or something that is guiding them through life in a positive direction. But the human brain does not rest. Instead, it wants to know where God might be."2

Vibration, Frequency, and the Teacher

A student benefits from their relationship with a teacher when the teacher is already vibrating at the frequency the student wants to experience. The teacher's guidance can entrain you to that frequency and then assist you to evolve so that you can sustain it for yourself and, eventually, develop the ability to entrain others.

When you awaken and start living the Holistic Lifestyle, your frequency of vibration, which has been imbalanced, begins to adjust. As it progressively shifts, your whole database of thoughts and beliefs, which are also vibrating forms of energy, must update to become harmonic with your new and more holistic frequency of vibration.

Things change. Suddenly, you might have the thought: "This food is too greasy for me." Or, "Why am I watching this violent movie?" The vibration no longer matches where you are. If you ignore the messages you are getting and forge ahead with old habits you will immediately feel polluted, heavy. Before, the frequencies matched, but now they don't and you will feel the disharmony on all three levels: physical, mental, and emotional.

Awakening radically shifts your values and behaviors. It will also shift your friendships, your peer groups, even (or especially) your family relationships. As your vibrational frequency changes, you will discover that you are simply no longer compatible with certain people, for instance, those who remain where you used to be or have shifted in a different direction than the one you have chosen. Friendships change, acquaintances change, work relationships change, your likes and dislikes change, your whole world changes from the inside, creating an outer reflection of this inner signature frequency adjustment.

Let's Get Physical

What do you learn in school about your body? What does your doctor tell you about what food you should eat or what exercise you need to create optimum health? Not much. In fact, many doctors barely acknowledge a connection between what you eat and health. If you show up in their office with some malady, they won't educate you about how to adjust your diet and exercise. They will often recommend tests, drugs, and surgery, but virtually nothing that could address why the illness developed. Here is a sadly accurate portrayal from *Healing Myths* by Donald M. Epstein:

"Hospitals are rarely places where we become empowered in our healing process. Nor are they known to be places where we can discover trust in the human body. Instead, they reinforce old healing myths that further disconnect us from healing magic. Patients in hospitals are generally not encouraged to laugh, touch others and be touched, or eat fresh food. They are rarely given dietary supplements to support their health and to help neutralize the harmful effects of medical treatment. Fresh air and sunlight are rarely available to hospital patients.

"Often isolated from their emotional support system, patients spend most of the day and night under some form of sedation, and bathed in high electromagnetic radiation while resting in the hospital bed. A hospital stay reinforces the dark myths that tell us that we are alone and helpless, that our bodies are stupid, and that the only way to heal is to do what a professional tells us to do. The modern hospital is the temple of these mythologies. It is generally not a place, regardless of treatment, where the contact you have with staff nurses and doctors will reduce your stress level, enhance your immune system, allow you to express your inner self, or inspire you to feel joyous to be alive. Yet the population of patients within hospitals becomes the basis for a doctor's clinical judgment as to how we will progress." [3]

Remembering that the real value of guidance is to empower you and that our fundamental principle is always balance, let's explore at the physical level, where we seek to establish balance with diet, exercise, and breathing. With a health care system in this country that is collapsing because it is overloaded by sick patients who have never been educated on prevention, it is increasingly essential that we learn how to become our own primary health giver and use medical professionals as supporters not saviors.

The Holistic Diet

Many of us already know that a moderate diet of fruits and vegetables (lightly cooked or raw), healthy proteins, some fat and very little sugar, caffeine, or alcohol, and with adequate amounts of water taken separate from meals, is the basis of a healthy, balanced diet.

Based on that simple formula, are you creating balance or imbalance with what you eat? If not, adjust. If you are eating chocolate bars every day, drinking three cups of coffee, and vegetables have become strangers, you are creating physical imbalance. You can change that. Or you can wait for disease to "strike" and then take your chances with the medical system. This is not rocket science.

Another important diet factor is to know where your food comes from. Mass produced food is usually over-processed and dead. Find out where your food is grown and who is growing it. What about your choice of restaurants? Who prepares your food there? Their vibration is going right into that food and into you when you eat it. The kitchen in Muktananda's ashram was like a temple, maintained as a place of silence and spiritual focus. His cook was handpicked and carefully trained. The holistic vibration of the food was empowering.

What is the current diet we follow here in our Sanctuary? We balance the amount of protein, fat and carbohydrates, and also the overall amount of food consumed each day. We track caloric intake and use the best ingredients and supplements available. We base our decisions on scientific research, not taste or fads.

Exercise and Breath

The flow of your life energy balances the biochemistry of your physical body. Medical science validates that. How much exercise do you get in an average day? All of us need a certain amount of exercise every day for oxygenation, to deliver health and wellbeing at the physical level. We recommend what medical science recommends, a good 45-minute cardiovascular workout every day. That is the most basic requirement. If you incorporated that into your daily Holistic Lifestyle, it would do a great deal towards creating and sustaining balance.

Dr. David Perlmutter wrote, "Laboratory rats that exercise have been shown to produce far more brain-derived neurotrophic factor (BDNF) in their brains compared to sedentary animals. And there is a direct relationship between elevation of BDNF levels in these animals and their ability to learn, as one might expect.

"With this understanding of the relationship of BDNF to exercise, researchers in a report in the *Journal of the American Medical Association*, entitled 'Effect of Physical Activity in Cognitive Function in Older Adults at Risk for Alzheimer's Disease,' found that elderly individuals engaged in regular physical exercise for a 24-week period had an improvement of an astounding 1,800 percent on measures of memory, language ability, attention and other important cognitive functions compared to an age-matched group not involved in the exercise program.

"The mechanism by which exercise enhances brain performance is described in these and other studies as sitting squarely with increased production of BDNF. Just by engaging in regular physical exercise, you open the door to the possibility of actively taking control of your mental destiny."[4]

We recommend this exercise pattern in each 24-hour period. Not every other day, or once a week, but every single day. Many people are resistant to this. To get them to walk for even ten minutes is tough. They just don't have time. Apparently they will have time later to go the hospital, have operations, and miss work. Your alternative: at least forty-five minutes of cardiovascular workout daily to maintain physical balance.

In the classical traditions, hatha yoga provided good cardiovascular exercise and movement, a healthy flow of energy through the chakras and meridian systems. This was combined with what was called a sattvic (pure) diet, which included a certain amount of protein, carbohydrates, fat, plus the third component in maintaining physical balance: breath.

Monitoring your breathing habits is another good diagnostic. You can immediately determine whether you are balanced or imbalanced depending on the comparative time of your out-breath and in-breath. If the out-breath is longer, which it usually is in our culture, you are fragmented. But you can easily correct that with simple breathing exercises.

One of my students recently moved to the woods and his only source of heat now is firewood. Every day he stokes the stove and notices how important oxygen is for robust combustion. Adjusting a lever that increases or decreases oxygen intake changes the burn rate instantly and dramatically. He told me that this has really helped him change his own breathing habits. Watching the flames flare up or die down ... it's an image that he's applied to the processing of food in his body. And since he became conscious to breathe more deeply, a number of irritating "allergies" have begun to clear up.

Rest

How much sleep a person needs is very individual. Some people are comfortable with six hours while others need eight or even nine. Some people sleep less but nap every day. Others sleep for long periods to catch up whenever they have the chance. You know your own biorhythms; it's just a matter of adjusting your lifestyle to get the rest you need.

I do recommend meditating briefly before sleep, to set up the meditative EEG in your brain. Actually, the brain is surprisingly simple in this regard. It retains patterns associated with experiences and one of those patterns is meditation. Another pattern is sleep; another pattern is your waking state. If you are meditating every day and then just before sleep time you meditate again, your brain selects from that menu and, expecting sleep, brings up a meditative EEG. There is not that much difference between sleep and meditation, so establishing the meditative EEG pattern before sleep is relatively easy. Your sleep becomes a meditation with all its benefits.

Balancing Your Emotions

You can apply the self-diagnostic to your emotional dimension by checking in periodically to observe how you feel. Just ask yourself, "How do I feel, right here, right now? Am I anxious, fearful, and negative or am I feeling positive, loving, compassionate, contented, and joyful?" Based on that simple diagnostic, you know what to do. If there is a dominance of the negative, emphasize the opposite to create balance. Easier said than done? Perhaps. Let's explore.

All feelings stem from the two master emotions of love as the positive and fear as the negative. Also on the positive side are feelings such as compassion, contentment, joy, gratitude, and forgiveness. On the negative side are feelings such as anger, hatred, resentment, greed, and jealousy. Learn to become quickly aware of whatever you are feeling that is negative and then immediately identify and express the opposite. For instance, what is the opposite of anxiety? It could be peace, so to balance anxiety, you would focus on being peaceful. You could use your imagination to visualize a peaceful setting for instance—sitting by the beach or in a forest on a quiet day with sunlight filtering through the trees.

Someone who is chronically anxious may need the help and assistance of a medical diagnosis, to determine if they need therapy or medication. Exploring how the anxiety started might take them back into their childhood enculturation. This illustrates an important component to the balancing process: making the unconscious conscious. For instance, you can bring a "feeling" to conscious awareness and then shift it. If it turns out that a person is chronically and unconsciously identified with anxiety and having difficulty shifting it, then I would certainly recommend a medical diagnostic.

It's a radical concept to most people, the idea of consciously creating a feeling. It's certainly not something we learned in school or from our parents! The norm is to react. This happens, so you have that feeling. That's what the media assumed about us in Mumbai. Because we were attacked, we should automatically feel fear and then anger, plus the "natural" desire for revenge. Instead, we wakefully interrupted that process. We certainly felt what we felt, including fear. Our choice was to balance our feelings by consciously expressing the opposite—compassion, understanding, love, forgiveness.

People asked, "How could you do that?" Well, it's second nature for us. It's natural for us because we have practiced it for years as an essential part of the Holistic Lifestyle. Now that you are adopting that lifestyle, let's practice.

What are you feeling right now? Scan your emotions. Identify what you are feeling. Can you name it? Now, what would you like to feel? Because this may be new to you, I'll suggest a feeling ... peace. Peace is something most of us would like to feel more of. It's easy to feel more peaceful when you learn how to express peace, regardless of what's going on in your environment. In truth, you don't actually need anything or anyone to be peaceful. It's a choice. Just slow down your reading, become aware of your breathing and think about what peace means to you. If it helps, picture a peaceful nature scene, perhaps a childhood memory. Feel what that feels like, notice your attention on this feeling and deliberately intensify that. It can help to breathe right through the feeling. As you do, notice how it is increasing. The power of your attention and intention, focused on a feeling that you choose, results in your experience as you express it. How amazing!

Balancing Your Thoughts

We can't completely separate dimensions because they are intricately intertwined. The emotional and mental dimensions affect the physical. The physical affects the emotional and mental dimensions. The mental dimension has the same two polarities, with a fear-based or life-negative perspective as the default dominant. And the same balancing act applies. You start with observing your thoughts, your patterns of thinking. Most people are on autopilot. Their thinking is habitual and unconscious, because they are identified with the content of their mind.

You can begin to shift this by consciously thinking positive, life-affirming thoughts. Esther and Jerry Hicks, who present the Abraham teachings, write about this in their book, *Ask and It Is Given*: "Any time that you are thinking thoughts that cause you to know your true nature, you are in alignment with who you really are, for this is the state of absolute alignment. And the way those thoughts *feel* is the ultimate emotion of connection. When you think in terms of the fuel gauge on the vehicle, the state of alignment would be the same as a full tank.

"In other words, imagine a gauge or scale with gradations or degrees, which indicate the position of the (fullest) allowance of your connection with your Source Energy all the way to your (emptiest) most resistance disallowance of your alignment with your Source Energy."5 They follow this with a chart that tracks feelings from love down to fear.

The first step with mental balancing is to simply observe how you think. How automatic is your thinking process? How identified are you with it and what is the content? If it is life-negative, full of illusion, this is an imbalanced mental dimension and it is fragmenting your experience. Once you recognize this, you can acknowledge that you are the creator of it, which allows you to responsibly proceed to change it. How do you change it? You emphasize the opposite. Although you had "help" from parents and teachers and life experience, you were the one who programmed the negative and you can likewise program the positive.

You write some truthful software. You, the programmer, get into the system and repair it. You turn it around. This is precisely where an affirmation—which is a truthful thought or statement—can be helpful. You emphasize the positive polarity and the more you emphasize it the more it substantiates in your database to create a balance between the existing negative and the new positive data. Holistic awareness expands progressively so that what is incongruent with that new level of self-awareness is adjusted or cleared right out. This process begins with the diagnostic followed by practice which, in this case, is thinking positive thoughts.

Wholeness

What we are talking about are balancing techniques, bringing your multi-dimensional consciousness into a state of relative balance. What is the result of that? Wholeness. The measure of wholeness is self-awareness. Does your holistic awareness increase? Yes. Does your wakefulness increase? Yes. Do you become more present and more fully alive within your experience? Yes. Are you less automatically unconscious, caught up in your mind and feelings and physical body? Yes. Are you more present in the here and now moment rather than lost in memories or fantasies about the future? Yes. Self-awareness expansion is the result, and that is the guiding criterion.

When there is expansion in your awareness and you are more whole, you are also more able to fully experience the essence of yourself as consciousness. What is the nature of that essence? It is joy, the delight of life, the self-delighting consciousness that you are. Your happiness, your joy, your bliss increases. You become happy for no reason at all. You don't have to do anything or have anything to feel happy. Joy is not a result of something happening to you, because of something external to you. You become more content within yourself, within your own experience. This is the most tangible result of adopting the Holistic Lifestyle.

In Living Your Unlived Life, Robert A. Johnson and Jerry M. Ruhl, Ph.D. address why we tend to turn our backs on the real thing. "We often refuse to accept our most noble traits and instead find a shadow substitute for them. For example, instead of living with spirit, we settle for spirit in a bottle. In place of our God-given right to the ecstatic, we settle for temporary highs from consuming something or possessing someone. At first it is puzzling why we would look for our potentially best qualities in something or someone else. From the point of view of the ego, the appearance of a sublime trait or quality might upset our whole personality structure." [6]

All the great masters enjoyed blissful experience, without requiring sex or drugs or anything else to achieve it. Life itself produces the high! Creating and integrating natural peak experiences consistently is the journey of evolution in consciousness and as it increases wholeness it brings more pleasure. Ultimately, the Holistic Lifestyle grows into an orgasmic experience moment-by-moment, not dependent on external stimulus from the world of content.

Obviously, when a master is having this experience, many people want to be with him or her. Here you have someone sitting there day after day, radiating their amplitude of holistic power from an orgasmic state and everyone in the audience is being affected by it, basking in the vibrating waves of scintillating energy. Because many in the audience still experience separation, they will assume that this influence is coming **from** the teacher, and that to have it more consistently it is all-important to get as close to him or her as possible. That's why women throw themselves at gurus! They want that orgasmic experience. But, it's just training wheels. Yes, enjoy the entrainment from a master's energy field, but use the experience to evolve so that you can enjoy your own ecstatic field and entrain others.

Muktananda was a taskmaster. He insisted that we practice the Holistic Lifestyle 24/7. In this regard, he was like a drill sergeant. While his Sourcefield supported and nurtured us, he knew that one day we would be on our own. If we had not substantiated our own holistic experience, we would be lost when that day came.

Masters offer radical empowerment, to help you to grow through experience, not analysis, and they do it with their amplitude of power. Those who abandon themselves into oneness with an authentic master in his or her energetic field find that their lives change because of the experience not the analysis. This is an experience you can have on your own, not dependent on anything or anyone, including the guru, but being in the presence of an authentic master with that kind of energy field gives you the actual experience. There is no substitute for experience!

This is the experience we then take into every aspect of our daily lives. From this perspective, I will now examine some of them—those that deserve the most attention—because, while they can give us the most trouble, they also hold out the most promise for an ecstatic experience.

Relationships

Conflicted individuals create conflicted relationships; conflicted relationships create conflicted families; conflicted families create conflicted societies; conflicted societies create conflicted nations; conflicted nations create a conflicted world. This is why our world is as conflicted as it is. It is an accurate mirror of the individuals who comprise it. How do you change the world? Start with yourself. Find the balance in yourself and resolve the conflict there. Once you are balanced and whole, then you have something truthful to bring to any relationship. Relationship is supposed to be a journey of increasing wholeness, where the two become one. It is not meant to be an experience of two remaining two, fundamentally conflicted and disharmonious but not understanding why and using therapy and various techniques to endure the constant struggles.

Some suggest that I am anti-relationship. No, I am just anti-unconscious relationship. I want to see wakefulness within all relationships. To achieve that, first focus on yourself to resolve your own conflict and live in a balanced, wakeful holistic state of experience. Next, support your partner to do the same. Then enjoy the journey to increasing wholeness together that naturally results.

Most relationships begin unconsciously when physical attraction starts the ball rolling, sometimes delivering a feeling experience called "love." How long does this last? Until the honeymoon is over. If this feeling is all there is, it's going to be fleeting because it was superficial and often fueled by alcohol and drugs. I recommend a different criterion for starting any relationship. You can learn to bring yourself into relationship consciously by considering very carefully what you have attracted. Consider this other person. Do you share the same values? That's a simple question to ask before plunging forward, blinded by urges and the promise of feeling better.

Further questions are helpful. What is their history in relation to your history, in terms of family, enculturation, and so forth? Is there a reasonable possibility for balance, wholeness, harmony, growth, and transformation? What are the compatibilities, incompatibilities, and shared values? Knowing all this creates a much greater likelihood of success. It doesn't sound romantic, which is why almost nobody takes the time to do this. Romance is supposed to be like lightning; it strikes without warning. But those who explore what I am suggesting find that romance is really something that grows over time. Yes, there is bound to be that wonderful first spark, but use it to light a fire that lasts, rather than an intense blaze that flames out in a hurry.

One concept that especially interferes with balance in relationship is the hope of finding your soul mate and spending the rest of your life with them (happily ever after). Sorry, but all evidence points to the contrary, at least on this side of the movie screen! The fact in today's world is that most people don't spend their life with just one person. Furthermore, research and evidence more or less proves that human beings are not actually monogamous. That's a tough pill to swallow in our culture so it is rarely discussed. We're still programmed to want the fantasy: the house with white picket fence, 2.5 children ... such a wonderful fulfillment it will be!

Who really has that experience? If you are holding those values, even unconsciously, as you enter into a new relationship, it creates impossible demands and will likely sabotage your chances for long-term success. Also, regardless of where you are in terms of compatibility when you meet, divergence of experience is bound to happen because you don't stop evolving. Each individual will continue to develop in his or her own way. Obviously so, because each has their distinct life path, complete with karma. For instance, a couple may have some activity they initially share. At first, they are both into it. But, over time, interest drifts for one of them. Now one loves it while the other hates it. What do you do about that? How about talking about it?

Relationships that suffer and eventually fail often do so because those involved have underdeveloped communication skills. They project on each other and live out of assumptions and fantasies. They also avoid the difficult conversations because they don't trust each other with full honesty and hesitate to share their actual experiences fully—the good, the bad, and the non-orgasmic. There is virtually no real truthful communication. If you can make a commitment early to communicate consciously, that is a huge advance. Then, when a challenge arises, you have the tools to deal with it.

Here's another suggestion: you don't always have to do everything together. It's okay if one goes in this direction while the other goes over there. You can actually support each other in your individual evolution, while simultaneously supporting the relationship in its evolution. It helps when you understand that evolution is the purpose of the relationship. You are not together to make each other happy. That is as impossible as having your partner make you weigh 115 pounds. You make yourself happy. The purpose of being together is to support each other's ongoing evolution and to enjoy sharing the journey.

If a person truly wants to find and be with a partner, they should first invest in their own wakefulness. Seeking what you haven't got from another just perpetuates your not having it. Get wakeful and balanced first. Be still, watch, meditate, and someone will come to you, drawn to your frequency because they are resonating with that same frequency.

Then, know that the path of relationship requires a full-time focus. That's one of the reasons why so many relationships fail in our culture. They are not given sufficient focus. People just have too many things on their plate and relationship is not their primary priority.

Oneness

The experience of oneness is what we are journeying towards in all our relationships. When there is relative balance in each individual and then between the two, what emerges is true love. While this is magnified between two people, it starts with the individuals and you can obviously experience love within yourself. In fact, that is what gets magnified when you share it with another.

You can be loving without saying a word, simply because love lives within you. If a partner tries to change you, you can communicate from a place of compassion and loving kindness. Whether or not your partner resonates with this is their choice. The real question is, "Who do you choose to be, in every relationship?"

To set yourself up for a truly enjoyable relationship, be enthusiastic with your practice of the Holistic Lifestyle. As Katherine Woodward Thomas writes in *Calling in the One*, "While most of us know that we 'should' make the time to pray and meditate, we may not see how it can help us achieve our goal of actualizing love, and so we don't make it a top priority. Yet, there is a tremendous similarity between what scientific evidence indicates a daily practice of prayer and meditation provides a person, and the emotional maturity that demonstrates a readiness to create and sustain a loving partnership."[7]

Marriage

Human beings are not monogamous. Divorce rates are above 50% in this country now. Marriage simply does not work for most people. If we were to abandon family as the ultimate context for human relationships and embrace a larger context that family relationships fit inside, we would have a better chance to evolve a compassionate society.

I mentioned earlier how sabotaging it can be to labor under the delusion that there must be an ideal partner for everyone. This is not universally true. Some people are journeying on their own and will have no significant relationship in this life time because that's just not what their journey is about. Others journey together. I am a monk, so relationships are not a priority for me. For one thing, I wouldn't give it the commitment it deserves so I would fail at it. Therefore, I'm clear that it's not for me.

Sex

Sexual energy is designed to be pleasurable. Orgasm brings you crashing into the here and now. Everything is suspended and there is only now. It is so all-consuming that you are totally focused in the now and the moment is all there is. Orgasm stops the mind. This is why people crave it so much. The radical bliss of physical orgasm is overwhelming and absorbs the mind in its pulsating experience. When two people experience orgasm at the same time, they know oneness together. An amplitude of holistic power floods the whole of their beings with biochemical, hormonal and neurochemical releases and exchanges in an orgasmic pulsation that is truly the most pleasurable experience possible here in the denser dimensions. No drug can get close to it. Masters approach sexual experience as a meditation, because true spiritual intimacy brings an opportunity for the seeming two to merge into the truthful one.

The maximum power in human beings moves in their sexual energy. In the Tantric tradition, sexual energy is an intricate part of the "Kundalini." Where consciousness has been contracted and awareness forfeited, that energy has been reduced and becomes next to dormant. Only one quarter of the Kundalini energy is needed for metabolism. With awakening, fullness returns. This energy is seated at the base of the spine and its fuel is seminal fluid.

If you can learn to contain that energy to the point just before physical orgasm, then relax and, after a moment, continue, you will discover a moment where there is no longer any "downward pull." Men, this means you can train yourself to have orgasms without ejaculation. In fact, it's possible to continue this way, being thoroughly fulfilled and ecstatic but without any physical release, for hours.

The best way to begin learning this is to just slow down. Focus and share your attention, be there for your partner, be as wakeful as you can be. Experience true intimacy as the play of one consciousness. Relax into the stimulation and see how far you can go, stopping just before the point of physical orgasm. In the Tantric tradition they describe the unfolding Kundalini energy as it begins to move up and through the vortexes, until it gets to the top of the head where it finds unification with its opposite polarity in the crown. The result is holistic experience or oneness. Within spiritual relationship, this is when the two become one.

"Urdvareta" is the Sanskrit word that describes orgasmic experience without ejaculation, where no fluid is released externally. The man's physical passage closes so that both the fluid and the energy move upward, not downward. It's the same for women who also produce seminal fluid and can experience the same Kundalini process.

This Kundalini is the evolutionary fire within you and must be fed. If you don't provide the fuel of a healthy, rich diet, the Kundalini will start eating you. That is why my teacher insisted that we have a very balanced diet. If you wanted to fast or cleanse, he would say just eat one thing for a short period of time, like rice. But never fast completely. He was adamant about that. You must feed the awakening Kundalini energy.

As the Kundalini awakens, your experience of sexual orgasm expands throughout your body. One of our resident monks, Martin, described this encounter with the rising Kundalini during one of our chanting rituals. "I was sitting on one of the benches around the fire pit and preparing to meditate while the priests chanted. I got a bit restless and tried out different postures, finally settling into the half lotus. Within moments, I felt my whole stomach pulling up into my spine while the muscles in the groin and hip area contracted intensely and my chin was pulled down into my chest. These sensations intensified, completely beyond my control.

"Meanwhile, my breath became suspended. After a minute or so, I noticed that my breathing resumed, but in a very shallow manner and in short bursts through my nose. That only lasted a few minutes until I stopped breathing again. That's when the physical sensations got even more intense. After awhile, the lock in the neck area released itself, and I resumed breathing. Now my head moved upward and backward into a new position, and breathing suspended again. Energy was building inside me, like a rocket ready for take off! I began shaking. Then suddenly energy shot up from the base of my spine all the way to my crown and blasted out the top of my head. Wave after wave of sweet bliss showered over me and a profound quality of peace and stillness deepened within me. I felt fully connected to Source. This whole procedure repeated itself two more times, and every time I was blown out of my mind at how much stillness and bliss I was experiencing."

Career

Those who love what they do don't work, they play. When you are balanced and whole, your work becomes another expression of the flow of your consciousness and it must therefore be delightful. If it isn't full of joy, the problem is not with your job, it's in you. Of course, in America we are taught that we must work during the week so that we can play on the weekend. From early childhood we are taught—and our parents model it for us—that people work because they have to, not because they want to. Work is an obligation. It is **work**, commitment, and duty. Play is free time, when you get home from work.

Naturally, people who have bought into this belief system want to work as little as possible for as much money as possible. This breeds fraud, obviously, all the way from secretly doing something else while you are supposed to be working to outright cheating and crime. Unavoidably, you'll spend a significant number of hours working during your lifetime, so why not make that time fulfilling in itself? It's more than possible; it's natural. The moments of "working" are also moments when you can live in witness consciousness and bring your gifts into a waiting world. As consciousness, this is a delight. So much so that the idea of waiting for the weekend before you can enjoy yourself is seen for what it is, a piece of corrupted code in an outdated internal software program.

Money

If everything is consciousness, that has to include money. If you have negative concepts about money, that's your old data, another illusion. "Money is bad ..." some believe. Really? Who says so? All your stories about money are simply that: stories. If you take away those stories about money, it is just what is. Who would you be without your money stories? Just be a witnessing consciousness enjoying whatever money is there or not there. And don't worry about "them"—the crooks who are stealing money. That's where their feet are! Can you allow them their experience, even when it impacts your personal "bottom line?" I don't mean you should be gullible and trust everyone. The world is full of those living in scarcity who would rather steal than create, so watch your wallet! Watch your beliefs just as closely, because they may be stealing from you every day.

In our society, money is ranked as the ultimate value. We do need it to survive and to be secure but people make compromises based on their fear of scarcity. If so, what are you investing in? Money is more important than consciousness? Impermanence is more important than permanence? Most people think so and behave accordingly, prostituting their values for survival through the ego-directed drive to accumulate money.

Because there is such a fever associated with money, let's pause. Consider how wealthy you are. Feel your heart beating. Notice your breathing. Heighten your awareness of the sounds around you. Look up from your reading to take in the room. You're probably not starving, freezing, ducking bullets. You're privileged, blessed, and abundant. Breathe all this in and then exude gratitude as you exhale. Feel yourself living in the midst of plenty... know that this is your nature, what and who you are, not something you need to get.

Here's an interesting money story. Muktananda's guru was a naked man in the jungle. Literally. For years he retreated farther and farther into the jungle to get away from people. He would sit in trees so people came and prayed to him in the trees. He would pick a leaf from the tree and throw it down. Someone would catch it and give it to an ailing friend ... who would be cured. Eventually there were so many people that they coaxed him out of the trees. This, by the way, was in the middle of nowhere, eighty miles north of Mumbai. They invited him to live in their village, which was tribal and of the lowest caste. More and more people showed up and they persuaded him to wear a loincloth. Over time, a whole ashram with thousands of people grew up around him.

He was lying down most of the time, while people came and asked for things, sometimes money. There are many stories of him pulling money out of his loincloth, or telling them where to find it. He himself never had any possessions but I've seen pictures of the piles of gifts that people brought. He had no interest in such impermanence. But it proved useful to others in need and the point is that great abundance appeared without him having to try and get it. Material abundance was a reflection of his abundant consciousness. That, in a sentence, is the **true** economic system!

Money is merely another form of consciousness. If you are able to open to consciousness in that form, then you include it and you will attract money towards you. If you are seeking it, by fearing that you don't have enough of it, then you will experience yourself not having it. I've met people who amassed a fortune through cleverness or subterfuge while in that limited state of consciousness. Ironically, they had the money but their consciousness hadn't changed, so they didn't feel secure yet. They had to fight to keep what they had and worried about losing it, which is just the flip side of worrying about getting it.

I left India after my teacher died in 1982 with five hundred dollars that he gave me (and told me never to spend), plus two suitcases that contained all my belongings. Here we are now, almost thirty years later, and I am apparently wealthy. Well, since I am a monk, I don't actually own anything. The Synchronicity Foundation owns it all. But they give me a comfortable home to live in, clothes to wear, nutritious food, and a car and driver when needed. My advisors tell me that I could retire, that I don't need to work anymore. Retirement? I have never considered what I do as work. That is not a context for me. I will enjoy whatever I do within this human experience until the day I drop and I don't need any payment for it.

I started in a little cabin on a farm five miles from here. My economic strategy was to trust and watch. I had no money but I did have a shaved head and orange clothes, which went over really well in redneck rural Virginia! I had to quickly adapt and let go of all those Eastern Indian cultural trappings, even though I love that culture. It just didn't fit here.

What did fit was giving value and that's as true for you in your situation today as it was for me in that situation back then. The more you live as a giver the more your holistic amplitude increases. When you contribute in some way to those around you, rewards return in appropriate ways. All selfless service is an investment in consciousness. Because there is only one, it's circular and it all comes back to you. When it does, don't take it to use just for yourself. Reinvest and create something else of further service. That's what our community member

Kia is doing by developing the non-profit organization One Life Alliance that we birthed in the aftermath of our Mumbai challenge, inspiring people everywhere to honor the sacredness of life in themselves and all others.

That $500 from Muktananda was a symbolic seed that has grown into an abundance we now share with the world through our programs.

The Sangha

Sangha, in Sanskrit, refers to a community of like-minded, spiritually evolved people who live and interact together in community, supporting each other in the experience where their feet are. There is little of that here in the West other than churches which, for some people, have become little more than a once a week social club.

Some intentional communities, although well-intentioned, can become havens for the disenfranchised, especially the mentally ill, because it's a perfect environment for hiding mental illness. Once diagnosed and known, such individuals find it difficult to find employment, take care of themselves or get disability benefits. They can't hold jobs, so they seek people and places that can take care of them. Some show up on the doorstep of communities like ours, professing interest in our beliefs and our lifestyle. They will say whatever it takes to get in and be taken care of. We have a detailed application process but sometimes a person like this can slip through. It takes about a month and then we start noticing the tell-tale signs: depression, anger, resistance, the inability to live the Holistic Lifestyle. It all becomes apparent within a month or so and then we have to inform the person that this is not what our place is for. We are just not qualified to take care of them.

What we **are** qualified to do is provide a spiritual home for those interested in learning and practicing the Holistic Lifestyle, expanding their amplitude of power and becoming increasingly able to help entrain visitors who come for our retreats. We provide this service together here and I am deeply grateful for the residents who share this delightful "career" with me! We enjoy blissful, honest relationships and a totally different kind of "family" experience together.

ৡৡৡ

JOHN:

We arrived home just in time for Dad's 88th birthday on December 1st. We had planned to have the family come over to his assisted living place but it turned into a "Welcome home, thank God you're alive" party. My wife flew into Dallas to join us.

Everyone sure wanted to hear our story. We told it, but it was surreal. I felt frozen and it seemed that the story was about something that happened to other people, not to my Dad and me.

When my wife and I returned to Palm Springs I realized that I had my life back now. I felt very lucky to have survived because, by all accounts, I should have been in that restaurant when the shooting started.

The whole thing has helped me increase my appreciation for life. Also, to know that there really is no safety, not really. I don't have to go around protecting myself to make sure something bad doesn't happen. That would be living in fear. It's more of an acknowledgment about what can happen to you, just out of the blue.

How it all pans out is beyond us. When is our moment of passing from this life supposed to be? That's unknown to us. But I believe now that it is known on some other level. And I feel a kind of acceptance about that. It's not giving up or anything, just acceptance. Truly, this feels more and more like a dream that I will wake up from one day. Maybe that's what death really is, waking up from this illusion. I don't know. But I'll get to find out some day.

MASTER CHARLES:

My house was the same when I got home, everything was the same, and yet I felt completely different. The experience had radically

expanded my state of being. Sitting at my desk, finally alone, I realized in a deep way what was really important. It sure wasn't any of
this "stuff" around me. I could easily reduce everything in my life
by half! I immediately began to do just that.

❧❧❧

To better integrate the meaning of this chapter, please visit
www.synchronicity.org, go to the "Forgiving the Unforgivable"
section, and use the password "one" to access additional material.

CHAPTER 10

Trust and Watch

Last night my teacher taught me the lesson of Poverty:
Having nothing and wanting nothing.
I am a naked man standing inside a mine of rubies,
clothed in red silk.
I absorb the shining and now I see the ocean,
billions of simultaneous motions
moving in me.
A circle of lovely, quiet people
becomes the ring on my finger.
Then the wind and thunder of rain on the way.
I have such a teacher.[1]

—Rumi

In media interviews and conversations with family and friends, survivors are pressed to condemn the terrorists. They don't. In fact, they remain consistently compassionate, expressing understanding, not judgment, and they refuse the call for punishment.

Kia, mourning the death of husband and child, says: "Forgive them … they didn't know what they were doing."

One terrorist survives. When confronted with the bodies of his fallen comrades and faced with the reality of what he/they did, he breaks down, confessing that he had no idea … He had been brainwashed, programmed.

As Kia had said, he didn't really know what he was doing.

Fear not.
What's the worst that could happen?
Death, or life unlived?

You cannot be destroyed
because your essence is eternal and incorruptible.
Embrace your true nature,
and when you grieve for what is gone,
celebrate what can never be lost.

You.
Life, which is forever,
in one form or another,
and formless in between.

It is all consciousness,
delighting in its play,
trusting and watching
as what will be, will be.

ༀༀༀ

LINDA:

One persistent reporter found an old phone number on the web and called. This was in the early frenzy of reporting the story, before my kids knew what was going on. This reporter managed to get through to my son directly and asked him: "So, how do you feel about your mom being shot?" That required some healing, as thoughtlessness always does.

I've learned that reporting is very fictional in these cases. One magazine never spoke to me yet quoted me talking (inaccurately) about my injuries. I knew where I was shot, and it wasn't the arm like they reported! They had no interest in facts. I thought the truth was frightening enough, yet the media had to exaggerate and create their own drama to make better headlines.

After the first story went out through a British newscaster we opted for no other media exposure at all until my children saw me in person. Here's a story we never gave them. (Who knows how they would have distorted this?) My oldest son had a premonition that I was in danger in India. He awoke from a nightmare and e-mailed, urging me to be careful and please come home safely. We found out later that he sent that e-mail about the same time that I was shot in the restaurant.

PHYL:

The media met me at the Sydney airport. They seemed to be looking for sensationalism but I just gave them the facts. They were pretty surprised that I was not being negative but I was genuinely grateful to be home and thankful for all the support I had received. They asked about my husband who, ironically, had been trapped in Thailand at the same time! What were the odds of that? One fellow Mumbai survivor, a businessman from Sydney, saw us on TV and called to say that his wife thought she would take up meditation now.

When people suggest to me that this was a terrible experience, I tell them about the support I received from Master Charles, the people of India, my family and friends and even the Australian Government. I told the media, "Love is stronger than terrorism." This is the message I always give and it went out over national TV.

LARRY:

Once we arrived back in Canada we were inundated by the media. It was like a three ring circus. We had no idea that we had been splattered across the newspapers and TV for the week prior. We did interview after interview and they all felt the same. The media was only interested in the body count, the gory details and the visuals of our warlike experience. That disappointed me. They asked us how it felt to be victims but we had never felt like victims. In fact, we have come to see our experience as a blessing. We were able to live through an extreme, life-threatening situation and understand it as part of a much larger plan.

We know that we went to India and to the Oberoi Hotel at that exact time for the purpose of offering a positive influence into a negative situation. We survivors were there as lightning rods for all the collective positive energies, the good wishes, the blessings that poured in from around the world. Alan and Naomi were there to serve as guides for all those that lost their lives so tragically, helping these poor souls pass with love, care, and affection.

By the end of our ordeal we had been transformed, from fear and uncertainty to balance and acceptance. I remember that our hotel room even became tranquil! Imagine that, with constant gunfire and explosions all around us. We just surrendered and allowed whatever was to be, to be.

KIA:

The first questions of that early morning press conference were directed to me. A reporter asked, "Kia, what's on your mind today?" I answered something like, "It's not so much what's on my mind, but what's in my heart. In fact, I'm not in my mind at all. I can only feel, because the emotions are so deep and so strong and contain so much—all the way from the deepest grief and pain I have ever known, to the most love and support I have ever received."

The next question was, "Kia, what are your thoughts on the terrorists?" I replied, "We must send them our love, forgiveness and compassion, we must. As Jesus Christ said long ago 'Forgive them they know not what they do.' They are shrouded and clouded by so much fear that we must send them love, because love overpowers fear. That's my choice."

MASTER CHARLES:

I appeared on the *Today Show* and *Good Morning America*. Then Kia and I hosted a large press conference in the Sanctuary. When they asked what we thought of the terrorists and what sort of revenge we wanted Kia voiced it perfectly. Love, compassion, and forgiveness: that's what we wanted. There were some in the media that cried when we told our story.

❧❧❧

*"People are all born with a love of learning, but the fixed mindset
can undo it. Think of a time you were enjoying something—
doing a crossword puzzle, playing a sport, learning a new dance.
Then it became hard and you wanted out. Maybe you suddenly felt
tired, dizzy, bored, or hungry. Next time this happens, don't fool
yourself. It's the fixed mindset. Put yourself in a growth mindset.
Picture your brain forming new connections as you meet
the challenge and learn. Keep on going."*

—Carol S. Dweck, Ph.D.[2]

In chapter one I encouraged you to focus on each word, even the spaces between them, to savor the learning experience of the moment. In fact, I jested that "What you seek is not in chapter seven." That is true. It's not in chapter seven; it's here in chapter ten.

"How did you do it?" This book was inspired by that one question, asked by people all over the world who saw us on the news and were inspired by our response to the Mumbai terrorist attack. Even some in the media admitted their curiosity. How could we be so positive in the face of such hatred? Two of our dearest friends in the world were killed. Four others were wounded. All of us were traumatized. Yet, without exception, we responded with compassion and understanding. None of us demanded revenge; none of us saw ourselves as victims, none of us blamed.

How did we do it? Here in chapter ten we answer that question by focusing on seven themes from Mumbai that seem to be the most relevant and important. Obviously, there were countless aspects to the experience but these seven cover the range of what most people would tend to experience in a situation like ours, from fear to grief. We certainly had to deal with them all and in this chapter I explore how we did that, from the standpoint of our Holistic Lifestyle. The seven are:

1. The fear of others
2. The fear of death
3. Survival
4. The fear of abandonment
5. Revenge
6. Being a victim
7. Grief

All that you have read so far has built a foundation of new understanding, so that you can now go far beyond intellectual enlightenment to have a real experience of what the words mean. This—your new experience—will help prepare you in very practical ways to handle the challenges coming your way, most likely not as dramatic as ours in Mumbai, but you never know.

You now know that witness consciousness is the first step. When you are constant in witness consciousness you don't react. You remain a detached observer. You are wakeful, watching the experience that is happening and being well informed about it before choosing a course of action to take. Instead of "Don't just stand there, do something," it's more like "Don't just do something, stand there!" Be still and know ... be aware of what is happening and **then** learn what to do.

That's how we did it.

Contrast this with how the average person reacts in an emergency. Adrenaline takes over. Old patterns trigger and panic directs them unconsciously. There is no witnessing, no ability to witness, just automatic responses uninformed by what is happening on subtler levels because that can't even be perceived.

The Holistic Lifestyle is designed to deliver witness consciousness and wakefulness, the inevitable result of balance. That's why every practice is centered on this one primary principle of balance. Balance, balance, balance. The more you can sustain balance, the more consistency of witness consciousness you have, the more consistent your wakefulness, the more natural your wise action will be in challenging circumstances.

Although the media and curious questioners assumed we were prisoners and victims in Mumbai, we were actually always at choice. Because of witness consciousness, we could experience something like, "I am a witnessing consciousness in a Mumbai terrorist attack. This is an experience that is really happening and I am watching it. What are my choices here and now?"

The knee-jerk, normal response would be a mind running at warp speed, adrenalin pumping up the metabolism and creating a state of hyper alertness. Alertness is vital, but fear-motivated alertness censors your perception from anything other than quickly determining what physical action to take. The mind just frantically searches for the information it needs to survive.

Witness consciousness is a stepping back from that frenzy to expand holistic awareness and perceive what is also happening on the subtler dimensions of experience. Remember, the human trinity of physical, mental, and emotional are not the only dimensions. Witness consciousness has a perspective on the whole picture, not just the most obvious parts.

Be still. Trust and watch. Of course, you can only trust if you are wakeful, because what you are trusting is something beyond the obvious dimensions. You are trusting in the play of consciousness, knowing that the terrorists are not orchestrating the show—consciousness is. There is something greater than you and them and all that you can see on these dense levels. So, yes, your adrenaline is rushing, your heart is pumping, everything that is instinctual and primal has been activated and that is appropriate! It's a life and death situation ... it's real! But, you are not lost "within" it. Someone lost within it is freaking out all right. "This is terrible, wrong, it shouldn't be happening, why me, what's going to happen ..." But that voice is not you.

In witness consciousness you allow everything to be the way it is. You accept; you don't resist. You flow with what is happening as the absolutely appropriate momentary happening of consciousness. This is an experience whose time has come. There is a reason for it then, hosts of reasons. This awareness doesn't mean you don't feel fear. We were afraid, obviously! Fear is appropriate when your life is in danger! Who wouldn't be afraid? We could die in the next moment. I hope that you understand from what we have presented on the two polarities of relative reality: that if fear is present there must be the opposite polarity, love. Love must be present and the two will inevitably oscillate together in some way. As far as this world of relative reality goes, there will always be fear, just as there will always be love. And from a truthful perspective, fear in a situation like this is an alarm going off in your emotional dimension that calls your attention to the moment. Fear is a gift request saying "Love is needed here!"

In his remarkable book, *The Gift of Fear*, Gavin de Becker writes about the difference between fear, as a gift, and the dangers of worry. "After decades of seeing worry in all its forms, I've concluded that it hurts people much more than it helps. It interrupts clear thinking, wastes time, and shortens life. When worrying, ask yourself, "How does this serve me?" and you may well find that the cost of worrying is greater than the cost of changing. To be freer of fear and yet still get its gift, there are three goals to strive for. They aren't easy to reach, but it's worth trying:

1. When you feel fear, listen.
2. When you don't feel fear, don't manufacture it.
3. If you find yourself creating worry, explore and discover why." [3]

"Explore and discover why." What a wise instruction. An alarm has gone off, you are feeling fear, but—because you are experienced in witness consciousness—you remind yourself to be wakeful. You pay attention. You explore and discover why you are feeling the fear. Don't worry about it; keep your mind clear and focused. And let the other dimensions feed you information as well. Don't close down, open up.

The subtle dimensions are always dominant for me, so it is natural that I explore those levels. This means that under pressure from the outside world my consciousness will elevate to minimize the physical, emotional, and mental dimensions. This helps me cope better, through reduced identification with physical, emotional, and mental levels of experience. I will remain still, saturated with peace, and focused within my own energy field which becomes even more expansive, opiated, and intoxicated in a threatening situation like Mumbai.

Most people demand information from the denser levels: "Where is the fire, is the hotel going to explode, who should I call on the telephone, what can I find on TV, **where do I get the information!**" What they don't get is any reassurance from a transcendent place. "Wait a minute, you are here and it is now, consciousness is orchestrating the show, trust and watch." That message is real and I've learned to trust it more than I trust my mind. One source of information is flowing from the connected wholeness of All, the other is disconnected and driven by an ego's need to survive at all costs.

There's a charming example of this in the film *The King of Hearts*. [4] Alan Bates's character is frantically trying to figure out where a bomb has been hidden that will blow up the whole town. Genevieve Bujold's character just wants to make out. Fighting off her advances, Bates finally exclaims, "Don't you realize that we only have five minutes left?" Bujold bats her long eye lashes at him and whispers seductively, "Five minutes would be wonderful." Bates gives up. He collapses in her arms, enjoys her embrace and, a moment later, jumps up, inspired. "I know where the bomb is!"

Intuition or subtle dimensional insight? The same awareness saved lives in Mumbai. My associates were not identified at the denser levels where fear would have blinded them. Their subtle dimensions were actualized, but it didn't just happen magically somehow. They took specific steps: they focused. Some were chanting, others were meditating, generating a peaceful state of experience. This is natural for them but totally radical in that sort of situation. It brought them moments of subtle intuitive insight. "Don't go to the Business Center. Go through this door, not the other one. Stay in your room." Where do you think that information came from?

Danger also triggers old data. Ben almost died in an airplane crash many years ago. When he heard an explosion and smelled fire, up came that data. Suddenly he was right back in that airplane. And now the fear doubled, tripled. Was Ben freaked out in the beginning? Yes, but he knew what to do. And he had two evolved people with him that kept helping him focus. This was an experience whose time had come for Ben. Because he knew that, from years of knowing it in low-stress situations, and because he has a well-developed, foundational experience in the Holistic Lifestyle, being thrown into that traumatic situation actually helped Ben face and deal with a past fearful experience in ways he hadn't been able to before. Others in our party will testify to the same thing. Mumbai did not leave deep scars; it healed old wounds. Such is the truthful nature of evolving consciousness. It creates precision experiences through which we grow and progressively delivers us to ever more evolved wholeness.

Before we begin exploring the seven specific issues I have chosen to focus on, let's take a balance break. You know the drill by now. Pause, slow your reading, become aware of your breathing and your heartbeat. Recall a memory, a time in your recent or distant past when you have been frightened, even terrified. Sink deeper into this memory, even though it may be difficult. Now, as you are recalling it (and take a moment away from the reading to really get into it if you wish), deliberately step back from the memory and focus on the feeling of peace. Savor this new feeling and experience yourself directing that feeling "towards" the painful memory. Notice what happens. Notice how the introduction of a positive feeling immediately brings relief, as it restores your emotional equilibrium.

The Fear of Others

We are surrounded by other people whom we illusorily experience as separate from ourselves, especially those whom we perceive as "obviously different." This can create fear, what I call "the fear of others." In *The Muslim Next Door*, Sumbul Ali-Karamali writes, "I have two Christian friends who tell me they are afraid to say anything positive about Islam because of the angry reactions such simple statements ignite in their acquaintances. ... If we add media stereotyping to all this negative medieval mythology about Islam, the result is a picture that resists erasure. Add also the confusion about what is religious, as opposed to cultural or socioeconomic. Add the tangible language barriers. Add the extremists who use Islam to commit horrifying crimes. The sum total is an impregnable misunderstanding of Islam and Muslims." [5]

Separation is illusion. In the holistic model of reality there is no one else out there. It is all you, reflections of you, multiplications of you. There is no separation of subject and object. If you are wakeful in that understanding, you are whole. You are broadcasting a completely different frequency of vibration, empathy in its purest form, which means no separation.

What affect does that frequency have on the fragmented world around me? The nature of what I vibrate is the nature of what I attract. Fragmentation attracts fragmentation. If you are afraid someone will hit you on head, they will—in some form or another—because that is what you are broadcasting. If you are whole and unified and radiating a field of positive holistic harmonics, don't you think the same is going to come back to you? You know from your own experience that it does.

Applying this logic, one could ask, "If those Synchronicity people were all broadcasting love, why did they 'attract' a terrorist attack?" Good question. Why do bad things happen to good people? That's a book title and an interesting question. But it hinges on judgment, this being good, that being bad. For those of us at the center of this Mumbai storm, our experience remained consistent. I won't go as far as to say that it was just another day at the office. It was extraordinary! Our choice was to use the same balancing techniques there that we always do. From our standpoint, what came to us was the experience whose time had come, the happening in consciousness, and we could evolve through the experience. We didn't need to understand all the reasons and we still don't. Our reaction in the heat of it? We generated the frequency of peace. Why? Because that could create balance within the situation and increase holistic awareness. I seem to recall some master facing a much worse personal attack saying, "For this reason came I to this hour." That was our attitude.

The real question in a situation like Mumbai is always, "Who do you choose to be?" Not, "Who is this 'other person,' what are they doing **to** me and why?" When you collapse separateness and embrace oneness a gift arrives: an experience to grow from. No judgment, just conscious choice. That is wakefulness.

Fear of Death

"As a well-spent day brings happy sleep,
so a life well spent brings happy death."[6]
—Leonardo Da Vinci

The holistic response to the fear of death is this: "If I am wakeful, what difference does it make?" If I am truly wakeful, I know that this human form of mine is impermanent. It will entropy, decay and die; that's its nature. If the time has come to die today, that's fine. But since I am not this body, I am not what is dying. The average person would tend to say otherwise. "I **am** this body and when it ends, I end. This body is all that I know; beyond is only speculation, so I must cling to what I know."

When you are whole—in experience, not theory—you have an existential conviction about what lies beyond the death of this human form. Fortunately, we haven't seen the trailer, so the surprise remains intact! But we know that the journey goes on, after a quick change of clothing. That is the holistic perspective, the bigger picture of who I really am and what life really is. It's not based on accepting some theory of reincarnation; it's an experience that is natural to all of life when life is fully experienced. Holistically experience the nature of life and you will know—you don't theorize, you know—that you will **never** end.

Japanese Samurai seek to die honorably. Great masters are renowned for it. They have everything in order and have usually chosen their successor to ensure the continuation of their work. When the moment comes they simply withdraw and make a peaceful transition.

A good example is Ananda Mayi Ma, perhaps the greatest Indian female saint/guru/master, who was first written about in the book, *Autobiography of a Yogi*.[7] She was a contemporary of Muktananda and they were friends. She had ashrams in every city of India and constantly moved around, staying a short time in each place. She had thousands and thousands of devotees. When she was in her eighties, she went to her ashram on the Ganges River by the foothills in Hardwar, lay down, and wouldn't get up. Attendants came to feed her but she refused to eat. They thought she was sick and summoned the doctor but nothing was wrong. She remained mostly silent, gazing out the window at the river. All she would say is, "They are calling me home." She slowly transitioned, dying six weeks before Muktananda did.

"They are calling me home." She was totally conscious of the process. There was nothing wrong with her; it was just her time to go. There are also stories about masters and students who choose to experience conscious death together. One was a disciple of my guru's guru, the man everyone thought would become his successor. About six months before the guru died, this disciple said "I don't want to be here after you leave; I want permission to take live Samadhi (conscious transition)." The master agreed. So, when the appointed time came, he simply assumed the yogic posture and left his body consciously.

Ram Das's guru, Neem Karoli Baba, did the same thing. Three days before he died, he gave his assistant his daily journal as a personal gift. She opened it after the funeral and found a single word repeated on every page: Ram. Ram means God.

When you are holistically aware, physical death is a continuation of this great journey. It looms ahead for all of us, unavoidably. How wakeful can you be as you complete life in your physical body?

Survival

The primal drive to survive is strong in all living creatures. Living the Holistic Lifestyle prepares you to handle even life-and-death situations in ways that conserve your energy. Stress is an alarm that signals imbalance. Stress burns up essential nutrients, therefore remaining calm and peaceful and detached gives you a better chance of survival. That describes the material level of experience. From a spiritual perspective, whatever is needed for survival can literally manifest out of thin air.

Once a great master was describing his lofty plans and a disciple couldn't help but interject to say, "But master, this will cost a lot of money. Where will that money come from?" The master smiled and answered, "From wherever it is right now." That level of confidence arises from true faith, natural to holistic experience. We expect miracles … and they happen. If we are destined to survive, we will.

Survival mechanisms are in place within every human being and they kick in during moments of danger. The primal part of the brain becomes operative. Unfortunately, if that is all you have actualized and you are governed by it, you get sucked right into the intensity of a high-adrenaline adventure, full of fear. That's not healthy.

The mind gets involved, diving into its fearful fantasies, rather than staying present in the moment. By contrast, when you bring wakefulness to the fear around survival, you can remember that your physical body is just one part of you. If it goes, hey, there's more of you than that! You will still be "here." You will always be here. In the ultimate sense, the fear around survival is an illusion. You are an eternal consciousness. When you live the truthful model of reality, you may not want to give up your body in some violent way—I would prefer not to!—but if you lose it, you're not losing everything.

There is a great story about a general and a master. The General says, "Don't you know that I am someone who can run you through in the twinkling of an eye?" The Master responds, "Don't you know that I am someone who can be run through in the twinkling of an eye?"

The Fear of Being Abandoned

We are all connected; we are all one. In holistic consciousness we are always together, as one, unified within our diversity. Fear of abandonment stems from the primary illusion of separation. If this illusion is operative via your ego, then you harbor the illusion that you are separate and different. If so, then you can be either accepted or rejected. This, then, is really an issue of self-worth. Are you good enough, acceptable, or could you be rejected, abandoned? Most people struggle with their self-worth constantly. They are always seeking approval and acceptance.

But the whole issue of abandonment is an illusion. In terms of the truth, you have all your worth by virtue of existence. Just the fact that you are alive ... that's it! That fact establishes your worth. The rest is illusion, powerful illusion that the ego proves with all kinds of data. Sadly, when you believe that you are separate and different, in one way or another that's exactly the experience you create. But it's not the truth; it's just what you (or rather your ego) created.

Of course, the great hope is to find someone who loves you and promises never to leave. "Til death do us part," it says in the traditional marriage ceremony. Of course, this is usually love with an illusory partner who is separate from you. On that basis they will most certainly leave you! That is guaranteed. Or, you will leave them. All form is impermanent! "Til death do you part." If you believe in separateness, you will create it. Ultimately, you will be abandoned. And, believing that at some unconscious level, you will live in the shadow of that fear. It's coming—somewhere up ahead on the road of life that horrible separation and loss is coming. Notice: you are the creator of it!

How can you abandon yourself? It's illusory madness, there for its own radical entertainment, by the way. So many people get caught up and suffer, until they are willing to wake up and realize, "I am creating this experience. There is no place I can go. I can't get away from myself. I cannot be abandoned because I am all and all is one."

Anger

From the holistic perspective, life is neither fair nor unfair. It is as it is. What's variable is how you interpret it. If "Life is so unfair!" is a story you choose to tell yourself, that will become your experience. This might make you angry, but your anger is a reaction to a story that you created. The fact that reacting this way is habitual and is backed up by a lifetime of practice doesn't make it legitimate.

From a holistic perspective, I don't even engage in that debate. I observe the situation and acknowledge that this is what is happening. I notice my data, what I am feeling, and the story that I begin to tell about it. Then I minimize the story and just be with it the way it is, without making it wrong, right, unfair, or "should be other than it is." This challenges one of the major default settings in our relative reality software—that the situation, my life, "should be different than the way it is." No, it should be exactly the way it is! Why? Because that's the way it is! What happens to anger when you open to that truth?

In some situations it is appropriate to get in touch with your anger in some deliberate way. You might slam a pillow, acting out your anger to release it. A skilled therapist is useful for navigating these potentially healing waters. Some people have buried and suppressed data that needs surfacing and reprogramming. Most people can learn how to become aware of an emotional reaction like anger and come to understand how they are creating the experience and even to an awareness of the causative data. By bringing it to awareness this way the field can be cleared.

For some, venting their anger can be healthy. What we call anger is just a very intense flow of energy orchestrated by your consciousness. For example, Muktananda was a very fiery person. He shrieked and yelled and screamed and smacked with a stick. Did his vibration change? Did the holistic amplitude of his power shift when he was expressing this way, which would mean that he dropped out of the unified state? No. He remained the same. When you looked in his eyes, they remained dilated with bliss. He was able to remain in that detached witness consciousness whether he was shrieking, quietly talking, eating, or riding in an airplane. It was all the same consciousness. Then ask the person who he was directing his intensity towards. They experienced empowerment! All his energy was focused on them, lasered right into them, and it often blew them wide open into a corresponding state of wholeness. Tough love, powerful entrainment!

Revenge

This was something the media expected us to want. We tried to convey that from our holistic perspective there is no one other than me who could hurt me. I am one with all these diversified forms, all people, including the terrorists. We are one consciousness in essence and if I can perceive and experience this essence, then I can celebrate the diverse expressions of that consciousness and know that everything and everyone's experience is valid. I don't know why a terrorist is a terrorist; that is the person's whole history expressing in the moment because of how their consciousness is evolving. Who am I to sit in judgment of that?

Instead, I can eliminate the terrorist in myself, the one who invests in illusory stories of fear, hatred, and revenge. I can choose to be truthful and fill myself with love, compassion, kindness, and forgiveness.

The whole "eye for an eye" concept only makes sense when there is a right and a wrong. But every person is simply having their appropriate experience. I probably can't understand theirs, just as they can't understand mine. But when anyone is suffering I am compassionate because they are a part of me. If they hurt me, I am compassionate. This is different than the concept of dualistic forgiveness. Compassion is the expression of a unified state of consciousness. Forgiveness—the way it is often conceived—requires something to be wrong, which then needs to be forgiven. "Some person injured me; I forgive them." But they didn't, they couldn't injure me, because I'm not giving them that illusory power over me. That means that there is actually no need for forgiveness. Not forgiveness like that and certainly no need for revenge. Not for someone in a holistic state of consciousness.

In a fragmented state of consciousness, revenge makes perfect sense. It's a predictable egocentric response. Somebody other than me did something to me that hurt me and therefore I must cause him or her pain in return. There it is again: the illusion of separation and victim identification. Reacting that way may seem to balance the score but it will only increase separation and fragmentation in consciousness. Just look at what happened post 9/11 because America sought to punish the "evil-doers." No lessons learned at all, no expansion of holistic awareness.

Being a Victim

Some people love to show off their scars. This is egocentric. Look how quickly tragedies turn into bestselling books with authors exploiting their tragedy for sympathy and profit. Identities spring up, victim identities, all based in how "somebody did me wrong."

It's been three years since our Mumbai experience (as of this writing in 2011). All of us have had time to let the experience season, to heal and evolve. Now, with some positive initiatives launching like the One Life Alliance, it is time to tell our story, not as victims identified with our suffering, but to share the holistic perspective so that readers who are interested can learn and take some first steps towards having the same liberated experience for themselves.

Fragmented people crave attention which they confuse with love and acceptance. Some people even fake a tragedy to create an identity more likely to be loved than their own, or so they think. Some of these strategies developed during childhood, ways to get attention when a parent wasn't really there. They keep repeating that program, adjusting the strategy to get what they lacked, which is love. But it's an egocentric manipulation. They may scream, get angry, bitch, complain, whatever might get them noticed and elicit a response. It's a negative strategy to get attention but at least it's attention. In a warped way, it reassures them that they are noticed, that they are loved. It may take them back into childhood, giving them some version of what was missing way back then.

It was never our intention to go before the media to get attention, to inflate our egos. We didn't say, "The media is over here, let's go tell our story and get a lot of attention." We never drummed up a press conference. Actually, we asked, "Do we really want to talk to them?" And, if so, what do we want to say that is wakeful and truthful? They have a role to play, informing their audience about a world event, and we have direct experience. What is our responsibility? Is it not to remain truthful to our experience? OK, what would that look and sound like?

With that intention, we became doubly watchful for ego stories that might creep in. We considered that carefully as a group here in the early days of creating the One Life Alliance organization. But once we saw what happened as a result of the media interviews, this worldwide response that came to us, and how people were inspired and wanted to know more about how to answer hatred with compassion, we saw that we could make a positive difference in the world. That's when we created a name and an organization, but it was a measured, natural progression, a wakeful approach.

A selfish, wounded ego will try to get maximum attention out of victimhood. That just exposes the depth of egocentric identification. "I am going to hang onto this story and milk it for all it's worth because I need the attention." Who would you be without your stories? If you let those stories go, all of them, who would you be? That is the holistic perspective. We are certainly not interested in **adding** another illusory story to our database. A holistic person simply doesn't see the value of investing in that kind of a story, or any illusory story for that matter.

Grief

There is a story about a master at the funeral for one of his young monks. Another student noticed the master crying and was puzzled. "I don't understand. Why are you crying when you know that life continues after death?" The master answered, "When else do I get the opportunity to cry?"

Grief is a natural human feeling. We cried when Alan and Naomi died. During their funeral we all felt a natural, deep sorrow to have lost them from our experience in this dimension. At the same time, we experienced grief from a wakeful state. By the way, wakefulness means full engagement. If you are wakeful, you are much more fully engaged in your experience than a person who is not wakeful. The person who is not awake is disassociating. Awake, you feel it all but you don't identify with what you feel. You watch and flow with the experience that is happening.

Wakeful Nothingness

In *Naked Buddhism*, David Deida wrote, "Your life is adorned with various gains and losses, pleasures and pains. In the midst of every present moment, you are either opening or closing. You are either feeling all, while giving your deepest gifts of love, or you are waiting."[8]

How about you? Are you opening or closing? You can find out by watching the stories you tell about your life because that is such an important diagnostic of wakefulness. When you do this, you will discover that you are the creator of your reality, you **are** the fabric of those stories you tell and those stories become your experience. That doesn't mean they are real, it only means that you **believe** they are real.

What **is** real? In all the wisdom traditions throughout the history of humanity we learn that the ultimate reality is a mystery that must remain a mystery. No human will come to know the totality of it within his or her finite human experience. "Wakeful nothingness," what is called "no-mind" in Zen, is the closest we can get. This is witnessing consciousness watching nothingness ... emptiness ... stillness in duration.

Mumbai was a special opportunity for us to experience whatever we could that increased the possibility for us to come close to this ultimate state of wakeful nothingness. In that sense, it was a test. Not a test to pass or fail but a strengthening test, a growing test. The Holistic Lifestyle is the same thing, living day by day, moment by moment, witnessing your life experience without your illusory stories, meeting tests with gratitude and learning, growing, evolving towards the experience of wakeful nothingness and ultimate wholeness.

࿔࿔࿔

BOBBIE:

Life is not unfair; it is what it is. As Master Charles always says, your experience is based on where your feet are walking at the time. This means that everyone's experience is okay, whatever it is. Even people who are expressing hate. That's where they are walking. When they are not supposed to have that experience anymore, it will shift.

This whole thing made me really look at who I am, at who I've become in my practice over all these years. As a young person I would have been totally stressed out, but I handled this OK.

I'm at peace with it all.

PHYL:

When I first arrived in Mumbai I was very nervous and afraid, even though I know that I probably came across as being calm. Now all of that anxiety and fear is just part of my database and it's not so up front. Before, I had known these teachings on a conceptual level. This event turned concepts into experience. Sure, fear is still there inside me from time to time, but I am more detached from it now. What you see on the outside is more of what is actually going on inside.

LARRY:

What did I learn? Well, with each bomb blast, a rush of fear literally exploded inside me. At the same time I felt love and was able to keep shifting myself back into the place of calm balance that I have nurtured all these years in my meditations.

I really felt unattached to anxiety. After all, there wasn't anything I could do to fix the situation. I just resigned myself to whatever was happening and concentrated on my spiritual practice. This allowed me to consciously experience what was going on without creating a whole lot of stories about it. That's what we usually do, manufacture projections and struggle with illusions, but that just creates more suffering and conflict. I chose to not do that and so I was able to feel calm, like being at the center of a storm.

AMY:

I knew I could die in that hotel room. And that would've been okay. Well, maybe I did die and this is what my life is like afterwards! Actually, I find myself reaching for those memories now and it seems like such a long time ago, but it also seems like it was meant to be, that there were no mistakes. It seems like time stood still during that madness.

There is a bond between us now, something that feels stronger even than family. We were like puzzle pieces that all came together for some very odd reason. Even Alan and Naomi ... especially Alan and Naomi.

After all, this human form is just a shell and what lies beyond is incredible. I can't prove that but it's what I believe. It's what I've felt. The soul never dies. Death follows birth. Life is eternal.

JOE:

I have been meditating since 1979 and I met Master Charles in the late 1990s. I'm 90 years old now and I can tell you that Mumbai was a capstone on the climax of my life. It was truly a focal point that allowed me to apply everything out of my past in the present, because the present was so urgent. I was actually able to re-think what it means to be a human being.

Here's my conclusion: Forgiveness is the foundation of the universe. Every moment is an act of forgiveness. Every moment is a gift of love. All is love. I am love, no matter what happens. I can respond compassionately. When I do, the next moment brings me even more understanding of wholeness and just wipes away the past.

That's my story and I'm sticking with it.

MUREEN:

I am more grateful now. Possessions don't mean as much to me as they used to. My husband and I were planning to build our dream home. I have absolutely no desire to do that now. It's good just to be alive. I'm also a more loving person, I think. Happy, wherever I am. Imagine what can come of a seeming tragedy!

MASTER CHARLES:

On my second day home I met with the whole community for two or three hours and we collectively grieved for our lost friends. Soon thereafter we held a funeral service for Alan and Naomi which was packed with friends and neighbors and associates from all over the world. It was a truly beautiful service and was simultaneously web cast so that all of our international associates could participate. The service concluded with the lighting of an eternal flame in Alan and Naomi's honor at our Shrine of the Heart, the site of the apparitional manifestation of the Blessed Mother within Synchron-icity Sanctuary. Several days later, we interred their ashes in the Grotto, our most sacred place, where She originally appeared.

ళ్ళళ్ళ

To better integrate the meaning of this chapter, please visit www.synchronicity.org, go to the "Forgiving the Unforgivable" section, and use the password "one" to access additional material.

CHAPTER 11

Your Human
Broadcast System

"Between a stimulus and response there is a space.
In that space is our power to choose our response.
In our response lies our growth and freedom.
The last of human freedoms is to choose one's attitude
in any given set of circumstances." [1]

—Viktor Frankl

Survivors reflect on their last moments with Alan and Naomi, missing them and celebrating their transition to subtler dimensions. Some sense them still near and communicate on subtle levels. All understand that this was their choice, the experience whose time had come for them.

Sadness mingles with fulfillment, and life goes on, now expanded and even more multi-dimensional for those who knew each other in one way and are now learning to know each other in another.

In this moment
and in every moment
you are receiving and transmitting energy.
What message do you send?
Love or fear?
What messages do you receive?
What channels do you select
from the endless array of available programming?
Love-based content or fear-based content?

Each moment offers you a choice:
what to receive and what to transmit.
According to your choices, you create the world you inhabit
and invite others to enjoy or endure.

༄༄༄

HELEN:

I remained in a state of extended bliss for quite a while after I returned home. I kept wondering, was there anything I could have done differently, anything I could have done to change what happened?

Then it began. Alan started showing up in some of my meditations and in my dreams too. He was always comforting and I got that no, there was nothing I should have done differently. They didn't need saving. Even this was an experience whose time had come, for them and for all of us. What peace came with that deep realization, not as a theory but as a truthful experience. In one visitation Alan told me that he and Naomi "had gone to scout ahead. Not to worry." That was a comfort.

PEGGI:

I knew Naomi when she was a very young child. What a free spirit! She seemed more like an angel than a human, spiriting along on her bicycle through the idyllic setting of our Sanctuary.

I'll tell you, Naomi had her eyes wide open in Mumbai. This was her first time away from home like this and she was like a kid in a candy store. Everything interested her. I remember her telling us over breakfast: "I'm going to get my nose pierced today!" It got postponed a couple of times so we heard her say that again and again, always with this angelic delight—never any complaint about the delays, just renewed enthusiasm and anticipation.

I think of Naomi now and just can't imagine how that spirit could have ended. She's sparkling somewhere else, I know that.

AMY:

I remember Naomi strolling up beside me one day on the street and asking, "So, where are all the cute guys?" Phyl was with us and she answered, "Oh darling, they are everywhere, don't you see them?"

We figured Naomi was looking for a blonde-haired cutey, the sort of guy she would probably never see at home in the Sanctuary. Well, she wasn't going to find him in India either!

MIRIAM:

A few of us were shopping and this guy kept giving me scarves to try on. Naomi walked in and I showed her a green one. She loved it, so I said, "It's yours." You know what she said? "This will be for my mother."

The shopkeeper, who was a very spiritual man, looked at the two of us and said, "You two have the same eyes." As Naomi was thanking me, Alan arrived. She showed him the scarf and he smiled at me. I hardly knew Alan, really. In fact, that may have been the first time he ever smiled at me. After Mumbai, Alan has come to me in meditation and our interactions have been characterized by clearance and guidance.

I really didn't know Naomi very well. I remember one day after she had her nose pierced (she was so proud of that) when a shopkeeper who had been a devotee of Sai Baba took one look at her and said, "She's really clear, this girl. Nothing left for her to clear."

LINDA:

One morning at breakfast we looked at the pats of butter and I thought that I saw the image of Jesus on one of the wrappers. Sort of like the shroud of Turin only with food and Jesus. Every night after that we would lift the top off the butter dish and describe what we saw. It got pretty funny!

I guess that's one of my biggest lessons from Mumbai, that we kept discovering meaning one moment after another. And here's the thing: they were all the same moment, really, just like all our moments are—moments to choose love, and laughter, even in the face of fear.

All of us are human broadcast systems. We transmit and we receive. Under pressure, we tend to revert to our "default settings" and transmit in reaction to what we are receiving. In other words, if we are fearful as a matter of course and then suddenly find ourselves in a frightening situation, that fear will erupt to the surface and broadcast. On the other hand, if we are peaceful, then the pressure of a fearful situation will tend to focus us all the more on peace and that's what will squeeze to the surface and be expressed. It isn't the situation that is causing the fear or the peace; that is already within us. The situation is just the trigger. After all, when you squeeze an orange you always get orange juice, you never get vinegar.

We got a good squeeze in Mumbai. Reporters expected us to retaliate with anger, because that's what is habitual and they know the experience in their own lives. But our lives are different. All of us had been practicing for years, just as you are beginning to practice now (and probably have already been practicing for many years, which is what led you to this book). As they say, practice makes perfect. We are perfecting our ability to express what uplifts and nourishes our environment and those in it, regardless of what comes at us.

Tests

Tests come in life, and with them, emotional challenges. In a truthful holistic model of reality, tests are simply the oscillations of polarities. The relative polarities are always oscillating and you can't have one without the other. Even when truth dominates illusion, illusion is still present. When negative polarity oscillation increases, illusion presents itself and you have a test of some kind. What is important is this: "Who do you choose to be within those tests?" That often relates to managing your feelings and none of us have received much training for that!

Most people are largely unconscious of what they are feeling; in fact, feelings seem to be something that happen to them, either in an obvious way (I drink this wine, I start to feel happy) or more subtly (I wake up with a sense of dread, don't know why, and hours later I am called into the boss's office and fired).

Where do feelings come from? Feelings are an interaction of energy flowing from universal consciousness into what is present in individuated consciousness, or are arising in reaction to what is happening in the environment. Both result in what you feel, moment by moment. Ideally, you are a witnessing consciousness, watching, experiencing and enjoying. You are also the general in charge of your army. You can pick any feeling and fill yourself to overflowing. "My cup runneth over." That's your "broadcast." It's one thing to have an unconscious broadcast of some kind, we all do. But this chapter explores what it means to consciously broadcast the feelings you choose, to balance your momentary experience and expand your holistic awareness.

How to Flow Your Emotions

In order to deliberately flow specific feelings you must first experience them. Start by becoming wakeful of your existence in the moment. This moment. Notice your breathing. What are you feeling? What is your broadcast in this moment? Pause in your reading to find out. Notice, as you search within yourself, how this automatically emphasizes your interior. Balance comes and holistic awareness expands. Remarkable! You didn't even flow a positive feeling yet. Just the act of interrupting your unconscious experience with a moment of interior focus created a change in how you feel. Now what are you feeling? Whatever it is, see if you can "flow" it. Just pay attention to the feeling and let your focused awareness expand it. Then use your breath to move it beyond your body.

There are an endless variety of feelings to experience and express. All of them emerge from the two primary emotions of love and fear. You'll feel enough from the default fear side just by being alive in this relative reality, so we'll concentrate on the love side! As you read the following feeling descriptions, use the same process we just introduced. Take your time. You can return to this section of the book and practice further whenever you wish.

Forgiveness

It's paradoxical that forgiveness is such an important part of ending the escalating cycle of violence on our planet yet, in the end, forgiveness is really only necessary when a judgment has been made! Forgiveness actually becomes irrelevant when you recognize that there is no "other." And, that there is no right and wrong. What needs forgiving is yourself for your investment in the illusion of separation and the suffering that has caused. Also, can you forgive yourself for your limiting beliefs, for your "mistakes?" Can you know that from the truthful perspective there are no mistakes? All experience is valid. You couldn't be here now except for all the experiences that preceded this moment; everything has grown you, including the confusion, delusions, even your guilt. All of it has brought you to this moment and, in this moment, you are more than you have ever been. Such is the true nature of evolving consciousness.

Talking forgiveness to egocentric people is useless because they simply can't get it. Why not? Because they are locked into illusory separation, right and wrong. In separateness, everyone is wearing a mask and competing with each other. It's this belief versus that belief and everyone is invested in his or her position. It's insanity and crazy people hurt each other, then struggle to forgive. Imagine a world where there is no need for forgiveness because that primary judgment is simply not actualized? Instead, compassion flows constantly between individuals experiencing their oneness together.

Contentment

Existence itself is self-delighting. Who you are in this moment is already content. It needs no other, no object or person to bring it contentment. All contentment is arising from it. Be aware of innate self-contentment and let it flow in you and through you and out into the universe. Picture yourself as the sun radiating contentment ... the joy of being.

Gratitude

Be thankful. Be grateful for the life that is empowering you in this moment, without which you have nothing. "I am alive. I am having the experience of being human in this moment." It is as it is, through all its expressions. Count your blessings, not your lack of them. Start with the feeling essence of gratitude which lives within as who you are and then flow that essence into the content of your life—what you observe in your surroundings, external and internal.

Acceptance

Acceptance begins with self-love. "I love myself as I am. Right here and right now I accept myself as I am." This may sound simple but it is routinely overlooked in our culture as a deliberate, conscious acknowl-edgement. It requires that you really grasp it and know that although we are indeed part of the same human consciousness, no two forms of con-sciousness are expressed exactly the same way. Each of us is totally unique and complementary; comparisons that judge make no sense because they are illusions. In this moment, can you love, accept and honor your unique expression of consciousness and celebrate the same in others?

Appreciation

Again, start at home. Appreciate yourself. Can you fully appreciate the consciousness that you are and can you appreciate the experience of life that you are having, complete with all its imperfections and fundamental impermanence? When you can, you will notice that the deliberate flowing of appreciation increases value. Appreciation is truthful celebration.

Peace

Peace is the nature of your formless interior which is always quiet and still. Peace is fulfillment. If peace is elusive to you, it is because you are looking for it outside of yourself where it doesn't exist (unless you flow it there). Peace does not have to be manufactured somehow. It is always here, it is our essence. What's required is to be aware of it and flow it. That's how we create a peaceful experience and a peaceful world.

Compassion

Isn't everyone doing the best they can? Haven't I done that my whole life, tried to do the best I could? That is compassion. I am a human being doing the best I can and so are you. From the saint to the terrorist to thieves and good Samaritans, corporate raiders, dishonest politicians, teachers, and social workers, everyone is doing the best they can.

And, obviously, you can't understand anyone else's experience. You barely understand your own. Judgment about someone else's experience is more of the same supreme delusion. Keep it simple; be compassionate. Compassion means allowing everything and everyone to be just this way, the way it is. It doesn't mean that you must choose it for yourself.

Note that compassion is fundamentally different from sympathy. Sympathy starts with a judgment: "This shouldn't be happening, I'm sorry that it is, how sad for you." Compassion doesn't judge. Compassion honestly acknowledges what is happening. Someone dies and you have compassion for the survivors because they are grieving. You honor their grief but you don't sympathize with their suffering by commiserating about how unfair life is. That's how the media started with us, sympathizing in our plight as victims. After they heard from us some shifted to compassion. They felt compassion, not just for us but also for the terrorists. There is no "other."

Your Own Broadcast System

You are a human broadcast center. You transmit and receive frequency bands of information. If you are unconscious and egocentric, you transmit and receive illusory fragmentation. If you become conscious of what you are transmitting and receiving, your programming content changes. You accept responsibility as the program director of your own broadcast system, transmitting and receiving the truth. The more wakeful you become, the more truthful your broadcast becomes. Let's conduct a programming review. During any day, what percentage of your broadcast is life-negative, fear-based, illusory data? What percentage of the day are you broadcasting truthfully? That covers the transmitting side. Now, what do you receive from people, circumstances, the environment around you? That depends on what you open yourself to. You have a choice as to which channel you watch! It is interesting to me that most meditators progressively tune out mainstream media. They don't have time for illusory data; it is no longer congruent with who they are and what they are broadcasting.

Programming

Mainstream media panders to the 90 percent majority that resonates with negativity and escapism. If you want the 90 percent perspective on life, turn on the TV. As you sit there watching, with the screen providing a focus, your brain waves decelerate. This balances the brain. But that's a problem in this case because the gateways of your database then open and whatever content is presented goes right in, programming and brainwashing you. At least they are honest by calling it programming!

The mainstream media does this knowingly because it is comprised primarily of fragmented, egocentric individuals who are focused on the default dominant polarity that is life-negative and fear-based. No surprise, then, that this is exactly what the media presents—life-negative, fear-based illusion. You don't turn on the news to find them talking about love and compassion. News is mostly bad, often moment-by-moment updates on some disaster which, as the details are endlessly repeated, makes you even more fearful. Remember the television coverage of 9/11? What percentage of the broadcasts covered the heroism and courage involved? At the time, almost none. The bad news was just too riveting.

No wonder younger generations in droves are turning their back on mainstream media. They prefer internet sites that share information which is less biased and fear-based. This accurately reflects the evolutionary shift in our collective consciousness and we can expect it to continue. The cycle is inevitable in its progression ... and that's good news!

I had an associate many years ago who wanted to start a newspaper called "The Good News." It turned out that virtually no one was interested because most people need their daily "fix" of bad news. This habitual regurgitation of negative-dominant data creates a biochemical, hormonal, neurological response and, if you don't get that every day, you just don't feel like "you," your illusory identity, that is. Of course, it probably doesn't occur to you that you are an addict, addicted to the perpetuation of your life-negative, fear-based data that supports your illusory egocentric identity.

I have had many years of experience with negative reporters looking for dirt in the name of "devil's advocate" journalism. They can be nasty. But they are forced to come from that position of negation and fear because that is what their audience wants. If they don't provide it, ratings plunge and they lose their jobs.

The media was completely different on Mumbai. Why? At first, it was because they saw us as victims. Kia lost her husband and her daughter; they could relate to that. What human being wouldn't be sympathetic? It opened their hearts and softened their approach. They listened and some of them actually heard what we said. Often media simply doesn't hear what you say and misquote you all over the place. This time they reported what we said, word-for-word.

When that broadcast went out through the international media the response that came back was uniformly the same: empathetic and love-based. People reached out to us from all over the world, thanking us and saying how inspired they were by what we were saying, by our wholeness and our authenticity. They were responding to our internal broadcast which was carried by the news broadcasts. Viewers, listeners, and readers could tell that we were genuine about this. We really did feel compassionate towards our attackers. And viewers resonated with that, by the thousands!

This says a lot about our collective consciousness at this point in time. When the truth is presented, a noticeable number of the population resonate with a positive message. It becomes a new option on the menu and some people will order it. Why? Because they want it and it's available.

As we evolve, we naturally gravitate towards the kind of media that resonates with our own personal broadcast. Our tastes change and we probably find ourselves reading and watching less news, or certainly being selective about our sources. Of course, it's not really the "news" anyway. What's new about it? It may be a breaking story but only the details have changed. The theme remains the same—people struggling in a fragmented state of consciousness. What is really new are stories like ours and thousands of others that go largely unreported, individuals who choose a different response, who answer negativity with something positive.

༄༅༄༅

BONNIE:

I know that it must have been our evolutionary destiny to come to Mumbai, because I know that at some level all of us choose our life experiences. That being said, who are we to judge what happened to Naomi and Alan? This was their choice, not consciously of course. I mean, who would wish for something like that? At some other level, though, this *was* their destiny. Master Charles said that Naomi and Alan were experts at this, and that they had been martyrs before, that at a soulular level they knew exactly what they were doing. I think about what blessings might come of this, the message of love that can be shared with anyone who hears or reads our story, how it could help them respond differently if they were to face a crisis like ours.

As a group, we certainly have been the recipients of a tremendous amount of love and compassion. It brings tears to my eyes, how loving we all can be to each other. This tragedy is the kind of dramatic wake-up that most people in our world seem to need from time to time, just to consciously recognize that we are all connected. Subtlety doesn't disturb deep sleepers!

Alan and Naomi haven't left; they've just changed form. I can interact with them anytime I tune in to their energy fields. I do miss those human forms. I miss them both and always will. I can close my eyes and see Naomi right now. She's up on a beautiful Mumbai rooftop with me at a birthday party and she's a translucent angel.

I'll always remember her that way.

AMY:

A year later, I was watching a documentary about the incident and learned that the one surviving terrorist had been sold to a terrorist organization as a child for dowry money to marry off his sisters. How could I judge or condemn this boy? It was not a choice for him at that age. I am an adult and at choice in my life. Shouldn't I choose to try and help these people rather than condemn them? This is human brotherhood with everyone. After all, we share the planet together, all of us. And this is where the real answer to terrorism resides—in all of us taking responsibility and helping each other. Therefore, no revenge or punishment for them, at least not from me because I know that they were just "pawns" in some terrible game. Worst of all, this is happening every day in our world.

LARRY:

Looking back at the experiences of those forty-five hours, I am truly compassionate for those that suffered and perished.

The terrorists were just kids. They were brainwashed to believe that they were doing the right thing. Actually, they were victims of an organization that holds no value for human life, programming them to kill innocent men, women and children in the name of their God. That's just such a perverse sense of "right."

Humanity must learn from these tragedies. Hate simply begets more hate and seeking revenge is absolutely not the answer. No, we must work together as a collective community, hand-in-hand, to accept that our differences can never be resolved by war or aggression. If we are to survive as a species we must learn to accept each other as equals. And love each other! That is the only way.

BONNIE:

I know that I have a more expansive awareness of the sacredness of life now. And I feel a deeper connection with others. Mumbai deepened me somehow. Not that I'm more serious, just ... life is deeper.

I think about those terrorists once in a while, and I wonder if any of us were born over there in some little village and sold by our families when we were kids, brainwashed like they were, would we have done what they did? I honestly don't know.

I'm not condoning what they did. I just don't think that they had any way to know what they were doing, not really. I think about the people who did know, who planned the whole thing out and took advantage of those kids. That's who we should be more concerned about.

Punishing the terrorists? Well, haven't we proven pretty conclusively that more fear, hate, and war, doesn't really change anything? That makes it worse. When are we going to try something else? Well, we are. That's been our response to Mumbai, to be loving and to treat other people the way we would like to be treated ourselves. That sounds familiar, let's see: "Do unto others, as you would have them do unto you." Haven't we heard that before? You see, this isn't really radical at all! What's radical is actually doing it, not just saying the words on Sunday. That's what can help heal the world.

Helen:

When we were reunited at the Four Seasons Hotel someone said something about the need for forgiveness. I said, why? What's to forgive? It's all Source. Perfect orchestration. It's all the eternal play of duality in consciousness: light and shadow.

I read in the paper that the parents sold these young boys to help buy dowries for their daughters. I just can't begin to understand that and I certainly can't judge it. And, here's a thought that has haunted me: if I had walked in that poor boy's shoes, I would probably have been the one holding the gun.

Joe:

Terrorists. Turn that around. We send our people over to Iraq and Afghanistan. We brag about how stalwart we are. We're convinced we are doing the right thing. People over there don't see it that way. Most of them see us as intruders trying to take away their lifestyles.

Those terrorists were doing what they thought was right. Doesn't everyone think that way? The problem is that most people think their idea of "right" is the only one that really is right. I say, honor everybody for who they are. Life is always going to be ambiguous. That said, sure, I was hoping the Black Cats would get those guys. That's what was best for me. But to want revenge, to hate those terrorists? Well, that would be going along with their whole belief system. It may be right for them but it's sure not right for me and I'm not going to change just because they show up.

PHYL:

I remember thinking that the terrorists were the real victims and at no time did I ever feel anything negative towards them. I just wondered, what is it that drives people to behave like that? Our rescuers were very young too. They could've been my children, both the terrorists and our rescuers. And they all believed they were doing what was right.

You know, when you look back on the history of the West, it's clear that we have done some appalling things. I can understand why there might be people here and there who would hate us. What sort of lives have they had, in part because of what we have done to their home countries? What were they really trying to achieve by killing people in Mumbai? Who has dug deep under the surface to find out why they did it, the historical reasons, I mean?

In the end, I feel the need to address the terrorist in myself. That's been the biggest lesson for me out of all this and I'll probably keep studying that for the rest of my life.

MASTER CHARLES:

Because of how people have chosen to see Alan and Naomi's death, especially Kia, their deaths can inspire millions of people with a truthful message. As for Alan and Naomi, they lived their lives in service and manifested a way to expand their service to the whole of humanity.

This greater vision is what has sustained Kia. Her years of meditation have cultured a heightened self-awareness that enables her to hold a greater vision and this is what her life is all about for her now.

With Alan and Naomi's death her real work has begun and she has been able to step fully into it.

There are no mistakes. The reporters kept asking how we could forgive the terrorists. What really puzzled them was when I said that everyone is a gift. Everyone you meet presents you with a possible experience to have. Of course, each of us must determine who we will be in relation to what shows up.

In this case, the terrorist arrived, bringing hate, violence, and fear. I was not having that experience before he showed up and I did not choose to have it just because he showed up. It was appropriate for him because that is where his feet were. I couldn't understand it, but it was appropriate for him. If I chose that experience for myself then I would have filled myself with it, but that would have been my choice. He then would have become my teacher.

Or, I could say, as I did: "I honor that this experience is appropriate for you, but it is not appropriate for me. Here is what I choose for myself instead: love, compassion, gratitude, and forgiveness." The reporters were at a total loss for words when I explained it this way but they got it because it is so very simple. Yes, I can choose my experience, no matter what experience anyone else is choosing. I am always at choice. I am the creator of my experience.

That is the full truth of forgiveness. Not to "forgive" someone for how they mistreated me or you, but to be for giving. To give. To be for that, for giving, not for hating. Imagine a world filled with all of us making that choice. It can happen, it is happening, one person at a time. It begins with you.

❧❧❧❧

To better integrate the meaning of this chapter, please visit www.synchronicity.org, go to the "Forgiving the Unforgivable" section, and use the password "one" to access additional material.

CHAPTER 12

Grace and Miracles

"Waking up this morning, I smile.
Twenty-four brand new hours are before me.
I vow to live fully in each moment
and to look at all beings with the eyes of compassion."[1]

—Thich Nhat Hanh

Life moves on for the Mumbai twenty-five.

None consider themselves to be victims or survivors. Each counts their blessings, enriched by the experience, more whole and fulfilled than before.

Increasingly, their personal shifts in consciousness begin to appear in the world as projects, collaborations, non-profit foundations, books, and media.

Because of their choices there is more love in the world.

As within, so without.
The world is a reflection in consciousness,
for each of us.
Live your life,
moment by moment.
Choose to express and experience
that which truthfully celebrates
the joyful nature of Life.
You are the power.
By your choices, so shall you live.
In this way, you create your "world."
When you connect with Source
individual and universal consciousness merge
into one undivided whole.
Grace and miracles
become your way of life.
This is life holistically lived.

࿎࿎࿎

BEN:

I had grief counseling sessions after I got home and cried for hours at a time. That really cleaned me out. Time would go by where I felt fine, then all of a sudden I would get irritable and cathartic. A whole rash of really intense feelings would come on strong, for no apparent reason. Something was happening within me and I would check the calendar. Yes, right on schedule, just as the psychiatrist had predicted. I was processing Mumbai.

HELEN:

For a short while afterward I had reflex reactions to sudden noises. EFT (Emotional Freedom Technique) helped to clear it. I notice that I now prefer to sit in restaurants with my back to the wall and facing the door. The shots and gunman had come from behind me in the hotel restaurant and I couldn't see what was happening.

Once, about six months after Mumbai, I rolled over in bed, half asleep, and the crinkling of the starched sheets crackled like gunfire. This brought me right back to that moment. Another time, I realized I was really sad. I looked at the calendar. It was November 26th, one year later to the day.

PHYL:

I have occasional dreams about it but no flashbacks. Once, my son-in-law opened a bottle of champagne and I really jumped. So I guess that my general awareness is heightened now. Whenever I am out somewhere I always check everything out, which is highly amusing to my husband. For instance, when we stay in a hotel I always look over the balcony. It's not that I am seriously fearful; I'm just being careful. Out here in the country where we live, if I hear gunshots, you know, from some hunters, I am immediately very attentive and ready to act fast.

BERNIE:

A friend who is a Vietnam War vet asked about our experience. "What are your thoughts about it?" he asked. I said that I don't really have many thoughts now, but added that if I remember anything it's the smells, the sights, and the wonderful people. He was surprised. He said that most traumatized people have a lot of thoughts, and that they really hang on to their fearful memories. I said to him, "Meditate, my dear!"

PHIL:

I'm a retired physician and I've spent my adult life in stressful situations. I know that my ability to have the kind of experience I did in Mumbai was a direct result of the evolution of my own consciousness. And now, in the aftermath, I have no lingering residue.

We were destined to be in that experience with Master Charles at this time. He trained us perfectly.

ॐॐॐ

As the banks of a river lead it unto the sea,
so is discipline to liberation.[2]

—Amrit Desai

As we begin the final chapter of this book, this much is clear: You can increase your actual experience of wholeness by practicing the Holistic Lifestyle which is based on the principle of balance. This means bringing a focused, wakeful awareness into your daily life. You do this by starting right where you are, looking at your current lifestyle, and bringing a new level of holistic awareness to it.

Where can you begin to implement the principles of balance you have been reading about? When is the best time for regular meditation, balance breaks, affirmations? Where can you schedule exercise? How can you improve your diet? How can you begin flowing positive thoughts and feelings to balance negative ones?

This all might seem overwhelming. Without some sort of system and support, it usually is. Fortunately, both are available. You can download a Personal Holistic Lifestyle Tracking Form from our website at www.synchronicity.org. Go to the Forgiving the Unforgivable section and use the password "one."

Start exactly where your feet are. Commit to what is possible and natural for you as next steps. If—even with local support and our help online—you cannot sustain your practice on your own, don't give up. This is what masters, teachers, mentors, are for. Not everyone is going to India and not everyone will have a guru, but everyone needs guidance. What is most helpful here in the West where we live? That's been the focus of my work since I left India and moved to Virginia in 1983. We've learned a great deal about how to offer support through mentoring programs and retreats (offered here in our Sanctuary) and courses online (through the Synchronicity School of Modern Spirituality). What we provide is part of a rapidly expanding menu of support offered by many other teachers and their teams throughout the world. Find what/who you resonate with and welcome what best empowers your ongoing evolution. When the student is ready, the teacher appears. Simply open yourself to the possibility.

By championing daily discipline I am not in any way suggesting that grueling work is required. Expect grace and miracles. Grace is the appearance of unexpected blessings in your life. Miracles are the impossible happening. When you practice the Holistic Lifestyle regularly, you will be positioning yourself to experience the extraordinary midst the ordinary. Universal consciousness interfacing with individuated consciousness opens the door to limitless possibilities.

Let's pause for a moment to let that sink in. In fact, feel yourself embracing the possibility for grace and miracles in your life right here and right now. Think of one problem you have. Focus it clearly in your mind. Now, simply observe it and let it go and, with a few breaths, welcome in the abundance of universal wisdom that surrounds and permeates you. Acknowledge that you live in a friendly universe and as you ask so shall you receive. The secret is to ask with "nothing wavering," as a Biblical text advises. This refers to faith. And real faith is based in experience, not theory. Recall the grace and miracles that have already blessed your life. Just pick one ... and contemplate it. How did the impossible happen in your life, bringing resolution to something that had seemed absolutely hopeless? All of us have at least one of those examples. Well, if it happened once, it can happen again. Living the Holistic Lifestyle opens you up for more miracles.

Prayer: What Works and What Doesn't Work

One of the first messages that I remember receiving from the Blessed Mother was, "Don't pray to me. Prayer separates you from me. Don't supplicate. I am everything, including you. We are not separate. Meditate rather than pray."

Prayer is about asking for what you do not have. It's about egocentric seeking. Meditation is about trans-egocentric being, being the experience you choose to have. Prayer belongs to the involutionary cycle, meditation to the evolutionary cycle.

Dr. Larry Dossey describes prayer this way in *Prayer is Good Medicine*: "In its simplest form, prayer is an attitude of the heart—a matter of being, not doing. Prayer is the desire to contact the Absolute, however it may be conceived. When we experience the need to enact this connection, we are praying, whether or not we use words." [3]

I agree that true prayer is "a matter of *being*, not doing." At the same time, having a desire to contact "the Absolute" could be evidence of not being one with the Absolute already. Living the Holistic Lifestyle is about being one with, not separate from. That said, there are moments when a need arises and calling on that connection can increase power. Note the difference between intensifying an already existing sense of connection versus seeking to make a connection where you believe there is none.

Here at the Synchronicity Foundation, we convene a weekly Healing Circle. A small group of community members—all of them advanced meditators—gather to generate a specific field of energy. They show up as the experience rather than praying for change. Various associates from around the world tune in from wherever they are for a group meditation. As awareness increases and focuses, a healing transmission occurs.

"Success" depends upon elevating, increasing, and sustaining awareness at subtle holistic levels. There is no story and no limitations. No one talks about symptoms and no one tries to heal them. The prevailing affirmation is: "I am ... all is ... one consciousness. I open to the possibility of health and wellbeing." The meditators hold that focus and generate a substantial energetic field, while those connecting from afar do exactly the same.

Let's say that one of those in a remote location is suffering from a headache. If she is able to elevate herself out of her limiting data that is contributing to the headache (without having to analyze it) and tap into the greater amplitude of power that is radiating from those in the Healing Circle in Virginia, the group energy field can dissolve her data and release those limitations that are causative to the headache. Or, the symptoms might not diminish, but her awareness could expand so that she was drawn to explore what might be causative to her condition, like eye strain from too much computer work or stress related to a family issue. In that case, it might take longer to achieve physical relief because the healing is occurring first on other levels through holistic awareness and then needs to be actualized through specific actions.

"People appear to receive healing deep in their bodies by being returned to the more coherent energy of the healer's intention. During healing, it could be that the 'orderly' energy of the well person entrains and reorders the sick." This is from author Lynne McTaggert in *The Intention Experiment*, indicating that the effect depends on the state of the one who offers healing: "In order to have the most powerful effect, a healer or sender needs to become 'ordered' on some subatomic level, mentally and emotionally."[4] Our meditators live in that orderly state and often their healees report back that they experienced a change in their condition during the Healing Circle session.

Sarah is one of our associates. She has Lou Gehrig's disease which she contracted from years of working in the mining industry where she was constantly exposed to heavy metals. When Sarah first showed up on our doorstep she had resigned herself to dying within two years. There is no known cure for this disease and her doctors held out no hope for improvement. But Sarah opened herself to a new possibility, acknowledging that she has the power to create her own experience. Before long, she found herself in Greece undergoing stem cell therapy with adult-harvested stem cells, a process now licensed by the FDA. She returned to the United States with a radical improvement in her health and wellbeing. In fact, before long I heard her say, "I have never felt so good!" Sarah believes that her healing actually started through her participation in our Healing Circle. She has recently resumed swimming and is now reporting a noticeable increase in muscle strength.

Donald Epstein writes about healing phenomena in *Healing Myths, Healing Magic*. "Medical literature is replete with case histories of individuals who have spontaneously recovered from virtually every type of hopeless situation, including heart disease, cancer, and AIDS. Those who have healed commonly report a change in their priorities and perspectives on life. They find themselves reaching for and affirming a purpose in life that is greater than the normal administration of their daily lives. This shift in consciousness seems to be inspired by the power of life itself, or that field of primary intelligence from which all things are created and to which all things return."[5]

The power of group meditation is easy to understand. Holistic individuals support each other and distant associates by combining their amplitude of power, which transcends geography. Our Healing Circle is not a prayer group. Praying for someone is actually an act of separation, if it's a prayer like "I want healing for their medical condition." In that case, what you are really saying is, "They don't have healing now." That is your actual prayer ... and it is always answered. The one you are praying for gets exactly what you are praying for: they are not healed.

Consider how profoundly different it is when a group simply sits together and shares the intention to create a field of health and wellbeing together in themselves, then opens that experience for the benefit of others. This field expands to surround the "healees" in a virtual bubble of health and wellbeing, without any asking or seeking at all. According to their receptivity, they will experience the immediate "preferred" energetic environment of being healed, and then later in form (for instance, the headache actually clears up) as the energetic blueprint translates into those denser levels, according to whatever timetable is universally appropriate.

A New Relationship with Mother Earth

In our relationship with the Earth, humans have been takers, not givers, for many centuries. "Rape and pillage" has been the primary human strategy, taking as much as possible while putting virtually nothing back. This is obviously egocentric and selfish "me first" behavior. We've acted like greedy children and elected leaders who behave the same way. In fact, most politicians look out for themselves, line their own pockets and those of their corporate puppeteers.

Recently the BBC reported on the impending world water crisis. One in five humans now has no access to safe drinking water. In a November, 2010 article in *The Telegraph*, Ambrose Evans-Pritchard wrote, "Stanford professor Donald Kennedy said global climate change was now setting off a self-feeding spiral. 'We've got droughts combined with a psychotic excess of rainfall,' he said."[6]

I won't attempt to duplicate the work of authors who are raising the alarm with details on just how critical our global situation is. It is true that every crisis, whether so called "natural" or man-made, has one thing in common: imbalance. Our human systems are chronically imbalanced. Balance cannot be created "out there" without first establishing it "in here." Einstein said that problems created by one level of consciousness could not be solved by a consciousness at the same level.[7] A change in consciousness must precede real and lasting change in the world. That's why I so passionately believe that learning and living the Holistic Lifestyle—which brings personal balance—comes first. Repeating Gandhi, "You must be the change you wish to see in the world."[8]

Since we have arrogantly resisted learning what we needed to learn and adjusting our behavior relative to Mother Earth, we've brought what I call the "sledgehammer effect" upon ourselves. Crises are arising on every hand now. Those who have made the connection between inner and outer and are proactively increasing balance in their own lives will welcome each challenge as an experience whose time has come and the future will become a powerful growth and awakening opportunity for them. Those who try to manipulate change in the results of imbalance in consciousness without addressing that imbalance will grow increasingly frustrated. We've reached a fork in the road as a species; this is how human consciousness is evolving itself in the twenty-first century and it comes down to personal choice for all of us. When I look at the world scene, I say, "Great. Change, evolution in consciousness ... and it can't be stopped! What's the nature of my contribution?" You might wish to ask this same question: what's **your** contribution?

That's a very different question from, "How will I survive?"

Energy

The world is approaching a power shortage. There is an exponentially increasing demand for energy and petroleum production has peaked. There is no alternative fuel on the horizon that can replace petroleum within the next twenty to thirty years, at least not on a large enough scale to allow for a smooth transition that would permit the uninterrupted continuation of our current lifestyle. Expect disruption; it would be denial to believe otherwise. Of course, most people choose to remain largely uninformed about the facts and our anaesthetizing media offers up a daily menu of distractions to obscure reality. Of course, repeating often and loudly that the Titanic is unsinkable wouldn't have changed what happened when it hit an iceberg.

Given our situation, how exactly do we prepare for the future? Invest in self-awareness; then you can flow with whatever happens. Invest in self-awareness, evolve your consciousness! Become wakeful enough to trust that whatever is happening is appropriate. This is an experience whose time has come, because it is all the orchestration of consciousness. You may not be able to understand why, but flow with it, accept what it means for you, and—here's the pay off—discover what to do next.

Looking at the world situation it becomes obvious that the primary issue is values. We can't just blame the oil companies, big banks or other "evil" corporations. We the people want the lifestyle that cheap oil and stock profits provide. Here are a few actual solutions: Disgusted with big oil profiteering? Carpool! Upset with the mainstream media? Turn off your television. Enraged by dishonesty in politics? Quit reading the news and focus on being absolutely honest yourself. If it's your calling, run for public office, on a platform of personal integrity!

Until we have a shift like that, where individuals refocus on maintaining their own holistic state of being rather than trying to change or save the world out there, we can make no real progress. The good news is that if enough holistic individuals maintain personal balance, we would see radically positive progress in the world very quickly. That big transformation starts small, with you and me.

Start. In this moment, as you are reading, reflect on the true energy source. It's not oil. It's not electricity. Pause ... breathe ... be aware of the power within yourself. Place one hand over your heart, feel it beating and ask this question, then close your eyes: "What is beating my heart?"

The Source of life is beating your heart in this moment just as it is beating mine. It's the same life in all human beings, in all living forms. Just be aware of that, right now. Without having to "do" anything, you are One, all is One. How magical! What a miracle, to have this experience, even a fleeting glimpse of it, so easily. Imagine sustaining this, expressing it within all your worldly activities? Could that bring some positive change, do you think?

From the evolutionary perspective, fear is appropriate right now. Fear alerts us to be wakeful and create balance, but the solutions we need won't come from the same level of consciousness that created the problems. Rather, we must access another level, a level of holistic awareness, then witness the unfolding of the experience whose time has come.

Every individual is at a different level of evolution in individuated consciousness and some of us can handle the "news" better than others. All of us can be selective, training ourselves to pay attention to what is really important. That's being wakeful and it prepares us for the shift in consciousness that is increasingly called for. It's possible to remain wakeful rather than completely immersing ourselves in what are really just stories about what is happening. Those stories solve nothing; but they do serve to keep us distracted and emotionally charged, blaming this oil company or that government official. What goes largely unreported is the momentum of evolutionary transformation in our consciousness.

Lynne Twist writes in *The Soul of Money*, "The job of our time is to hospice the death of the old unsustainable systems and structures and to midwife the birth of new sustainable systems and new ways of being. To hospice those systems that have reached their limits and are unsustainable is not to kill them, but with some compassion and love, to witness their disintegration, and then to midwife with compassion and love the development and creation of new structures, systems, contexts, and constructs that support and empower sustainable ways of being. These ways are based in the reality and understanding of a world in which there is enough, in which we can all thrive, not each at the other's expense, but in collaboration and cooperation."[9]

2012?

All prophets of every wisdom tradition seem to say the same thing: a great shift is coming. Signs point to 2012, but the shift is already happening, from fragmentation to wholeness, from material myth to spiritual myth.

2012 is a literal date (the end of one phase of the Mayan calendar) and also symbolic (a quantum leap in universal consciousness, also experienced in individuated consciousness). This evolutionary shift towards increased wholeness is already happening. The structures and systems of our material myth are crumbling around us, and increasing numbers of us are turning inward for value. There is a growing recognition of impermanence and a celebration of what endures and grows: consciousness.

This is the real news and, ultimately, there is nothing to fear about it.

A New Leadership

Like attracts like. People who are balanced and whole (let's call them masters) are going to congregate. They are inevitably attracted to each other. It is simply the mechanics of consciousness. As there are more people experiencing wholeness, masters will gather with each other. This is already happening with networks of leaders meeting to create something specific or just to share wakefulness together. The result? An increased amplitude of shared, transmitted, holistic power. Those who have mastered their own holistic lifestyle are now showing up as a new breed of leader and they are exerting a transformative effect in "the world," courtesy of their evolving consciousness.

Wakefulness is even coming to some aspects of the corporate world. Paul Hawken writes in *The Ecology of Commerce*: "This turbulent, transformative period we now face might be thought of as a system shedding its skin; it signals the first attempts by commerce to adapt to a new era. Many people in business, the media, and politics do not perceive this evolutionary step, while others who do understand fight it. Standing in the way of change are corporations who want to continue worldwide deforestation and build coal-fired power plants, who see the storage or dumping of billions of tons of waste as a plausible strategy for the future, who imagine a world of industrial farms sustained by chemical feed-stocks. They can slow the process down, make it more difficult, but they will not stop it. Like a sunset effect, the glories of the industrial economy may mask the fact that it is poised at a declining horizon of options and possibilities. Just as internal contradictions brought down the Marxist and socialist economies, so do a different set of social and biological forces signal our own possible demise. Those forces can no longer be ignored or put aside."[10]

Of course, the force that cannot be put aside is the evolution of consciousness. It is beyond our control because it operates according to cosmic cycles of inevitability. Living the Holistic Lifestyle synchronizes your individual life with this "life in the universe" and positions you as one of these leaders-by-example in the grand transformation of these times. There is room at the top, so to speak. You are welcome ... based on the evolution of your consciousness.

The True Secret of Forgiveness

It's easy to see the urgent challenges in our world and agree that a responsible person should be concerned to help the world become a better place. Those who get active with social causes and work on the "real" issues can become increasingly depressed and desperate, realizing from hands-on experience just how intractable many of our chronic problems are.

Likewise, those who choose an inner path can become increasingly convinced that nothing **should** be done about all that. They retreat deeper within themselves to find peace in meditation.

The new world leaders are different. We—and I am including you now, because you have succeeded in navigating to the end of this book and, I'm sure, are seeing and knowing things very differently now— express into the outer from the inner, knowing that all is one. We understand there is no separation.

Formlessness and form are connected by ... us! We get it. We witness ourselves in that space between. This is who I am, what I am! I am this space, you are this space. All is One in this space. This space is holistic consciousness.

From this space, compassion emerges through you and me to heal our world, starting with what is closest to us. As we know this in our experience, we finally understand that true forgiveness, compassionate forgiveness, is not coming to terms with someone else or even with yourself. The secret of compassionate forgiveness is hidden in plain sight, right within the word itself: forgiveness, for – give – ness. To be forgiving is to be for giving. For giving, not taking. Consciousness is always compassionately giving of itself. It selflessly empowers all and everything. Consciousness compassionately gives and gives and gives ... of itself ... to itself ... for the sake of itself ... because there is no other ... there is only One. To experience yourself as the compassionate and eternal giver is to become a master of the Holistic Lifestyle. It is to be consciousness itself. In truth, it is ultimate mastery ... the mastery of being human.

๛๛๛

KIA:

It has been challenging this year. There was so much to do at first, but after things settled down, that's when I really experienced a lot of grief. Now I am transformed. I live simultaneously with pain and the possibility to contribute something of value.

I often feel like a very, very small person and that there is nothing new, that it has all been done by people more skilled, more famous, and even more dedicated than I am. Still, a voice within me says that I can join them as a junior partner! And the fact is that when even one person's heart opens because of someone's sharing, lives can change.

I'm not special. My experience isn't even that unusual. Tragedy strikes every day. The choice to answer hatred with compassion is unusual, and that reaches people. That's it.

BEN:

Things are very different than the way they looked on the surface. We all sensed that Alan and Naomi knew exactly what they were doing. We all embraced this, not as a concept, but as real. And our lives have been radically changed for the better because of what we experienced. Now we get to share our story and have a positive impact on the world because it's a real love story.

There was so much love for such an extended period of time that it just pried my heart open. I'd never encountered such strong, loving energy. It transformed me. I hope that people who find out about this experience will be able to feel some of this love too.

RUDOLPH:

As a psychotherapist for over thirty years, I've had a great deal of experience with patients suffering from post-traumatic stress syndrome. I noticed a profound difference with the five Synchronicity members that I counseled. Two weeks after the incident they presented less obvious disturbance than usual. All remained accessible and spoke openly about their experiences, without hatred or anger.

One survivor communicated a single incident of shock, following a sudden noise at home. She felt this triggered her memories of gunshots in India. She recovered from this quickly and did not report anything further.

Overall, I am most impressed with how the survivors are dealing with the trauma related to this terrorist attack. It suggests to me that their holistic lifestyle and meditation practice has established an inner stability and that this is what is making the difference.

MASTER CHARLES:

One night, shortly after returning from Mumbai, the house alarm went off in the middle of the night. I was immediately catapulted right back into that hotel room. An automatic, primal instinct arose. It turned out to be a faulty sensor. That seemed ironic, like a metaphor of some kind. How many other faulty sensors do I have, right inside me, causing me to react in one situation because of trauma from another?

A few months later I was traveling and I heard a door close and some commotion in the hallway outside my room. There I was, immediately alert, sitting up in bed. The psychiatrist predicted these milestones in our post trauma healing process. It's the way the brain works. Still, from all I have observed, those of us who went through this experience are in remarkably stable shape. Yes, there is appropriate trauma for us to deal with, but I notice that we have all blossomed in unique ways, especially Kia, who lost the most and by all accounts should be suffering the most. No, even she has been enriched and transformed by this experience.

That is how it should be, always, whenever we fully and truthfully embrace the experience whose time has come.

ॐॐॐ

To better integrate the meaning of this chapter, please visit www.synchronicity.org, go to the "Forgiving the Unforgivable" section, and use the password "one" to access additional material.

Epilogue

"Even if you've forgiven that person 99 percent, you aren't free until your forgiveness is complete. The 1 percent you haven't forgiven them is the very place where you're stuck in all your other relationships (including your relationship with yourself)." [1]

—Byron Katie

From my holistic perspective, most human beings are terrorists, although only a few are violent. We terrorize ourselves with our thoughts and beliefs, our illusory stories about who we are and what life is. Then we terrorize each other with the same madness. In order to successfully eliminate terrorism from our collective expression, we must first eliminate it from our individual expression. Socrates said, "The unexamined life isn't worth living." [2] I like to say, "The unexamined mind isn't worth having." We must each take responsibility for what we think and believe. We must determine whether our stories are truthful or not. As wakefulness dawns, we can eliminate those illusory stories and relinquish our own personal brand of terrorism. If one person chooses it, that makes a difference. If a thousand, a million, a billion choose it ... That's how we transform first ourselves and then our world. The holistic truth is that life is what has ultimate value. Life is sacred. This is our common ground of being and the unity within all our diversity. Without life, we have nothing. As Neale Donald Walsch wrote in Conversations with God, "If not now ... when? If not you ... who?" [3]

The Holistic Model of Reality and the Mechanics of Consciousness can be reduced to this simple statement: We are here to learn how to love. This is the real bottom line—everyone wants to receive love. Yet universal law states that you cannot receive what you do not give. Love is the blissful expression of holistic truth. It is the non-dominant polarity, the emphasis of which creates balance, wholeness and fulfillment ... the mastery of being human. Begin with yourself. Love the life that empowers you and be grateful for all its personal blessings. Then be grateful for everyone and everything else, in the same awareness. Be relentless in this focus ... moment by moment ... day by day. What you give is what you get... multiplied by a million. In this regard, my teaching is extremely simple... Choose love ... live love ... be love. It is your very salvation.

*   *   *

Twelve of us returned to Mumbai in November, 2010, for a two-year anniversary celebration. Yes, it was a celebration! We were able to show up both as individuals and also as representatives of the organization we have founded, One Life Alliance. O.L.A. is a nonprofit organization dedicated to the sacredness of life and it was birthed through a combined focus from all of us, as a direct response to this event. Our associate Kia Scherr has now taken the lead and risen to the global opportunity to grow this service organization, which has meant stepping into a radically new life. How would you feel if you were suddenly plucked from your familiar environment to find yourself living for months at a time in India, answering the phone one morning to receive a request that you join a welcoming party for the French President and his wife! Such is Kia's new life.

She went to Mumbai months before the event to help organize it and met with U.S. President Barack Obama and his wife Michelle when they visited. Kia is demonstrating how to turn the tragedy of losing a family to terrorist violence into something life-affirming that immediately resonates and inspires everyone who meets her.

O.L.A. can indeed provide a great service in the world and we clearly observed that during the Memorial Program. Holistic truth which includes forgiveness, true forgiveness, is needed everywhere in the world. But we didn't set out to create an organization. We simply continued to live holistically, remaining open to what would unfold.

O.L.A. is what showed up for us as our unique way to contribute. Everyone has the same opportunity to contribute, each in his or her own way. Here's one truly remarkable example:

"Mavis sat in her comfortable rocking chair as she listened to the evening news. Toward the end of the news she heard the reporter mention that in South America many newborns were being sent home wrapped in newspaper.

"Wrapped in newspaper?" said Mavis out loud. "That's terrible!"

"So Mavis went to her sewing room and went to work. Over the next few weeks she made more than 200 quilts and receiving blankets. As she finished each blanket, she gave it an affectionate hug before placing it in one of the boxes to be taken to the Church's Humanitarian Services Center.

"There's something you should know about Mavis: She was 91 years old and legally blind. But Mavis was an amazing individual. She said, "There is something I can do," and she wanted to make a difference for newborns around the world."[4]

The question is, what can, what will, *you* do? What will your unique contribution be? The choice is always ours.

☙☙☙☙

KIA:

I had never been to India and it was very odd that my first visit was to Mumbai and the hotel where my husband and daughter were killed. Actually, as it turned out, there was so much work to do leading up to the second anniversary memorial program that I didn't really get into the personal side of this right away. It was like being thrown into the deep end of the pool! I quickly learned that in India everything comes together at the last minute. We ended up with a ballroom full of five hundred-plus people, including businessmen, educators, representatives of both government and non-government organizations, Muslims, Christians, Hindus, Jewish people, and others. It was remarkable to witness the diversity of individuals who joined us to celebrate creating a positive outcome from this tragedy that had claimed the lives of so many innocent people.

There were some remarkable presenters during the memorial program. The Vice Chancellor of Mumbai University, the Sheriff of Mumbai, religious leaders from the Jewish and Catholic faiths, a Muslim Imam, and two Hindu Mahamandaleshwars, who each offered examples from their wisdom traditions about the sacredness of life. Between speakers we played thirty-second film clips of Synchronicity survivors on two Jumbo screens, talking about what the sacredness of life meant to them. And we introduced One Life Alliance.

LINDA:

Mumbai taught me to expect nothing. Expectation creates limitations, lines drawn in your thinking that restrict what can happen. Friends had all kinds of lines drawn around me that caused them to feel terrified but I wasn't afraid to return, not even when I walked back into that restaurant where I'd been shot. I did think about the terrorists, as I followed the path they took that night, past the wall as it turned into windows and took a seat at a table right where it had all happened. Someone had sure drawn some lines for those men to follow!

As I sat there, I remembered our laughter together. It was a gentle moment with some sadness, too, and a deep understanding of how some experiences will endure to nurture us forever. How blessed we were in those magical Mumbai days! And today, I thought, beyond logic, the blessings continue.

I slept like a baby in that hotel.

PHYL:

As I prepared to fly back to Mumbai, I did feel some anxiety. But that changed the evening before I left and I was flooded with a sense of deep calm. When I arrived and went to my room I looked out the window and saw exactly the same view that I had in 2008. This was a little unnerving and I felt a sudden chill, but this soon passed.

I went for a walk the first morning and very strong emotions surfaced. I began to cry and just let go, just let it happen. It was surreal, being back there and seeing those familiar places again in such a different context. The Tiffin restaurant was especially challenging. I felt sympathy for the hotel shopkeepers who have been so negatively affected by that attack two years ago. But they all greeted us with such love; they really treated us like royalty and family.

I noticed that I felt a lot more confident about myself and realized just how much the experience had evolved me. It seems that I now value myself more, which helps me to value others without judgment. I am standing in my power.

HELEN:

My daughter Robyn accompanied me and we arrived at night during a downpour. They strapped our bags to the roof of the taxi in uniquely Indian fashion, which meant that our clothes were thoroughly baptized by the time we got to the hotel. Perfect for a fresh start.

It was early morning when we reached the hotel and our room wasn't ready yet, so we went straight to the restaurant, which had been renovated and renamed The Fenix. I don't know why they picked that spelling but it is pronounced the same way as Phoenix, the mythical bird that symbolizes rebirth. How perfect! The restaurant wasn't open yet but the staff let us walk around. I went right to the area where our old table had been and said my hellos to the essence of Alan and Naomi. It felt surreal but no obvious trauma. "This is going to be easy," I thought.

A day or so later we visited the ladies washroom where Naomi and I had often gone to freshen up. As my daughter and I chatted, I suddenly noticed her voice drifting off into the distance while the back of my neck and spine went ice cold and prickly. I was suddenly hurled back in time to join Naomi for one trance-like moment.

The moment passed and we returned to the lobby. Honestly, the staff were so incredibly friendly and respectful that I remember thinking, "Love lurks around every corner here, just waiting to share itself with us." I was especially thrilled to visit the perfume shop and discover they were stocking the unique fragrance that shopkeeper Sabina had made for Naomi. It was such a fresh scent. It really captured her essence and she wore it the night of the attack. My daughter asked if she could have a bottle of that fragrance so I happily bought her one.

CAROL:

I was apprehensive returning to the hotel, especially to the ballroom where I had been during the attacks, but I used an affirmation that Master Charles gave us: "I am here and it is now." This helped. As I walked through the hotel, had dinner in the restaurant, and shopped in the mall, I began to feel increasingly grateful. In so many ways I was the most fortunate one of our entire group because I got out of the hotel first.

I do miss our friends, I always will.

BONNIE:

The hotel was beautifully renovated and there is now a gorgeous red grand piano in the open lobby. Soft music drifts up and around the entire area. They replaced the dark rose marble floor with white granite, which is quite extraordinary. The rooms have been renovated, of course, but mine felt the same and this brought up fleeting memories of the attack. I was able to simply be with the experience and, overall, everything about my return was joyous. I felt comfortable and happy to be there with my old friends and to make some new Mumbai friends, so happy to be alive and able to celebrate life.

I've changed. I am more compassionate now, more loving, and more understanding. I feel a deep-rooted connection to everyone. I see the same God in their eyes that is in me. It is so beautiful that words can't really express how this feels. And now we have O.L.A.

282 FORGIVING THE UNFORGIVABLE

and our message about the sacredness of life transmitting into the world. I feel so grateful and honored to be a part of this and look forward to more trips to India. I will do whatever I can to carry this message to the world.

LINDA:

It all started with Naomi, when she asked me to draw a peace dragon with her. Well, she inspired me. I took over five hundred pieces of art to Mumbai with me, created by children all over the U.S.A. as part of my Peace Dragon project. And I returned home with one thousand pieces from kids in India. I have drawn over 6,000 Peace Dragons in the two years since the attack.

We also created a permanent Peace Dragon that now sits in the Oberoi Hotel. It stands about five feet tall and is covered in fabric, adorned with small hearts and has gold lamé wings. It was quite a moment when we unveiled it. I told everyone to listen carefully because we would hear the sound of hearts opening. A collective sigh filled the ballroom, followed by a standing ovation to celebrate what this figure represents, hearts from all over the world joined together for peace.

KIA:

At the end of our celebration, all the five hundred-plus people stood up and took the O.L.A. pledge. "Here and now and for the next thirty days, I will honor the oneness and sacredness of life in myself and in everyone I meet."

I will never forget that moment. I felt the power of it moving in my heart and through us all. How simple! I opened to the possibility of hundreds more taking this pledge and really living it. Thousands, hundreds of thousands, millions ...

MASTER CHARLES:

I had tea at the American Consulate with the Consul General and his staff. They were happy to see me, but when I began to thank them for everything they had done for us, they seemed surprised. I don't know whether they thought I had come to ask for something or to complain. It was quite a transformational moment, just sitting there with them having tea and feeling their hearts open. This might seem strange to say, but they really felt like family! That's the power of gratitude.

On another day I found myself sitting with the Vice Chancellor of Mumbai University. He is a lovely man who spoke at the Memorial Program. I listened to him talking about spiritual philosophy and relating ancient understandings to what we were doing with O.L.A. He kept referring to what was written in the scriptures and then saying that we had the opportunity to actually live it now. The experience with this man was especially significant for me because Mumbai University is where I lectured thirty years ago as Muktananda's representative.

One day Kia and I were interviewed by a Chinese television news reporter. She actually didn't know that I was a survivor until after the interview had started. That's when she really got into our conversation and extended the interview. On her way out, she mentioned that her broadcast would be going out to over a billion people in China. That blew my mind! Imagine, over a billion people being offered this simple message about the sacredness of life.

It was inspiring to me that twelve of our original group chose to return for the reunion. Joe was 90 years old and he brought seven members of his family!

HELEN:

I was hoping to meet Parumel, who had been the Oberoi staff member who took me by taxi to the hospital and watched over us all during that first night. I had never been able to thank him in person. I looked for him every day with no success. The last evening I noticed a man in a housekeeping uniform working near us who looked just like Parumel, at least from behind. As I approached him carefully he turned around and it was not him. Well, I burst into tears. He hurried over and immediately called the head of housekeeping who told us that Parumel would be working again at seven AM the next morning. We were leaving for the airport at eight!

At exactly 7:00 the next morning Parumel knocked on our door! I gave him a hug, which was very inappropriate in India, and asked if he remembered me. He said, "Yes, attacks." I thanked him for being there for me and gave him a gift to express my gratitude. My daughter Robyn took a photo of us. Even in the photo the light of truth shines through his beautiful face. I was so lucky to have an angel like this caring for me.

MIRIAM:

When I arrived at our familiar hotel in Mumbai I realized that I had left my address book in Singapore. How symbolic, leaving my past behind! Everyone that I met at the various functions we organized thanked me for coming back. They kept on saying that I was so brave, but in fact going back was a reminder of my decision to live when I escaped down those eighteen floors of the Hotel.

That was an external, action choice. Returning in 2010, I made an internal, spiritual one. For the two years since the Mumbai terrorist experience, I had been releasing the suppressed and angry Miriam, the Miriam who couldn't (or wouldn't) speak up when she needed to. When I saw my interview on the giant screen during the Memorial Program it was like looking at a new person! I saw that I was standing firmly in my truth.

My very life had been threatened by "terrorists" in 2008. This jolted me into the realization that I had actually felt threatened by "others" all my life. I had been terrorizing myself internally. Because of Mumbai I was able to let that go, to shed my negative past data and experience being fully alive.

I am less fearful now. I am more loving and compassionate towards myself and others. I am more giving and forgiving. I don't take what people do or say so personally. In fact, every day I seem to be growing into more of who I really am. I am now able to embrace and include my past, present and future. It is all aspects of the ONE expressed in different ways.

Yes, the Mumbai experience in 2008 shook my being to its core, so that in 2010 I can fully embrace myself as life and love, being present in the now of truthful reality.

KIA:

I decided to launch the New Year by honoring the sacredness of life in a very personal way. On January 1st, I went into the restaurant and found the area where Alan and Naomi had died. This was immediately overwhelmingly emotional for me and I began to weep. Waiters hurried over to me. I put my hands together in prayer and choked out, "I need to sit at this table, this one, right here." They understood. They knew.

My waiter turned out to be one of those who had often waited on my family and he said that I reminded him of Naomi. He had been back in the kitchen that night so he didn't get shot. He explained how the group usually sat at a front table but had come in late that night, so he'd had to seat them at the back. That's why some of them escaped, because the shooters came in the front.

I had lunch at their table. Just me. And it was New Year's Day. A new moment, a new year, a new life.

HELEN:

India has burrowed itself so deeply into my heart that it is almost physically painful not to be there. I know I will return many times. I love the last two lines of a poem called "My India" that Paramahansa Yogananda recited just before he died: "Where Ganges, woods, Himalayan caves and men dream God—I am hallowed; my body touched that sod."

ॐॐॐ

Be aware of this moment and its limitless possibilities. For one final time, slow your reading, notice the words and the spaces between them, observe your breathing and your heart beating, pause ... and be fully aware that you are here and it is now. In this wakeful moment, there is only One. Consciousness is all. Who am I and who am I choosing to be? Just hold that question. Who am I and who am I choosing to be? As you deeply relax into the fullness of this moment, know that you couldn't be more on schedule if you tried, and accept this holistic experience whose time has come. Invite understanding. Imagine that you are the one who has met the genie with three wishes but that you tell him you need only one: the gift of true understanding. Invoke that now, with your heart wide open and your mind focused and receptive:

"I welcome the understanding of true forgiveness which is oneness. I embrace the unified state of being in this moment, and as I do, I experience myself as one with all beings, all life forms, in all the 50 billion simultaneous universes. Life is indeed sacred."

"Here ... now ... always and forever ... I am ... all is ... one."

Now ... it's your turn. What is your epilogue?

"I read this book, and then I ..."

Afterword

You have just finished reading a book that I have no doubt has been called to you from the deepest place within your soul, that you may once again be reminded of the deepest truths of life and the most meaningful aspects of your Earthly experience.

As you turn the last page of this remarkable document, which has covered such a wide span within the human experience—from terror to death to sexuality to our experience of divinity itself—I hope and pray that you take with you the turning of another page and the closing of another chapter and the end of another story.

I hope that you take with you the turning of the saddest pages of your life, the ending of your most difficult chapter, and the finalization of any story that has separated you from the grandest experience of your highest self. That is the purpose of this book, and that was the purpose of the experiences that have been described on these pages.

No one could read of those experiences without being deeply touched and profoundly moved. The fact that the survivors of the incidents recounted here have found a place of forgiveness and love in their hearts is a glowing testament to the divinity that lies at the heart of each of us, and to the highest possibility that awaits its emergence in our daily encounter with every adventure of life, be it joyous or tragic.

Allow this book to inform you once again of Who You Really Are. Allow this book's message to not only reside deeply within you, but to be shared openly with all those who cross your path on this day and through all the days of your life. Tell everyone about it!

Obviously, of course, I don't mean to tell everyone you meet of all the stories you've read here. What I do mean is to take the gift that you have been given by these stories and place it into action as you encounter the people and events that will form your own personal story in the years ahead. Allow what you have read to inform what you choose to be. In this way, the book you are holding becomes *causal*—and that is the greatest gift you can give in return to all those whose stories are related here.

This book *is* a remarkable gift. But I hope it will not be taken as simply the first-hand account of a shocking and terrifying encounter. It hope it will be understood to be a great deal more. I hope you will hold it deeply in your heart not only as a testimony to the greatness of those people whose story is told here, but to your own greatness as well. If I had one wish for you as you turn the last page of this book it would be that you see *yourself* in the heroism, in the compassion, in the courage, in the forgiveness, and in the unconditional love that has been expressed, demonstrated and illustrated in all of the preceding chapters.

So I would invite this of you: Don't let the message of this book end here. Let this be just the beginning. Carry forward the notion of a forgiveness without end, combined with your own inner decision to express love for all of humanity, also without end, so that the events described in this book may be given more glorious meaning than one might ever have imagined could possibly result from such a calamity.

Allow this deeply insightful book to place you exactly in the heart space that is described by this wonderful author, and allow yourself to come from that deep place of heartfelt love in all the remaining moments of your life. In this way, your day-to-day experience will become a Conversation with God.

—Neale Donald Walsch,
Author of *Conversations with God*

Endnotes

Front Matter

1. Mark Twain, quoted in Lois Einhorn and Arun Gandhi, *Forgiveness and Child Abuse: Would YOU Forgive?* (Robert Reed Publishers, 2010), 162.

Introduction

1. Damien McElroy, quoted in "Amish killer's widow thanks families of victims for forgiveness", *The Daily Telegraph* (London, October 17, 2006) http://www.telegraph.co.uk/news/main.jhtml?xml=/news/2006/10/16/wamish16.xml.

2. Socrates, quoted in Plato, *The Apology, An account of the death of Socrates,* Apology 38a.

Chapter One

1. Sufi aphorism, quoted in Reynold A. Nicholson, *The Mystics of Islam* (Routledge, Kegan Paul, London, 1914), 7.

2. Jalal al-Din Muhammad Rumi, "The Ocean Moving All Night" quoted in John Moyne and Coleman Barks, *Open Secret Versions of Rumi* (Shambhala, 1999).

3. Ibid.

4. Hafiz, quoted in Daniel Ladinsky, "Before You Wander in Love's Street", The Gift (Penguin Compass, 1999).

5. Andrew Zimmerman Jones and Daniel Robbins, *String Theory for Dummies* (For Dummies, 1st edition 2009).

Chapter Two

1. Fritjof Capra, *The Turning Point: Science, Society, and the Rising Culture,* (Bantam, 1984).

2. Albert Einstein, quoted in Richard A. Singer Jr., *Your Daily Walk with the Great Minds of the Past and Present (*BookSurge Publishing; 1st edition, 2006), 194.

3. Ramana Maharishi, quoted in Dennis Merritt Jones, *The Art of Being: 101 Ways to Practice Purpose in Your Life* (Tarcher, 2008), 60.

4. Wilfred Cantwell Smith, *The Meaning and End of Religion, (*Fortress Press, 1991).

5. James W. Fowler, *Stages of Faith* (HarperOne; New edition edition, 1995), 4-5.

6. Ibid., 11

7. Amit Goswami, *God is Not Dead* (Hampton Roads, 2008), 52.

8. Eckhart Tolle, *The Power of Now* (Novato, CA: New World Library, 2004), 152.

Chapter Three

1. Eckhart Tolle, *The Power of Now* (Novato, CA: New World Library, 2004), 10.

2. Jean-Jacques (John) Rousseau, quoted in Jennifer Leigh Selig, *Thinking Outside The Church: 110 Ways to Connect with Your Spiritual Nature* (Andrews McMeel Publishing, 2004), 134.

3. Bruce Lipton, *The Biology of Belief* (Hay House, 2008), 156.

4. Philip Yancey, *The Jesus I Never Knew* (Zondervan, 2002), 37-38.

Chapter Four

1. Canon Lauren Artress, *Walking a Sacred Path: Rediscovering the Labyrinth as a Spiritual Tool* (Riverhead Trade, 1996), 21.

2. Paramahansa Yogananda, *Autobiography of a Yogi* (Self-Realization Fellowship, 1946), 275.

3. Andrew Newberg and Mark Robert Waldman, *How God Changes Your Brain,* (Ballantine Books, 2010), 142.

Chapter Five

1. Lydia Maria Child and Bruce Mills, *Letters from New-York* (University of Georgia Press, 1998), 173.

2. Max Planck quoted in Daniel Jappah, *EVOLUTION: A Grand Monument to Human Stupidity* (Lulu.com, 2007), 241.

3. Ken Wilber, *The Integral Vision* (Shambhala, 2007), 56.

4. Michael Talbot, *The Holographic Universe* (Harper Perennial, 1992), 79-80.

5. George Dvorsky, quoted in "Managing your 50,000 Daily Thoughts." *Sentient Developments.* March 19, 2007, http://www.sentientdevelopments.com/2007/03/managing-your-50000-daily-thoughts.html

6. Jonathan Haidt, *The Happiness Hypothesis: Finding Modern Truth in Ancient Wisdom* (Basic Books 1st edition, 2005), 5-6.

7. Ibid., 2.

8. Andrew Newberg and Mark Robert Waldman, *How God Changes Your Brain* (Ballantine Books, 2010), 163-164.

Chapter Six

1. Lao Tzu quoted in Stephen Mitchell, *Tao Te Ching* (Harper Perennial; Compact edition 1992).

2. Daniel Goleman, "Why It Can Matter More Than IQ", *Emotional Intelligence* (Bantam Books, 1995), 117.

3. James W. Fowler, *Stages of Faith* (HarperOne; New edition edition, 1995), 303.

4. Teri Degler, *The Divine Feminine Fire: Creativity and Your Yearning to Express Your Self* (Dreamriver, 2009).

5. Walt Whitman, *Leaves of Grass* (United Holdings Group e-book 2011), Book III # 52.

6. Emma Jung, *Animus and Anima: Two Papers* (Spring Publications, Inc.; Second edition, 1985), 87.

7. Ryo-Nen, Her Last Composition quoted in Aldous Huxley, *The Perennial Philosophy* (Harper Perennial Modern Classics, 2004), *138.*

8. Eckhart Tolle, *A New Earth* (Penguin; Reprint edition, 2008), "A Brief History of Your Life".

9. Count Leo Tolstoy, quoted in M. J. Rose, *The Memorist (The Reincarnationist)* (Mira, Reprint edition, 2010), 136.

10. Diane Hennacy Powell, MD, *The ESP Enigma* (Walker & Company, 2009), 172.

Interlude

1. Rumi, quoted in Camille Adams Helminski, *Rumi Daylight, A Daybook of Spiritual Guidance* (Threshold Books), Rumi II: 827-30; 116.

Chapter Seven

1. Alan Watts, *The Essence of Alan Watts* (Celestial Arts (1977), 47.

2. Jack Kornfield, *A Path with Heart: A Guide Through the Perils and Promises of Spiritual Life* (Bantam, 1st edition, 1993), 167.

3. Amit Goswami, *God is Not Dead* (Hampton Roads, 1st edition, 2008), 274-275.

4. Bruce Lipton, *Biology of Belief* (Hay House; 13th edition, 2011), xxix.

5. Henri Matisse, quoted in Ayamanatara, *365 Days to Enlightenment* (Hunt Press, 2007), 164.

6. Stephen Wright, quoted in *Stephen Wright's Deadpan Humor*, www.freemaninstitute.com/Wright.htm.

7. Victor Davich, *8 Minute Meditation: Quiet Your Mind. Change Your Life* (Perigee Trade, 1st edition, 2004), 94.

Chapter Eight

1. Sigmund Freud, quoted in Bruce Rosenblum and Fred Kuttner, *Quantum Enigma: Physics Encounters Consciousness* (USA: Oxford University Press, 2008), 171.

2. David Chalmers, quoted in Bruce Rosenblum and Fred Kuttner, *Quantum Enigma: Physics Encounters Consciousness* (USA: Oxford University Press, 2008), 171.

3. Rumi, quoted in Edward Henry Whinfield, *Teachings of Rumi: the Masnavi of Maulána Jalálu'd-Dín Muhammad i Rúmi* (Dutton, 1975).

4. Ann Weiser Cornell, *The Power of Focusing* (New Harbinger Publications; 1st edition, May 1996), 21.

5. Sri Nityananda, as quoted in http://www.colorhealing.com/quotes.htm.

6. Jean Houston, as quoted in August 1, 2011, http://www.listentoatale.com/quotes.html.

7. Daniel Pink, *A Whole New Mind* (Riverhead Trade, Rep Upd edition, 2006), 107.

8. Peter Levine, *Healing Trauma* (Sounds True, Pap/Com, 2008), 19-20.

9. Lynne McTaggart, *The Intention Experiment* (Free Press, 2008), 52.

10. Wikipedia: "RDF" http://www.wikipedia.org/

11. Wikipedia: "Prime Directive" http://www.wikipedia.org/

Chapter Nine

1. Ralph Waldo Emerson, *The Complete Prose Works Of Ralph Waldo Emerson* (Kessinger Publishing, LLC; 5 edition, 2006), 139.

2. Andrew Newberg and Mark Robert Waldman, *How God Changes Your Brain* (Ballantine Books, 2010), 244.

3. Donald M Epstein, *Healing Myths* (Amber-Allen Publishing, 2000), 46-47.

4. Dr. David Perlmutter, "Effect of Physical Activity in Cognitive Function in Older Adults at Risk for Alzheimer's Disease." *Journal of the American Medical Association* (JAMA, 2008), 300(9):1027-1037. http://jama.ama-assn.org/content/300/9/1027.short

5. Esther and Jerry Hicks, "Ask and It Is Given", *The Teachings of Abraham* (Hay House, First Edition, 3 book set, 2007), 116.

6. Robert A. Johnson and Jerry M. Ruhl, *Living Your Unlived Life* (Tarcher, 2007), 66.

7. Katherine Woodward Thomas, *Calling in the One* (Three Rivers Press, Later Printing edition, 2004), 183.

Chapter Ten

1. John Moyne and Coleman Barks. "Rumi of Open Secret", *Versions of RUMI* (Shambhala, 1999) 2075, 47.

2. Carol S. Dweck, Ph.D., *Mindset: The New Psychology of Success* (Random House, 1st edition, 2006), 53.

3. Gavin de Becker, *The Gift of Fear* (Dell, 1999), 303.

4. *The King of Fear*, videocassette, directed by Philippe de Broca (Culver City, CA: MGM/UA Home Video, 2000).

5. Sumbul Ali-Karamali, *The Muslim Next Door* (White Cloud Press, 2008), 246-47.

6. Leonardo Da Vinci, quoted in Vernon McLellan, *Wise Words and Quotes* (Tyndale House Publishers, Inc., 2000), 65.

7. Paramahansa Yogananda, *Autobiography of a Yogi* (Self-Realization Fellowship; 13th edition, 2000), 385.

8. David Deida, *Naked Buddhism* (Plexus, 2002), 73.

Chapter Eleven

1. Viktor Frankl quoted in *Learn/Practice the Power of Empathy*, http://www.cnrg-portland.org/node/19432

Chapter Twelve

1. Thich Nat Hanh, *The Heart of the Buddha's Teaching* (Three Rivers Press, 1999), 153.

2. Amrit Desai.

3. Dr. Larry Dossey, *Prayer is Good Medicine* (Harper Collins, 1996), 83.

4. Lynn McTaggert, *The Intention Experiment* (Free Press, 2007), 61.

5. Donald Epstein, *Healing Myths, Healing Magic* (Amber-Allen, 2000), 103.

6. Donald Kennedy quoted in Ambrose Evans-Pritchard, *The Telegraph*, November 23, 2010, http://www.telegraph.co.uk/finance/comment/ambroseevans_pritchard/

7. Albert Einstein, quoted in William Powers, *Twelve by Twelve: A One-Room Cabin Off the Grid and Beyond the American Dream* (New World Library, 2010), 49.

8. Mahatma Gandhi quoted in Richard Scase, *Global Remix: The Fight for Competitive Advantage* (Kogan Page, 2007), 86.

9. Lynne and Teresa Barker Twist, *The Soul of Money* (W.W. Norton & Co., 2006), 252.

10. Paul Hawken, *The Ecology of Commerce* (Harper Business, 1994), 2-3.

Epilogue

1. Byron Katie and Stephen Mitchell, *Harmony with the Way Things Are* (Three Rivers Ress, 2008), 266.

2. Socrates, quoted in Plato, *The Apology, An account of the death of Socrates*, Apology 38a.

3. Neale Donald Walsch, *Tomorrow's God: Our Greatest Spiritual Challenge* (Atria, 2005), 393.

4. Mavis quoted in Jo Ann C. Abegglen, "The Power of One: Selfless Service". *Speeches*, July, 2006, http://speeches.byu.edu/reader/reader.php?id=11421.

About the Authors

MASTER CHARLES CANNON is a leader in the field of modern spirituality, a visionary and pioneer in the evolution of human consciousness. He founded Synchronicity Foundation for Modern Spirituality in 1983 and developed the High-Tech Meditation and Holistic Lifestyle experience which have helped transform the lives of millions worldwide. His speaking engagements include: the United Nations; the World Health Organization; the National Institutes of Health; Columbia, Oxford, Tel Aviv and Bombay Universities; Westminster Abbey and the Vatican.

His primary inspiration occurred during early childhood when the Blessed Mother began appearing to him. He became a close disciple of Paramahansa Muktananda, one of the most acknowledged spiritual masters of our modern era and was ordained as a monk in the Vedic tradition. His monastic name is Swami Vivekananda Saraswati.

Master Charles and Synchronicity associates inspired world audiences in 2008 by expressing love, compassion, and forgiveness rather than condemnation towards Islamic terrorists who murdered two and injured four of their group during the Mumbai terrorist attack. In the aftermath of their rescue, they created One Life Alliance, a charitable, educational organization dedicated to honoring the oneness and sacredness of life.

WILL WILKINSON has written obsessively since childhood. "I cherish the unique challenges of collaborating with contemporary wisdom keepers to discover and express an authentic voice that sings harmony into the world."